The National Trust Guide to
New Orleans

Roulhac
Toledano

PRESERVATION
PRESS

JOHN WILEY & SONS, INC.
New York • Chichester • Brisbane • Toronto • Singapore

Library of Congress Cataloging-in-Publication Data:
Toledano, Roulhac.
    The National Trust guide to New Orleans / Roulhac Toledano.
      p.   cm.
    ISBN 0-471-14404-5 (pbk. : alk. paper)
    1. New Orleans (La.) — Guidebooks.   I. National Trust for Historic
Preservation in the United States.   II. Title.
F379.N53T65   1996
917.63' 350463 — dc20   956-42538

Printed in the United States of America

10 9 8 7 6 5 4 3 2 1

Contents

Preface

This guide is grounded in the sure knowledge that architecture provides the underpinning for the enjoyment of New Orleans. Architecture reflects the people, their needs and their tastes. Buildings also reveal the economy that provided for the material preferences of the citizens.

The French Crown, having established New Orleans in 1718, abandoned the city with its 3000 French citizens in 1762, ceding it to Spain to keep it out of the clutches of the hated British Protestants. Louis XV handed over the heartland of what is now the United States to his Bourbon cousin in Spain.

Forty years later with just enough time to settle in, Spain sailed away, forced by Napoleon to retrocede to France its colony with 10,000 creoles in the capital city of New Orleans. Twenty days later Napoleon presented to President Thomas Jefferson's representative the Mississippi Delta. The cost? A paltry four cents an acre. Napoleon's reasoning was much the same as that of Louis XV—hatred of the British.

What's left of those 100 years of sweat and agony by the French and Spanish is still here for you to see. New Orleans' eighteenth-century and early nineteenth-century colonial architecture is what's left, and there's nothing like it anywhere else in the United States. French Quarter buildings evoke the creoles and their exciting history.

On Jefferson's advice, hordes of Americans headed downriver after 1803 as fast as their keelboats and flatboats could bring them from Kentucky and Tennessee. Anxious to cash in on the great opportunity, others sailed from New England and New York, Virginia and North Carolina, down the Eastern Seaboard and into the Gulf of Mexico.

St Louis Cathedral from Jackson Square, Gilberto Guillemard, architect, 1789, rebuilt, 1849–1851, J.N.B. DePouilly, architect (see p. 24). Photograph by Clarence John Laughlin, 1945. Courtesy of The Historic New Orleans Collection.

Immigrants—clever and rapacious ones, refined and restrained ones—from Britain and France rushed to New Orleans as fast as the sails could carry them. They joined thousands of French creole émigrés who had filtered to New Orleans after the revolution had begun in St. Domingue. Another 10,000 French creole refugees from St. Domingue arrived in 1812, after an interim stay in Cuba. As Louisiana became a state these new people built upon the French and Spanish city that they found. The French-speaking population spread downriver and the English-speaking peoples latched onto the land upriver to build the busiest port in the Western world by 1840.

What they built remains an exhibition of cultural memory. In addition to having 14 National Register Historic Districts, there are 11 local historic districts, administered by the New Orleans Historic District Landmarks Commission. Two entire neighborhoods are National Historic Landmarks: the Vieux Carré or French Quarter, and the Garden District. Individual National Historic Landmarks abound, as do buildings selected as landmarks by the Orleans Parish Landmarks Commission, a state agency. Even these designations fail to cover all the 10,000 or more worthwhile historic buildings that you can enjoy.

Out of this vast inventory this guidebook addresses your driving and walking convenience. It also provides a cross section of types and styles of architecture for each neighborhood covered. Attention is given to architecturally important buildings that were inhabited by notable persons. Good condition is not a criterion of selection; many buildings discussed need stabilization or restoration; others are threatened. Since this book can serve as an armchair guide to New Orleans as well as a street guide to the city, images created by earlier building watchers are presented. Photographs, paintings, drawings, engravings and etchings as well as printed comment about the city by earlier observers can deepen your own observations.

Building watching can be heady stuff. A look at a building, a complex, or group of buildings that comprise a neighborhood provides as good a way to assess a society as can be found. Building watching puts the eye to work seeking aesthetic pleasure and gathering information, encourages the mind to compare, assess, and analyze the single building against neighboring structures and against a collected bank of general knowledge.

This guide offers an opportunity to observe selected buildings in their setting and to see them through the eyes of those who recorded them over the centuries. Historic buildings that are difficult to get to are included so that you may understand their part in the city's tapestry. Presentation of notarial information about the architects, builders, and residents can expand your understanding of cultural and social history.

For example, New Orleans abounds in Roman Catholic institutions. The prominence of churches, convents, and religious schools, colleges, universities, hospitals, orphanages, and homes for the destitute, illustrate a Roman Catholic City. The abundance of such institutions also indicates a port city situated in a hostile environment where the residents required spiritual sustenance as well as physical care. Yellow fever, hurricanes, breaks in the levee, and prolonged heat threatened seasonally so that fear and danger became a way of life. Photographs in this book, along with selected communal history, illustrate one of North America's few Catholic cities.

Only in New Orleans will building-watching, supplemented by archival findings, reveal the full spectrum of African culture in the South. A census today shows that African-Americans hold ethnic majority in the city, but

Lafayette Cemetery. Photograph by Betsy Swanson. Surveyor Benjamin Buisson's suburb centers today around the cemetery on Prytania Street, in opposition to his intentions.

only architecture and its accompanying records uncover the important role men and women of African heritage played in developing this port city.

Since 1726 talented architects and builders, ironworkers, and real estate developers have emerged from this community of *personnes de couleur libres*, free persons of color. The golden age in New Orleans for those African-Americans fortunate enough to be free was the 1830s and 1840s when they produced notable architects and builders, artists and musicians, as well as manufacturers and entrepreneurs in a wide variety of businesses. That golden age is captured in the buildings they built and lived in.

With the advent of the Civil War three-fourths of the building lots in Faubourg Marigny had been owned at least one time by *gens de couleur libres.* The numbers in Faubourg Tremé surpassed that. For example, Aristide Mary, a free man of color, inherited from his Caucasian father major buildings on Canal Street in the new American sector, and leased both residential and commercial property to prominent creoles and Americans prior to and following the Civil War. He used the profits in 1892 to instigate the far-reaching lawsuit *Plessy* v. *Ferguson,* led by Faubourg Tremé French Speaking creoles of color Homère Plessy and the writer Rodolphe Desdunes. Their efforts to test the constitutionality of the Jim Crow law resulted in the establishment of the separate but equal doctrine in public areas. In these ways and others, New Orleans persons of color profoundly affected American history. These men and women are gone, but their neighborhoods with buildings as solid as the social and legal effects of their endeavors remain.

House histories disclose that most persons of color who owned real estate owned slaves, too. These slaves were tied to the properties of their owners, rural and urban. In fact, slaves, like some real estate, often were included with the land title—not by law—but by tradition. Examination of property titles shows how slaves were sold or manumitted, how they bought their freedom or how they were exchanged in tandem with house sales and property settlements.

1436 Pauger Street. Dolliole-Clapp-Davis house, built ca. 1820 (see p. 56). Photograph by Eugene D. Cizek, Ph.D., A.I.A. One of the first restorations in Faubourg Marigny, this house, built by a free man of color about 1820 was restored by architect Arthur Davis of the firm Curtis and Davis, architects for the Superdome.

933 St. Philip. Dolliole House (see p. 56). Photograph by Frank W. Masson. A.I.A. Architect Frank Masson and his wife Ann, bought the Dolliole house in 1980 after it had been abandoned for 30 years, restoring the creole cottage as it would have appeared during the ownership of free man of color, builder Jean Louis Dolliole. Dolliole bought the lot in 1804 from his French emigré father, Louis Dolliole, built the house and raised his family in it. His wife, Hortense Dussau, free woman of color, died here in 1820, but Dolliole lived in the house until 1854.

Andrew Jackson emerged as a national hero after his leadership at the Battle of New Orleans on January 8, 1815, against British General Packenham's forces. His statue presides over Jackson Square. Thomas Jefferson, James Monroe and Robert Livingston deserve the kudos, though. Jefferson, as president, sent Monroe as minister plenipotentiary to Paris to buy New Orleans. He and Livingston, U.S. Minister to France, negotiated with Talleyrand and Napoleon, and Monroe sailed home with title to the Mississippi Valley. Jefferson felt that New Orleans would become the most important port in the Western world. His prophecy became reality in the late 1840s and 1850s, and opulent American New Orleans remains upriver from the French Quarter to prove it.

Anglo-American mentality created the foremost and best preserved historic residential neighborhood in America:The Garden District, a National Historic Landmark. It may also be the most static neighborhood in the country. From Scotland came builders; Irish architects and builders sailed from Ulster and County Cork, often via New York. In the 1830s some of these immigrants created the new American neighborhoods.

By the late 1840s poverty and the potato famine brought Irish Catholics in shipload after shipload. Their initial treatment was as bad as slaves endured in those first hard years; signs in nineteenth-century lithographs of architectural landmarks proclaim, "No Irish Allowed. Hod Carriers Only." They died of yellow fever and cholera by the thousands while laboring to dig canals. Slave owners would not lease their chattels to perform this same work, digging in the fever-ridden swamps to drain the area and thus provide more land for New Orleans developers.

One job was not proscribed to the Irish. They could run for political office, and, with their numbers, win. Thus the Irish overcame prejudice and discrimination to take their place in New Orleans' history.

The Irish rented spaces in new-built frame, classic-style housing close to the wharves where they arrived in the 1840s, giving the area the Irish Channel. They clustered in great numbers around churches such as St. Patrick's in Faubourg St. Mary and the Redemptorists' complex in the new upriver suburb laid out by Barthélémy Lafon. Irish neighborhoods in the Lower Garden District and the Irish Channel, and the neighborhoods they built for other English-speaking immigrants, are National Register Historic Districts.

A flood of Catholic Germans invaded the Lower Garden District near the Irish neighborhoods after the Professors' War, or *1848 mini-revolution* in Germany. These immigrants built St. Mary's Assumption Church in the 1850s and their Society of Turners built Turners Hall at 932 Lafayette in the Faubourg St. Mary in 1868. They and their descendants built much of Jefferson City and the suburbs through Carrollton. The brickwork on churches and affiliated buildings from Faubourg St. Mary through Carrollton attest to their talents.

This architectural guide reveals a culture as different from the rest of the United States as night and day. For example, Edgar Degas' mother was from New Orleans, and the French artist made oil sketches of house interiors and exteriors during a New Orleans visit in 1872. His cousin Norbert Rillieux, a *personne de couleur libre* from Faubourg Tremé and an upriver plantation, had 92 patents for the processing of sugar in 17 European and North African countries. He, like his cousin Degas, lived in Paris and is buried at Père Lachaise Cemetery.

New Orleans Notarial Archive documents show that Faubourg Lafayette was awarded to the young French general who fought beside Washington in the Revolutionary War. The signature of Guy Lemottier, General Lafayette, is inscribed with his 12 given names and lengthy titles alongside transfers of land to him from the federal government.

Other patterns are revealed at the Archives; one shows how often a man's fortune was made from his wife's inheritance, as in the case of Claude Tremé of Faubourg Tremé and Beltrán Gravier of Faubourg St.

Portrait of Don Andrés Almonester y Roxas (1725–1799). By José de Salazar, 1796. Courtesy of the Louisiana State Museum. Almonester came to Louisiana from Andalusia, Spain in 1769 as an officer in the Spanish colonial government. Appointed Royal Notary, he became New Orleans' wealthiest Spanish colonial citizen. He financed the rebuilding of St. Louis Church and the construction of the Cabildo and Presbytère at the Plaza de Armas and the Mississippi River.

Mary. The archives reveal that one Spanish colonial notary, Andrés Almonester y Roxas, and his creole daughter Micaela, Baroness, de Pontalba, created the architectural core of New Orleans. The Cabildo, Cathedral and Presbytère were conceived and financed by the Spanish father, while the creole daughter developed the Pontalba buildings and Jackson Square.

Title searches among documents from the 1890s and a look at names inscribed on building parapets announce the arrival of Sicilians in great

Portrait of Micaela Almonester, Baroness de Pontalba (1791–1874).By Eliza Appolina de Harme, ca. 1830. Executed in France.Courtesy of the Louisiana State Museum.When she was 15 years old this creole daughter of Don Andrés Almonester y Roxas and his young French creole wife, Louise de la Ronde married Joseph Xavier Celestin Delfau de Pontalba, son of a French baron who was descended from a distinguished French colonial family in Louisiana. In 1848 she planned and financed the two rows of storehouses flanking Jackson Square, the old Plaza de Armas her father had improved. Her home in Paris is now the American Ambassador's residence.

numbers to the French Quarter, where they settled from the lower Pontalba Apartments on Jackson Square to the Faubourg Marigny. A further look reveals that many came from Contessa Entellina, an Albanian refugee village founded in Sicily in the sixteenth century. At first they rented the worn-out historic buildings of the French Quarter and Faubourg Tremé. Stories relate the birth of both calves and babies in the 1850 double parlors of the lower Pontalba buildings.

These newest immigrants took over the lower French Quarter, but the building stock had been complete for decades, since about 1860. Once settled, by 1900, Sicilians influenced the business of eating: restaurants, factories for pasta and pastries, the fruit industry, and related import-export enterprises.

What was unique about New Orleans architecture had already occurred by the time of the Civil War, but the social and political structures of the city continued their dynamic development long afterwards. Architecture, music, food, politics, ethnic variety, Mardi Gras and the Roman Catholic Church articulate New Orleans and make it unique. This difference can be appreciated by observing the outdoor museum of buildings selected and explained in this book.

This entire book is an index of New Orleans, staccato accounts of a rich and varied history, of land development, architecture, artists, historic figures and events. Names of house owners and developers appear at the address in the text. Addresses appear alphabetically by street name, according to neighborhood. Names of architects, artists, and builders are listed in the index as well as individuals whose profession or accomplishment aside from house ownership informs the reader of book and index.

Dedication to
Samuel Wilson, Jr.

I once edited a little book, **Bienville's New Orleans,** that Sam Wilson and I had conceived for the Friends of the Cabildo. In those days working with Sam meant taking the streetcar down to his architecture office and waiting while he wrote out a section long hand; then I hauled it off to type. This time, Sam promised to edit my manuscript, to keep me out of trouble, since every fact about New Orleans' architecture had been interpreted in a least three different ways. Instead, sadly, he died.

But he left behind some 175 essays and books about New Orleans as revealed through its architecture. During a 62-year career as an architect in this city, Sam Wilson worked on 150 buildings in the French Quarter alone. We can enjoy these and many more elsewhere in the city and the Gulf south.

Sam had a discreet way of saving old buildings: first he synthesized records, presenting documentary evidence; then he renovated and restored the buildings in a conservative fashion, yielding his own imprint to the building's original footprint.

Because he was a pioneer in teaching regional architectural history, having developed the first course in Louisiana architecture at Tulane University, hundreds of New Orleans' historic buildings were preserved and our cultural memory enhanced before preservation was a civic consideration elsewhere. Because of his quiet scholarship and with the help of his talented associate, Henry Krotzer, the mansion in Paris, France, of the New Orleans' Pontalba family was saved from demolition to be carried out by our federal government. Now it's the U.S. ambassador's residence.

I said to a friend and one of his coauthors, "It's so restful to see a building that Sam has worked on. His circumspect attitude reveals itself without layers of dynamics."

"Oh, I prefer his scholarship," was the retort. "When I'm upset I always get out a volume of Sam's. His architectural and historical prose is wonderful for breakfast reading."

I thought about that. I haven't gotten to the point of reading Wilson at breakfast, but when I do, I may begin with the complex history of Faubourg Panís. Nobody much cares about this small strip of New Orleans history. He did.

Civilized, comprehensive, and functional, Sam Wilson's work, in architecture and in scholarship, has helped his students and his colleagues to catalogue, study, restore, renovate, and love the architecture of New Orleans.

Roulhac Toledano
June 2, 1995
New Orleans, Louisiana

Acknowledgments

This book would not have been possible without the contribution of time and talent by the staff at the Historic New Orleans Collection, particularly John Magill, and the use of their vast photographic archives.

As for individuals, everyone I know helped, at one time or another, for this is largely a volunteer project to serve and to save the built environment and southern culture. I am grateful for their company, hospitality, advice, and the understanding with which they joined in an effort to help the City That Care Forgot.

First to Mary Louise Mossy Christovich, with whom I have worked on six books and other projects. Her optimistic attitude, organizational skill, and perseverance in improving everything that we have ever written together have not been lost on me. Whether the objective was to write a book, to save a cemetery, or to block a projected expressway from destroying historic properties, she has always demanded diligence.

To Betsy Swanson, classmate at Newcomb College, a frequent coauthor with me and a documentary photographer, for demanding that I be more careful in my documentation, that I slow down to accomplish more. She taught me to see more as I joined her in selecting views as she photographed 6000 New Orleans buildings for our New Orleans architecture series.

To Lelia Washburn for her hospitality on Massachusetts Avenue in Washington within walking distance of the National Trust Office; and for listening to the book as I read it aloud to her for advice and comment. To Warren Robbins, founder and Director Emeritus of the National Museum of African Art, for his crisp and succinct use of words and for a computer and desk in his Capitol Hill office. To my mother, Phylis Gewin Bunkley, for providing hideaways for writing in Texas and Alabama. To Rosemarie Fowler for her thorough research and for checking every hotel, restaurant, and address in New Orleans that I considered presenting in this book. To Fred Starr for his index and footnotes in *Southern Comfort*, his volume on the

Garden District; his book made easily available much information I had run across in the Notarial Archives, but I didn't take notes.

For those who helped me cut down and clean up masses of information, I must mention editors and friends, Linda Hobson, Linda Blackford, Sharon Hinson, Jennie Williams, Jennie Kelland, Scot Hinson, and André King of the Alliance Française. Thanks to my daughter d'Arby for study photographs and to my son Macon for architectural analysis; my other two daughters, Cleanth and Gabrielle served as test-tourists walking the city of their birth and viewing it through my eyes.

Roulhac Toledano

New Orleans: City of Rhythms and Patterns

I n 1763, Louis XV ceded to England all the French land holdings west of the Mississippi River except l'Ile d'Orléans. France and Spain always referred to the Island of Orleans, and as the city developed through the decades, it became isolated culturally, too, generating its own special rhythms and patterns as distinct from the rest of the country as the Mississippi is from other great rivers. Today, New Orleans is still an island unto itself, geographically and culturally.

Water defines the city, bounded as it is by the Mississippi River and by Lake Pontchartrain. Cleared and drained cyprières or cypress swamps formed many neighborhoods. New Orleans is further cut off from its geographic surroundings by Lake Maurepas to the west and ribbons of water

2300 Block of Laurel Street between First and Second Streets. Photograph by Betsy Swanson, 1969. Classic- and Italianate- style galleries "civilize" modest one story double shotguns used as rental houses in the mid-nineteenth century. At the same time, similar galleries and cornices were applied as adornment to two-story side-hall Garden District mansions.

such as the Rigolets and Chef Menteur to the east. In the early years, bayous, such as Gentilly, Tchoupitoulas, and Sauvage, their beds now dry, divided the landscape while providing transportation to connect it. Bayou St. John, although closed in the downtown area, is still a waterway.

Ironically the water that isolated New Orleans caused Jean Baptiste Le Moyne, Sieur de Bienville, to build the city. The Mississippi River is the reason for New Orleans, and he selected a crescent for settlement in 1718 about 90 miles upriver from the Gulf of Mexico. Bayou St. John, named in Bienville's honor, was essential to his reasoning because it provided the five-mile water linkage from the Mississippi River to Lake Pontchartrain, thence east through the Chef Menteur to Lake Borgne, the Gulf of Mexico, and the open seas.

The runoff of 30,000 miles of waterways sweeps past New Orleans through the passes at the foot of the river, dumping into the Gulf of Mexico. Manufactured goods, raw material and agricultural products from 12,000 miles of the Mississippi River and its tributaries reach New Orleans. From the earliest years the economy rose and fell according to the seasons and the harvests, the climate and water levels.

The river weaves its own pattern, rushing and swirling against the levees and jetties that harness it. The crevasses that crash through the cut banks and levees have ceased, unless the River blasts through to the Atchafalaya, changing its course to bypass New Orleans entirely. No one stands on Canal Street looking anxiously toward the River to see a wall of sandbags against a higher wall of water ready to roll through the city. But the rhythms of the river are still there, and peril looms as a subconscious memory to the populace. Many Orleanians have never seen the river that articulates the city and drives the economy. Others ignore it, even hating it.

Yet the water creates the patterns of port life, carrying the sounds of the fog horn, the wail of the tugboats and ferries, and the bump of barges. As a port, New Orleans survives according to the age-old rhythms of the Gulf of Mexico's tides. The Mississippi River makes its own music, distinct from the lapping waves in shallow Lake Pontchartrain, the still waters of the bayous, or the swift rush of the Rigolets or Chef Menteur that cut New Orleans apart from the rest of Louisiana.

Approaching its tricentennial, New Orleans retains its island mentality, a city apart, now more state of mind than reality since the advent of bridges and machinery to drain swamps and pump out unwanted water. New Orleans remains distinct from other southern cities in its appearance, religion, ethnic mix, prejudices, and attitudes. Like the ebb and flow of the waters that bound and bind it, New Orleans follows its own cultural rhythms and patterns. These are manifested in a myriad of ways, especially in architecture, music, cuisine, religion and language.

New Orleans even has its own special aromas. On a drive in from the east, the scent of roasting coffee beans ascends to you at the top of the Industrial Canal bridge. Magazine Street is sometimes wrapped in the smell of coffee beans roasting. This wafting aroma provides a preview to the *café au lait* and *beignets*, the ultimate French doughnut, at the French Market on Decatur Street.

The sensory experience along Tchoupitoulas Street that Sir Henry Morton Stanley encountered in the 1850s during his boyhood in New Orleans is still available. In later years the renowned explorer recalled the roasting coffee beans imported from South America and the beer being brewed, with its sweet-sour smell of hops.

Baking French bread aromas drift through the air from Leidenheimer's at 1501 Simon Bolivar Avenue downtown. Gambino's Italian cheesecakes and layered Dobergé cakes continue to tease the senses at 3609 Toledano Street. Your nose can tell when the trucks delivering King's Cakes and brioche arrive at McKenzie's many bakeries. Dixie Beer is brewed in New Orleans today at 2401 Tulane Avenue, giving the same yeasty smell that Bienville noted when he visited the Dreux brothers' hops plantation in the 1720s.

These aromas fight with the pungency of fish, crawfish, shrimp, and oysters on sale at the market and on refuse heaps in front of restaurants. In New Orleans the diesel smell of the boats, and oil and chlorine off the water mingle with the smells of the best food in the country and the flowers, vines, and shrubs of a tropical treasure right here in the United States. In the Garden District and uptown the air is redolent with the heavy aroma of sweet olive, jasmine, gardenias, and ginger lilies in their seasons. Thick hedges of pittosporum and ligustrum serve as aromatic fences, and the leaves absorb car exhaust on the narrow streets laid out before the automobile was envisioned.

Like the scents, the sounds of New Orleans have always pervaded the streets. From the chant of the *Calas* (rice cakes) vendors to the strip joints' jazz ensembles, from the quadroon ball orchestra to the symphony, there's been music ever since the first parish church was dedicated with a musical accompaniment from the nearby ship's band. Dixieland jazz, big band sounds, and the blues are at home in New Orleans as much as Debussy, played on the Pleyel pianos at Loyola University.

New Orleans is the hometown of jazz, and its sound in cabarets, honky-tonks, nightclubs, and music halls, even in the cemeteries, is part of the daily pattern of the Crescent City. Euphonious names echo through the Jazz Archives at Tulane University and at the Jazz Museum in the United States Mint building like the Dixieland jazz and big band music they played: Leonard and Sidney Bechet, Alcide Pavageau, Louis Dumaine of the Tupelo Brass Band, Clarence Desdunes and Armand Peron of the Joyland Revelers, Lorenzo Tío of the Onward Brass Band, and Ferdinand Le Menthe, whom we know as Jelly Roll Morton. These and more are some of the 60 musicians who lived and played in the creole suburbs between 1880 and World War I.

New Orleans residents can easily conjure up a jazz band with a telephone call or a chat with the butcher, the mailman, or the garbage collector. A three- or four-piece jazz ensemble will play for a party, luncheon, dance, cocktail, or dinner party. No piano required, just a small space for the performers and a rolled-up rug to provide floor space for the dancers. Use a corridor for a snake dance, or just weave and dance right out the door into the city streets.

Parades during Mardi Gras season offer the easiest way to experience New Orleans Jazz. The Mardi Gras season kicks off on Twelfth Night or Epiphany, when tradition has it that The Three Kings of the Orient appeared in Bethlehem and, like Santa Claus, arrive symbolically in Hispanic countries to bring gifts. More than 60 clubs or "krewes" parade between Twelfth Night and Mardi Gras Day or Fat Tuesday, the day before Lent begins. Bands of revelers and orchestras ride on huge decorated floats, while marching bands dance and swing as they belt out music for miles and miles while weaving through the neighborhoods. Almost nightly, the beat of drums, the wail of trombones, and the blare of trumpets reverberate throughout New Orleans for a season of festivity.

St. Patrick's Day on March 17 is a chance for Irish bands to march in the French Quarter, Irish Channel, and Lower Garden District and to play in uptown bars. On the weekend before March 17, the Decatur Street Marching Club gathers at the French Market and travels through the French Quarter, and the Irish Channel parade begins at Race and Annunciation Streets.

St. Joseph's Day belongs to the Italian-American neighborhoods. March 19th brings parades and music and St. Joseph altars. These altars are lavishly decorated with food and bread to give away at the Italian-oriented St. Joseph Church that towers over the landscape near Charity Hospital at 1802 Tulane Avenue. Other colorful altars are located at the Piazza d'Italia, designed by architect Charles Moore, at the corner of Poydras and Tchoupitoulas, and at many other churches, charitable institutions, and private homes. All locations are listed in the *Times-Picayune* and are open to the public.

Listen, too, for the rhythm of language along the streets of New Orleans, in the restaurants, bars, and music halls. Listen as you swing along on the streetcars or sway on the buses. A New Orleans taxi driver does more than take you to your destination if you strike up a conversation. If he asks, "Doilin', an ya momma'nem?" that means "How do you do?", more or less. Another might add *et la bas* to the end of nearly everything; it means something like "over there." "Where y'at?" instead of "How are you?" is such a common greeting in parts of the city that some citizens call themselves "Yats"; and an "oldies" station WYAT can be found at 99.0 AM on the radio dial.

The kinship between the New Orleans and Brooklyn accents is said to be the commonality of County Cork ancestry. But there are many more accents special to New Orleans, like the English of the old creole families, totally different in sound and rhythm from the English accent of Cajuns, who began speaking their own French patois and now speak English with their particular accent.

Occasionally you find families, both African-American and creole, still speaking French on their front balconies in the French Quarter and the creole suburbs. Uptown you can find French or English with lots of *chères, tantes, cousines* and French endearments among ladies in their boudoirs while they sip demitasses of black coffee and chicory. From shotgun porches uptown and in the creole suburbs, the Waguespacks, Couvillions and Marmillions speak French, each accent a variant of a southern Louisiana region. The "German Coast" French accent of the Waguespacks, for example, differs in words, tone, and rhythm from the nearby Bayou Teche and Acadian parish French farther southwest.

Young men and women of Anglo-American heritage from Texas and the adjoining Gulf coast states graduate from Newcomb and Tulane, and from Loyola; they marry New Orleanians and enrich the complex sounds of New Orleans with more traditionally "southern" speech patterns. Only in New Orleans do natives give tours in Cajun, Louisiana's special patois, as well as in French, Spanish, Italian with its Sicilian variants, and other languages, including Vietnamese.

The water, the warm climate, and the Catholic religion attracted this most recent group to the city in large numbers. So many Hondurans have settled in New Orleans that it is said to be the third largest city "in Honduras," close behind Puerto Cortes and Tegucigalpa, the capital.

2915-2901 Camp Street at Sixth Street (see p. 148). Photograph by Betsy Swanson, 1969. Rows of late nineteenth century shotgun houses were habitations for the poor people, usually Irish and German immigrants and their descendants who settled on the fringes of the Garden District.

1424-1428 Royal Street. Carriageway of a *porte cochère* house (see p. 54). Photograph by Betsy Swanson, 1970. Courtesy of the Historic New Orleans Collection.

Semitropical New Orleans welcome the world with music, good food, and a relaxed attitude. The difficulty of life in New Orleans has made it a festive city, perhaps as a challenge to pestilence, hurricane, and flood. Even the funerals are celebratory, musical occasions.

With New Orleans' long growing season, flowers, shrubs, or trees are always blooming and most trees are green year around. Azaleas and camelias border the raised-house foundations and iron fences, while oleanders and crape myrtles line the streets and neutral grounds; Christmas brings poinsettias to the city fences. Live oak branches create tunnels of dusky green and the wisps of Spanish moss add atmosphere to streets edged with architecture that concocts by the repetition of shapes and forms yet more cadences in this city of patterns and rhythms.

New Orleans architecture—the buildings and their surroundings—represent New Orleans. The entire city is a public, festive, outdoor museum. Buildings function as artifacts or as outdoor sculpture filled with decorative art, with food or music or with the exotic people of New Orleans.

Each neighborhood remains, even today, an island or an entity of its own, with all the characteristics an urban place needs to be independent and self-sufficient. Each has its own civic, educational, and religious institutions. Public squares, parks and cemeteries, commercial districts, shopping enclaves and corner storehouses mix among the residential blocks of every neighborhood.

New Orleans neighborhoods also show the ebb and flow of interest in preservation. The Bayou St. John Improvement Association was a leader in 1927, but after working on City Park, it languished. In 1936 interest in the future of the French Quarter was caused by the demolition of a small Spanish colonial creole cottage across the street from the then-dilapidated Ursuline Convent. The Vieux Carré Property Owners, Residents and Associates was formed. A 1937 city ordinance protects, "the quaint and distinctive character of the Vieux Carré." Statewide preservation legislation followed in 1939, among the first in the country. Not until 1950, when the

1300 block of Chartres Street with the Ursuline Convent at the left. Etching by William Woodward, 1934. Courtesy of the Southeastern Architectural Archives, Tulane University Library. The demolition of this tile-roofed Spanish colonial building on Chartres Street beside the Ursuline Convent thrust the French Quarter preservation movement into action in the late 1930s.

French Quarter courtyard. Etching by Childe Hassam, 1927. Courtesy of the Historic New Orleans Collection. This scene recalls the way the French Quarter looked during the days when William Faulkner, Rouark Bradford, Sherwood Anderson and so many southern writers, artists and photographers rented cheap rooms between the world wars.

Mississippi River Bridge Authority threatened to demolish the 1814 Delord-Sarpy Plantation house in the midst of the urban Lower Garden District, was the Louisiana Landmarks Society launched. The battle was lost in 1957. The statewide preservation association has been successful with other efforts.

The internationally recognized series of books *New Orleans Architecture* published in the 1970s served as catalysts for the next progression of preservation associations and projects throughout the 1970s. The aggressive Preservation Resource Center, launched in 1974, serves as an umbrella for over 45 preservation and improvement associations.

Now, thanks to the volunteers who have saved and re-saved the city—because it's a constant necessity in the face of modern values and pressures—the rhythms and patterns, the festival of New Orleans history, its buildings, and its spirited and varied population remains to be enjoyed. *Laisscz lcs bons temps rouler*. Let the good times roll.

The National Trust Guide to
New Orleans

CREOLE
NEW ORLEANS

Royal Street, Ca. 1940. Courtesy of the Historic New Orleans Collection.

The French Quarter

T he New Orleans Metropolitan Convention and Visitors' Bureau is one of the best in the country. But it's not a patch on the job John Law did in Paris to promote the French colony between 1717 and 1720. Without Scottish financier John Law's scheme, outrageous in its gall and staggering in its conception, to promote the settlement of Louisiana and the establishment of its capital city, there would be no French Quarter, the place he called Nouvelle Orleans after the regent.

In August 1717, Law, the *protégé* of Le Duc d'Orléans, Regent to Louis XV, wrested the franchise on Louisiana from Antoine Crozat, a bibliophile and art collector who had amassed a fortune in Parisian real estate but had failed miserably to settle the colony. Law formed the Company of the West, called the Mississippi Company, to handle his 25-year monopoly over the commerce and trade of Louisiana.

Enrichissez-vous was his theme. Law garnered wealth for himself, but by selling shares in the colony and developing Louisiana, he meant to support the French Crown and to enrich shareholders willing to invest in the colony. This meant enticing investors to apply for land concessions in Louisiana; these investors, called *concessionaires*, were charged with locating and shipping workers to Louisiana on company ships, with sufficient provisions to support them until land had been cleared and a crop harvested. These men and their families, termed *engagés*, were promised their own land, supplies, and clothing after a three-year indenture. The larger concessions also employed, in addition to the usual director, a subdirector, a surgeon, and an apothecary, among other educated men of business.

Back in Paris, investors were crazed with excitement. Stock trading generated a new wealthy class who built their private mansions or *hôtels* on such elegant streets as the Rue de Grenelle and became known as *millionaires*, a word coined for traders in the Mississippi Company. For example, the Oglethorpe sisters, daughters of Sir Theophilus Oglethorpe and English exiles at the Court of James II at St. Germain-en-Laye, having acquired wealthy French husbands, the Marquis de Mezières and the Marquis des Marches, maneuvered them to purchase stock in the Mississippi company. They sold at a huge profit, only to buy more as it escalated in value. They also financed concessions in the colony, sending personnel and *engagés* to develop land on the Ouachita River and along the Mississippi.

To provide colonists, Law even convinced the regent to take orphans out of convents, dowering each with a trunk of clothing. They were sent off chaperoned by nuns to Lorient and La Rochelle on the west coast of France before setting sail for Louisiana. Unsatisfied still with the small numbers of colonists, Law had the regent's own guard abduct women off the streets and from the insane asylum and hospital of La Salpetrière to send to Louisiana.

This outrage made the headlines, and in response, artist Antoine Watteau, resident at Pierre Crozat's elegant home on Rue Richelieu, painted "Le Depart Pour les Isles," depicting these pitiful young women as they were forced to sail off in the Mississippi Company flutes and brigantines.

In February 1718, after three months at sea, John Law's first shipload of Frenchmen arrived, disgorging starving settlers and directors of proposed concessions. In 1719, Law sent other ships from France to Senegal and the west coast of Africa, where he had acquired the slave franchise. After leaving Cap Vert, loaded with Africans, the ships headed for Louisiana, seven months at sea from France.

Meanwhile, in Louisiana, Jean Baptiste Le Moyne, military governor for the Mississippi Company, seized upon the arrival of the ships with their cargoes of workers to focus on the establishment of his proposed post of Nouvelle Orléans. LeMoyne, a Canadian of Norman background whose family had been in New France for about a century, had conceived and promoted the idea for a trading post and settlement to be named after the Regent, Le Duc d'Orléans. Law grasped at the establishment of Bienville's New Orleans as a marketing tool for his financial scheme, soon to be known as the Mississippi Bubble. It burst when investors in Paris were unable to cash in their stock, risen to 40 times its original value. Nor was there gold or silver to back the paper money Law had induced the regent to have printed. This left Governor Bienville and the settlers stranded in the New World in a new *entrepôt* or trading post.

Jonathan Darby described the scene of New Orleans' founding in the summer of 1718. An English Roman Catholic exile in Paris, he had sailed to Louisiana to manage the Mississippi River concession of the Cantillon brothers, bankers in Paris. "In June, 1718," he wrote, "Monsieur de Bienville

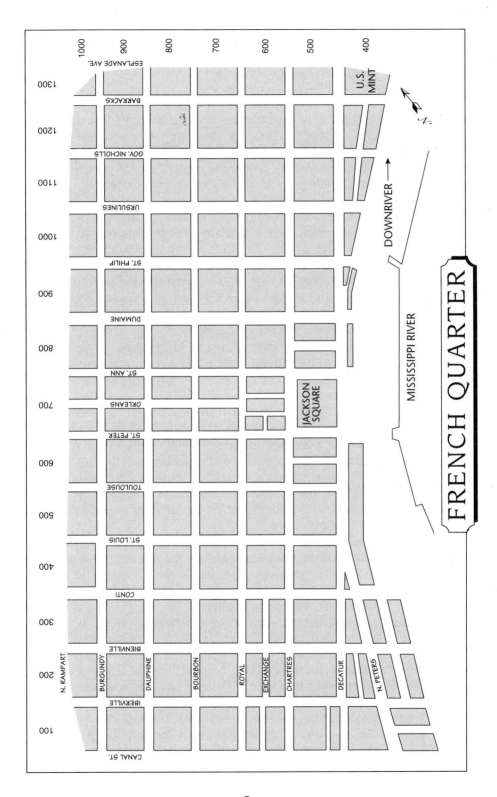

FRENCH QUARTER

arrived with six vessels loaded with provisions and men. There were thirty workmen, all convicts; six carpenters and four Canadians. M. de Bienville cut the first cane, Mssers Pradel and Dreux the second . . . to open a passage through the dense canebrake from the river to the place where the barracks were to be . . . .The whole locality was a dense canebrake with only a small pathway leading from the Mississippi to the Bayou [now St. John] communicating with Lake Pontchartrain." When one of the men thrust his knife into the marshy ground, a great howl and thrashing terrified the group as an alligator thrust his head and tail out of the bog, reported one of the participants.

Governor Bienville saw the entire settlement wash away in the flood of 1719, and in 1722 a hurricane leveled it again. Both engineers to the King Perrier and Le Blonde de la Tour, sent to lay out the city, died, the latter by yellow fever in October 1723. Adrien de Pauger arrived to finish the job according to the precepts of the French military engineer Sebastien Vauban. New Orleans proved too much for its third engineer, too, and de Pauger died in 1726, requesting in his will to be buried in his still incomplete parish church, site of St. Louis Cathedral.

By 1720 the slave ships began to land in large numbers, first on the beach at Biloxi. Most of the Africans were taken to New Orleans in light barks that sailed across shallow Lakes Borgne and Pontchartrain to enter New Orleans at Bayou St. John. There they collected: the Canadians, the newly arrived Africans, and the French, from nobleman to scapegrace and felon. Out of the swamp forest to survey the scene stalked the southeastern natives, tribes that were eventually so decimated that they are nearly forgotten: the Chitimacha and the Acolapissa. The natives immediately saw opportunity, leasing arms and powder from the Europeans and providing them with game, meanwhile learning to use the guns. The Indians also set up a market near the bayou outside the strange new European settlement on the Mississippi River.

Because of the avarice, the vision, and the determination of John Law and Bienville, New Orleans was established. The problems that began in 1718 are by and large the problems the city has today: corruption, prejudice, conflict among governing agencies over power and money, and a burgeoning bureaucracy, then in its infancy.

Law had to flee Paris when his scheme collapsed. Most investors in France were ruined, and he was dead by 1723. Bienville lived in New Orleans and Paris until 1768, in time to see his city and his colony fall into the hands of Spain. In November 1762, Louis XV had ceded, by the secret Treaty of Fontainebleau, that part of the French colony west of the Mississippi and the all-important Ile d'Orléans, where New Orleans was located, to Spain under his Bourbon cousin, Carlos III. It was an effort to keep French Louisiana out of British hands. At the subsequent Treaty of Paris, in February 1763, Louis XV was forced to cede the rest of the French colony, all the land on the east side of the Mississippi River except Ile d'Orléans (already ceded to Spain), to England. Spain, in turn, ceded West Florida with St. Augustine and Pensacola and all the country to the east and southeast of the Mississippi to England. New Orleans and the land that ultimately made up 11 states and more of the Louisiana Purchase became Spanish Colonial Louisiana.

Spain was stretched out over too great an area of the New World to rule Louisiana aggressively. Besides, New Orleans was not a favored post compared to the thriving island of Cuba or Mexico and Peru, where riches were available to the energetic. Most Spaniards who came to New Orleans arrived in some official capacity: as soldiers, customs officials, notaries, or government personnel, and most of those arrived without wives. This circumstance positioned the French to preserve their culture in Louisiana, beginning in the nursery after New Orleans French colonial women married Spanish men.

Spain replaced the French Superior Council with the Cabildo as the governing body, and law required notaries to record official acts in Spanish. In daily life, however, French prevailed as the spoken and written language of choice, as attested by memoirs and notarial documentation of family meetings. French culture continued in New Orleans, far more relaxed and sparkling, and far less religious than the usual Spanish colonial life across the New World.

Spain made its first notable mark in the Mississippi Valley when young Bernardo de Galvez arrived in 1777 as military governor. Like Unzaga before him and Miró and Gayoso de Lemos afterward, Galvez followed the Spanish pattern of marriage to French colonial women. Their children were *creoles*: that is, French and/or Spanish persons born in the New World. Galvez excited patriotism by expelling the English from Mobile, Pensacola, Baton Rouge, and Natchez in campaigns that are considered an essential part of the American Revolution. He did little, though, to develop the city and did not even have an engineer on his staff in 1778.

When a violent hurricane leveled much of the city in June 1779, rebuilding preserved the original French engineers' plan and the vernacular architectural customs. Spanish New Orleans remained French in character. Governor Galvez did build a home on Chartres street before he left to become viceroy of Mexico in 1785, but it burned in the fire of 1788, which occurred under the governorship of Miró.

Governor Miró reported in 1788: "In the afternoon of the 21st of March last, at one-thirty, the residence [site of **619 Chartres Street**] of the Army Treasurer Don Vincente José Nuñez caught on fire, reducing to ashes 850 buildings." During the city's reconstruction the Spanish Crown posted the Baron de Carondelet, a Flemish nobleman with holdings in Andalusia, Spain, to New Orleans as governor in 1791. Then on December 8, 1794, during his stewardship, a second disastrous fire started at what is now **534 Royal Street** (see p. 36). and spread upriver, destroying the southwest quadrant of the city. The new cathedral escaped and was dedicated two weeks after the fire.

Then in 1802, 40 years after European politics and the Seven Years' War had driven New Orleans into the hands of Spain, another set of politics, this time Napoleon's takeover of France, his defeat of Spain, and his war against England, thrust Louisiana into American hands. Napoleon sold what he had gained from Spain in the spoils of war, Louisiana, to Thomas Jefferson's United States.

Napoleon's thinking, ironically, mirrored that of his predecessor's, Louis XV, to spoil British plans. Napoleon arranged for Louisiana to be transferred from Spain to France on November 30, 1803, and on December 20 of the same year New Orleans and the remnants of the old French and Spanish colony became part of the United States. Jefferson appointed 26-year-old W. C. C. Claiborne, a Virginian active in Tennessee politics, as governor of the Mississippi Territory.

As a territory of the United States, New Orleans could have relinquished Spanish customs, but instead they reinstated French culture. As much of the Spanish population as could afford it left for Cuba. The language reverted to French both in official documents and in society.

Young Governor Claiborne, who didn't speak French, had some awkward times. His young wife, Eliza Lewis of Nashville, died of yellow fever September 20, 1806, the same day their baby succumbed to the disease and a year after Micajah Lewis, Claiborne's secretary and brother-in-law, was killed in a duel. Then Claiborne, like several Spanish governors before him, married a French creole and learned French. When Clarisse Duralde of Biscayan origin died, he married a Spanish creole, Suzanna Bosque, who luckily had a French mother, so she spoke the requisite French.

Ironically, the first clusters of immigrants to New Orleans in the Spanish colonial and then Federal period until 1820 were French-speaking peoples, most of them refugees from St. Domingue. They had a lasting influence on the French Quarter, by doubling its population and by building in their accustomed French colonial fashion. They more than doubled the numbers of *gens de couleur libre* or free people of color with up to 5000 such émigrés. These refugees also brought to New Orleans the forms of voodoo that had been prevalent on the island for generations.

French Quarter Architecture

With a few potent exceptions, the French Quarter today exhibits just about 80 years of architecture, from the 1780s Spanish colonial period to the 1850s. Yet these residential, commercial, and institutional buildings reflect almost 300 years of French, Spanish, and American history and building practice. The French Quarter packs into 80-odd squares a procession of buildings that reveals French colonial building method, Spanish colonial architectural customs, and the American influence on creole architecture.

1114 Chartres Street. The Ursuline Convent before its 1973-1978 restoration. Photograph by Betsy Swanson, 1970. The first Ursuline Convent was designed by Ignace François Broutin in 1727. The stairway was reused in the 1745-1750 reconstruction by Claude Joseph Villars Dubreuil, builder, planter and entrepreneur. The building is the sole survivor dating from the French colonial period, although the building traditions continued through the Spanish colonial period into the post-Purchase era.

The fires of 1788 and 1794 and subsequent demolitions have left just one French colonial structure, the oldest building in the Mississippi Valley, built in 1745, the Ursuline Convent at **1114 Chartres Street.** (see p. 27). This sole remnant is and always was the most important and largest of the French colonial buildings in the entire colony.

Madame John's Legacy, a private residence built in 1788 at **632 Dumaine Street,** (see p. 31). provides the key to Spanish colonial building attitudes in New Orleans. The Spaniards continued the French vernacular styles in residential and plantation complexes. The result is creole architec-

632 Dumaine Street. Madame John's Legacy, a Spanish colonial building that continues French colonial traditions, illustrated in a mid-nineteenth-century presentation. Watercolor by Boyd Cruise, 1940. Courtesy of the Historic New Orleans Collection. Now owned by the Louisiana State Museum, the house received its name when George Washington Cable set one of his late nineteenth-century short stories here.

ture. An American builder in the employ of a Spanish officer, used French colonial building methods and customs almost a century after the first Canadian and French settlers settled arrived at Bayou St. John.

At the other end of the time line, in 1850, the Baroness de Pontalba, Micaela Almonester, a creole of Spanish and French background, had Irish architects James Gallier and Henry Howard help her design 32 common-wall buildings in the American style, facing both sides of the old Place d'Armes that she, herself, renamed Jackson Square. This massive and creative effort to revitalize the French Quarter was conceived by a woman who had commissioned Ludovico Visconti to design a *hôtel particulier* in Paris in 1842 on Rue du Faubourg St-Honoré, now the official residence of the American Ambassador in Paris.

Both her projects, in Paris and New Orleans, were architecturally stunning. The Pontalba buildings were financially borderline and they did not achieve her projected goal, although she and her heirs collected rents from the 1850s until the 1920s. Nor did it stave off the development of American New Orleans outside the French Quarter. On the other hand, it gave New Orleans' French Quarter an order and coherence at its heart that makes the old Place d'Armes, lined by the Cathedral, Cabildo, Presbytère, and double rows of common-wall storehouses one of the finest urban places in the country.

Of course, other fine buildings went up after the Pontalba Buildings. Architect James Gallier, Jr.'s house at **1132 Royal Street** (see p. 40). was completed in 1857, the same year as his monumental French Opera House at Bourbon and Toulouse Streets. The opera house burned in 1919 while Tulane University owned it. By and large, though, the French Quarter was complete before the Civil War.

Why do we call the old city a French Quarter or Vieux Carré, Old Square, if it is all Spanish colonial or American except for the Ursuline Convent of 1745? First, French architecture, French taste, and French sentiment held fast during the Spanish years from 1768 when Spain activated its 1762 acquisition of the colony. Types and styles of architecture continued to be built in the old French colonial way even during the Spanish period and long after the Louisiana Purchase.

Refugees from Toussaint l'Overture's revolution in St. Domingue arrived in New Orleans in large numbers between 1792 and 1812, reinforcing French culture and architectural traditions. Among them were surveyors, including Joseph Pilié and the architect François Correjolles' family. By 1812 refugees from St. Domingue who arrived via Cuba were so many that Governor Claiborne ordered the troops to expel the boats trying to land—to no avail. The *émigrés* disembarked in the swamps and came through the marshes to the city, bringing with them their French ideas and building practices, thus prolonging French custom in New Orleans.

What had become creole, an acculturation of French and some Spanish building customs, continued after the Louisiana Purchase with a fresh influx of French taste brought directly from France. The French Revolution and the Terror, Napoleon's defeat, and the restoration of the French monarchy each brought waves of *émigrés*, including the architects Benjamin Buisson and Barthélémy Lafon. Others, including Claude Gurlie and Joseph Guillot and military engineers Jean Hyacinthe Laclotte and Major Arsène LaCarrière Latour were among a number of French architects, surveyors, and engineers who realized that New Orleans offered opportunity once the port and river traffic had been opened to the world. They knew, too, that they could find a place in the only French- speaking and culturally French port in the United States (the French city of Mobile had long succumbed to numbers of Anglo-Americans since Louis XV turned the city over to the British in 1763). In fact, New Orleans' most important architecture during the Spanish colonial years—the Cabildo, the Presbytère, and the Cathedral facing Jackson Square—was built in the late Baroque style by a French architect, Gilbert Guillemard, but financed by a Spanish colonial philanthropist, Señor Don Andrés Almonester y Roxas, a native of Andalusia, Spain who amassed a fortune in New Orleans real estate.

After 1835 the Greek Revival American taste conquered the front elevations of French Quarter architecture. Creole customs continued, however, centered on the rear elevations, service buildings, kitchens, and

courtyards. Both business and residences persisted in having service buildings and wings around an open court which served as outdoor living and
dining room. Exterior stairways rose beneath wide rear galleries or loggias.
Cabinets or small storage and service rooms, perhaps nurseries, perched at
each end of rear galleries in the French manner. French-style transoms and
elliptical openings across loggias on the rear elevation survived as the-
matic elements for decades. Often, even if a front elevation had double-
hung American-style windows with weights, rear elevations were
penetrated by casement openings and wide, lowered arches.

　　Buildings in the French Quarter continued to be set at the *banquette* or
sidewalk and to have front *abat vents* or overhangs held by iron bearers or
by decorative S-curve wrought iron brackets, made by local ironworkers or
shipped from Cadiz. Mixed residential and commercial use prevailed, with
elegant residences above first-floor commercials, or expensive creole
houses beside commercial buildings in the seventeenth- and eighteenth-
century manner of Paris and La Rochelle.

French Colonial Period Architecture: 1718–1762

Although it was built during the Spanish colonial period in 1788, Madame
John's Legacy addresses many French colonial building customs.
Colombage or timber framing was filled with brick-between-posts, called
briqueté entre poteaux. In some variations, brickbats were used between
the posts, or *bousillage*, mud-and-moss fill. Examples of each can be found
throughout the French Quarter, as the construction was used up to the
mid-nineteenth century.

　　The early French colonials used wide galleries covered by the roof
framing, extending from the front and rear of the buildings. This resulted
in the characteristic double-pitch hip roof, called West Indian, a misnomer
because it came directly to New Orleans with the French king's engineer in
the 1730s. The French roof was more effective against rain than the flat
terrace roofs the Spanish persisted in using.

　　These wide galleries across the front and rear elevation and sometimes around the house, covered by a hip roof, also characterized houses
along the St. Laurence River in New France. One can be seen at
Beauport, the Canadian ancestral home of Juchereau de St. Denis, who
left New France to come to Louisiana in the 1690s. In Canada the covered
galleries made possible storage of wood and other necessities under a
covered roof during the snowy season, and the steep hip roof collected
little snow.

　　The early French émigrés and subsequent colonials avoided construction of interior halls or inside stairwells. They used the galleries as halls
and stair-halls. Each room had access to a gallery or the outside by means
of casement openings, and transoms were used from the 1730s, as were
batten shutters.

By 1730 the French had learned the need to plaster the local soft river-sand brick manufactured by the *briquetèrie* of the Company of the Indies on Bayou Road from 1725, when it opened. The creoles developed the idea that buildings are vulgar if the brick is left exposed.

Settlers used flat tiles for roofs and round tiles for those of more pitch as soon as a *faiencèrie* or tilery produced them along Bayou Road in the 1730s. Kitchens often had tile for fire prevention even if the master house was covered in cypress shingles. Flat green tiles were imported from Nantes and Le Havre, but these have all disappeared.

The raised basement, like that at Madame John's Legacy, was used as early as 1730 in country houses outside the city. It became endemic for houses beyond the city walls, and a few appeared within the French Quarter, especially along the Rue de Levée, now Decatur Street, facing the river. These have been removed, symbolized today by the one remainder, Madame John's Legacy at **632 Dumaine Street**. (see p.31).

Spanish Colonial Period Architecture: 1763–1802

Spanish proprietorship brought few changes in building styles, but the economy improved and the squares filled with conservative one or one-and-one-half and two-story flat-fronted buildings. They had front overhangs, balconies, or even covered galleries and were built at the *banquette*. A wide band of stucco often outlined building doors and windows. A proportionately wider projecting band bordered the outer edges of the building itself, creating a wide cornice-like band that shows below the *abat vent* (overhang) or parapet and articulates the building edges.

French-speaking exiles from St. Domingue popularized the four-room, hall-less, one to one-and-one-half-story dormered creole cottage. Émigré builders and architects, including Louis Pilié and others as yet unrecognized, many of them *personnes de couleur libre*, built them, block after block, in just two or three variations. Gable ends prevailed except at corners, where there was a hipped end to the roof. Most had double dormers, front and rear. Over the *banquette* all had an *abat vent* or overhang.

These creole cottages were brick, *briqueté entre poteaux*, even plastered *bousillage*. Moreau de St. Mery described them as they appeared in St. Domingue in his book **Partie Française de Saint Domingue.** Spanish islands of the Caribbean and the old sections of Spanish colonial towns of Central and South America also abound with such inexpensive housing appearing in multiples.

These four-room creole cottages rest low, at the *banquette*, with four casement openings, the earlier ones having full arches or segmental arches and transoms. One door and one window access each of the front two rooms. A cottage has two chimneys, one to serve the back-to-back fireplaces of the two front rooms and the other for the two rear rooms. If the chimneys are set at the gabled ends, they are built in, so that the chimney breast affords a base for a wraparound or apron mantel with a fancy overmantel.

A *cabinet* gallery crosses the rear elevation. This central gallery with small rooms, or *cabinets*, at each end is covered by the roof of the house. Often the gallery serves as a loggia, with stairs to the dormers. Usually detached, galleried service buildings of two stories line the sides of the lot and cross the rear. The courtyard originally was paved in square tiles or bricks, and there was a *potager* or kitchen garden designed in a *par terre*.

The late Spanish period brought hundreds of new French Quarter houses after the great fires of 1788 and 1794. New fire regulations specified tile roofs for all. Only about three examples of Spanish tiled roofs remain in creole New Orleans because they were covered over with hip roofs to minimize leaks in the second rainiest U.S. city.

The creole townhouse, used also as a storehouse, or four-bay two-story building with a balcony at the second level, became a vernacular form. Those dating from Spanish colonial times had a flat roof, used for a patio as illustrated by architect Benjamin Latrobe. These townhouses often have four evenly spaced arched openings at the first level, with square-headed openings above. Those that adhere more closely to the French colonial style have segmental arched openings with French doors throughout.

The *porte cochère* house, appearing from the 1780s until about 1840, features a carriageway accessed through a wide, arched opening placed to one side of the front elevation or sometimes in the center. Above the carriage opening and the regular-sized arched or square-headed openings crossing the front elevation are balconies or sometimes galleries with posts supporting an overhang. Spanish colonial and post-Purchase architecture into the transitional period featured wrought iron balconies until cast iron became available for fancy covered galleries by 1850.

Architects today should observe how builders incorporated access and storage for vehicles into the building design to provide the distinctive aesthetic of the *porte cochère* house. The *porte cochère* leads through a vaulted corridor paved in flagstones to the courtyard, with a service wing bordering one side and a high wall or another service wing along the other side. Usually, a galleried building, kitchen, or stable crosses the back of the courtyard.

Entresol storehouses began to be built by the 1780s. Such masonry buildings are commercial below, residential above. The secret of the design is the *entresol*, the area for storage between the commercial first level and the residential second level. The *entresol* storage area is hidden behind transoms or upper sections of the arched openings. *Entresol* buildings can be identified by their elongated and attenuated first floors with a wrought iron balcony above.

Since all French and Spanish colonial houses are oriented toward the rear, the building philosophy contrasts with English or American traditions. Just as exposed bricks were unacceptable to French or Spanish colonials, so were ostentatious entrances or front gardens. French and Spanish colonial proportions are restrained, as is any ornamentation, and the facade is simple and flat. The only adornment may be a graceful expanse of local wrought iron work in balcony supports, railings, and hardware, perhaps by local smith Marcelino Hernandez. Individuality was within, where family life proceeded in its secluded fashion. Anonymity codified the street facade and created a sense of mystery.

Post-Purchase Period Architecture: 1803–1820

Building customs in the early post–Louisiana Purchase years continued, with the same French, creole, and St. Dominguan architects and builders under contract. A few classical forms derived from contemporary European neoclassicism appeared with the newly arrived French architects. These gave a more delicate character to forms than had first been used in the post-1788 fire replacements. Slender pillars began to articulate facades, dormers took on an attenuated look, and arches became taller and narrower, unframed punctuations in broad expanses of unadorned wall surface, always plastered over soft brick. More delicate, curved muntins divided the lights of the transoms above French doors.

The wide, slightly projecting stucco bands that outlined the Spanish Colonial buildings and fenestration fit well with the new federal gracefulness. These bands evolved into narrow, flat pilasters and stucco cornices, as seen at the upper story of such buildings as **413 Royal Street** (Dujarreau–Rouquette house, built in 1808), **541 Royal Street** at Toulouse Street (Vincent Nolte house, built in 1819; (see p. 37),* and **718 St. Peter Street** (Garnier house, built in 1818; (see p. 43).

North American and British-born architects, including Benjamin Henry Latrobe and William Brand, arrived in the early Purchase Period to introduce the American Federal style into the tapestry of French and Spanish architecture. Latrobe's 1820 building at **401 Royal Street,** (Manheim Galleries; (see p. 34) is an example. The English and American architects and builders imported red brick from Philadelphia or hard brick from Baltimore. They introduced white trim, and louvered shutters replaced the old batten ones, although they were still painted "Paris green." Americans contributed center halls, double parlors, and double-hung windows; they dared to fill the streets with three-bay, side-hall townhouses, even in the French Quarter.

Transitional Period Architecture: 1820–1835

1820 to 1835 brought American traditions in architecture that infiltrated the older colonial and post-Purchase types and styles. Even French architects Gurlie and Guillot, who had worked together in the city since 1795,

---

*In the sections on Creole New Orleans and American New Orleans, when a more detailed description of a specific location appears elsewhere in the book, the page number of that description is noted.

began using hard red brick from Philadelphia and Baltimore, and they left them exposed. During this golden age for French immigrant architects such as the DePouilly brothers, who arrived in 1833, clients with money commissioned sophisticated designs and wealth began to show from the street in the English fashion.

Architect François Correjolles, whose family came from St. Domingue, designed the Le Charpentier–Beauregard house at **1113 Chartres Street** (see p. 27) in 1836. He introduced new American ideas, such as the central hall, but adhered to creole practices with interior forms and on the rear elevation, with a *cabinet* gallery, detached outbuildings, and rear court.

By the 1820s a generation of New Orleans-born *personnes de couleur libre* had grown up to take their place as builders in the pageant of architectural development in creole New Orleans. Prominent among these was Jean-Louis Dolliole, *homme de couleur libre*, born in 1779, a second-generation builder. His father, Louis Dolliole, was a French builder from La Sène en Provence who had immigrated to New Orleans, where he was active in the industry. Myrtil Courcelle, *homme de couleur libre*, joined Achille Courcelle, his white relative, in the building business in the 1830s. Etiénne Cordeviolle, *homme de couleur libre*, born in New Orleans in 1806, was an active builder in the city with his father, Estebán Cordeviola, an immigrant from Italy to Spanish colonial New Orleans.

American Greek Revival Period Architecture: 1835–1850

New Orleans became American politically in 1803. By 1835 Americans prevailed in numbers and in buildings under contract. After 1835, Greek Revival became the standard vocabulary for both French- and American-oriented New Orleans. Although the style is universal, in New Orleans differences are detected between the Anglo-American and the creole or French interpretation of it. James Harrison Dakin and James Gallier, Sr.

Architect of the Arsenal, James Dakin, declared bankruptcy in 1841, as had Gallier earlier in London. His reversals were caused by the Panic of 1837, the death by yellow fever of major clients, and disastrous fires in Mobile that destroyed much of his work. The Louisiana State Capitol begun in 1847, was his last and major commission in Louisiana, in the "castellated style rather than the 'Grecian or Roman Order' because no style . . . can be employed with so little cost." Dakin died in Baton Rouge on May 13, 1852 at the age of 46. His death notices referred to him as a colonel because of his service in the Mexican War, and he received Masonic honors and ceremonies.

expressed the Anglo-American taste, and the French taste is seen in the works of the DePouilly brothers, Claude Gurlie, and Joseph Guillot.

Newly rich citizens, whether American, French, or Spanish in background, demanded that homes and churches reflect their success. This trend coincided perfectly with the Greek Revival style of architecture and ornamentation that raged across the country, landing in the French Quarter with the arrival of James Gallier, Sr. and William Brand.

French Quarter property owners of all backgrounds succumbed to the new style throughout the 1840s. The 1850s saw renovation and additions in the new style, especially of cast iron galleries, which were applied to older buildings. By the end of the 1850s it was over. The architectural development of the French Quarter was complete. Creoles of wealth and affluence looked to the newly cut-through Esplanade Avenue. Americans and British-born citizens who remained in the French Quarter usually had creole connections in business or family, including John Slidell, Judah P. Benjamin, Zachary Taylor's sons and nephews, Henry Clay's brother John, and architect James Gallier, Jr. Others moved upriver to the new American suburbs.

Touring the French Quarter

You may guide your own walking tour, with frequent stops at the numerous coffee houses, restaurants, and bars. Antique shops in the old buildings have enormous inventories, well selected by dealers, some of whom represent the fourth generation on Royal street.

Visit the long-established Royal Street shops, such as Rothschild's, on Royal Street since 1933, at **241 and 321 Royal Street;** Royal Antiques, since 1899 **(307–309 Royal);** Keil's **(325 Royal Street);** Henry Stern's, who brought English antiques to Uptown New Orleans over 65 years ago **(329–331 Royal Street);** Waldhorne's **(343 Royal Street);** Moss Antiques, affiliated with Keil's **(411 Royal Street);** and Rau's **(630 Royal Street),** with the elder Mr. Rau presiding over the oldest antique store specializing in American antiques—all offering more aesthetic pleasures than you would have thought possible in antique furniture, decorative arts, and jewelry. At **407 Royal Street** behind a discreet facade, the internationally recognized Raymond H. Weill Company has offered rare postage stamps since 1932.

Chartres Street has the reputation for less expensive antiques, where a "sleeper" might be discovered among the casually displayed array of antiques. Don't miss Whisnant's and Zula Frick's Button Shop, among many others. Chartres Street and the side streets have shops worth a careful visit.

I start with breakfast at Croissant d'Or at **617 Ursulines Street** or La Madeleine on Jackson Square at Chartres Street. If you are energetic enough to enjoy the French Market at dawn, go to Fiorella's, where the market vendors eat a hearty breakfast at **45 French Market Place.** Take a break later for some pralines at The Old Time Praline Shop at **627 Royal Street,** the eighteenth-century Antoine Cavelier house; pass to the back to see the courtyard of one of the two oldest buildings on Royal Street. Or try Italian granita at Angelo Brocato's in the Lower Pontalba at **537 St. Ann Street.**

If you proceed on the Bourbon and Burgundy Street sections of your tour after a good po–boy or muffuletta, you will probably hear jazz music emanating from any number of the historic buildings after two o'clock in the afternoon. Traditional restaurants and bars are described on pages 199-204.

For the focus a professional can give, take a guided tour of the French Quarter led by the Friends of the Cabildo. Go to the Presbytère at Jackson Square to register. Jean Lafitte National Park also offers French Quarter tours from their headquarters in the French Quarter.

Bourbon Street

238 Bourbon Street

Absinthe House. This 1806 post-Purchase storehouse, built for the 1806 purchasers of the lot Pedro Font and Francisco Juncadella, natives of Cataluña, charac- terizes the *entresol* style with its high first story. The first-level commercial section with its arched openings is elevated to contain an *entresol* or intermediate ser- vice floor lighted by the fanlight transoms of the ground floor. The second, shorter level, remains residential. The originally

238 Bourbon Street. Absinthe House, 1806. Etching by William Woodward, ca. 1934. Courtesy of the Southeastern Architectural Archive, Tulane University Library. The *entresol* is the storage space behind the glazed arches above the door. The building type began to appear in the late Spanish colonial period and continued in the early post-Purchase years.

tiled, nearly flat, terraced roof with a ter-race is typical of the Spanish colonial period and is a holdover, as are the wrought iron balcony and its supporting consoles.

In 1866 the Juncadella heirs had returned to France, and their local rela-tives and agents, Jacinto and P. O. Aleix, opened a coffeehouse here, employing Cayetano Ferrér, from Barcelona, as chief bartender. In 1874 Ferrér took over the lease and called it the "Absinthe Room," and when the Ferrér sons ran it from 1890, they called it "The Old Absinthe House." The marble bar was moved to another site during Prohibition.

327 Bourbon Street

St. Martin–Benjamin house. This three-story American-style side-hall town-house was built for Auguste St. Martin around 1835. His daughter Natalie mar-ried Judah P. Benjamin, who came to New Orleans as a young lawyer, went into business with John Slidell, became U.S. senator and later served in the Confederate cabinet. Afterward he be-came king's counsel to Queen Victoria and in 1884 died in Paris. Note the bow–and–arrow design of the cast iron balcony. A bracketed cornice crowns a decorative frieze.

409 Bourbon Street

Jean Louis Isnard, a refugee from St. Domingue, had the three-bay creole-style house built about 1801. The design is attributed to Frenchman Barthélémy Lafon. Casement openings below seg-mental arched transoms characterize the style. Although this building has been renovated, the overall proportions, with segmental arched transoms above French doors, flat surfaces, and con-servative appearance, reflect its creole heritage.

In 1809 the Louisiana Lodge No. l, F&AM, leased the building and Edward Livingston, former mayor of New York City, was the first Worshipful Master.

Livingston became U.S. senator from Louisiana and Secretary of State from 1831 to 1833. His brother Robert R. Livingston was minister to France and negotiated the Louisiana Purchase with James Monroe.

522 Bourbon Street

The Jacques-Philippe Meffre-Rouzan house, designed by Irish architect James Gallier, Sr., probably dates from 1838–1840, soon after Meffre-Rouzan bought the lot in 1838 from the notary Marc Lafitte. The granite-faced townhouse, in English Regency style, recalls James Gallier, Sr.'s years in the Grosvenor estate, London, where he designed and built. The rusticated first level and the sculptural pediments are high style for New Orleans. Up to 1884 it was the townhouse of Meffre-Rouzan, who had plantations in East Baton Rouge Parish. He and his brother Antoine-Julien were New Orleans creoles, sons of an *émigré* from Chateau Roux, France, and Rose Felicité Rouzan of New Orleans.

711 Bourbon Street

Built for Dr. Joseph Adolphe Tricou, this house was designed in 1832, during the Transitional period, by French architects Gurlie and Guillot. A central, creole-style *porte cochère* has two full–length arched openings on each side. These and the dormer windows, decorated wood cornice, wrought iron balcony, and *garde de frise* are characteristic cre-ole amenities of this period. The exten-sive galleried service wing still has its wrought iron bearers. A traditional cre-ole elliptical arch and a tightly curving stairway are notable.

941 Bourbon Street

Lafitte's Blacksmith Shop. This hip-roof creole cottage reveals its *briqueté entre poteaux* construction, which should be plastered over. The cottage is almost square and had been, like all creole cot-tages, divided into four rooms, each

941 Bourbon Street. Jean Lafitte's blacksmith shop. Watercolor showing a mid-nineteenth century presentation by Boyd Cruise, 1940. Courtesy of the Historic New Orleans Collection. The building's association with the pirate and hero of the Battle of New Orleans, Jean Lafitte, may be literary. However, the corner creole store illustrates the influence of the French colonial refugees from St. Domingue on New Orleans architecture toward the end of the 18th century.

having two French doors to the exterior, patio, or street. The date is unknown, but this type of construction was used from 1730 until 1845. The building plan became popular after 1782. *National Historic Landmark.*

1132 Bourbon Street

Mme. Julie Duralde, the widow of John Clay, Henry Clay's brother, had this American-style Greek Revival side–hall townhouse built sometime after her 1835 purchase of the property and owned it until her death in 1861. The diamond–pattern second–level balcony railing (the iron cresting on the overhang was added) is a delicate feature on this solid, Greek Revival house. Photographer Frances Benjamin Johnston lived here from 1940 until her death in 1952. Johnston, a Grafton, West Virginia native, received a Carnegie Foundation grant to photograph southern architecture. These photographs are now in the Library of Congress. *Orleans Parish Landmark.*

Burgundy Street

901 Burgundy Street.

This corner building is an example of eighteenth century house moving. A 1781 contract between builder Mauricio Milon and house owner Gabriel Peyroux, specifies that the builder was to preserve every nail, brick, and piece of wood in the move from Peyroux's plantation on Bayou Road to this site, owned by Madame Gabriel Peyroux, Suzanna Caue, since her father had bought the square in 1754. The Bayou Road house, standing when Peyroux bought the plantation in the 1770s, was of *colombage* construction, and the spaces between the framing were filled with mud and moss, a process called *bousillage.* It was altered in the 1781 move to Burgundy Street. The contract specified that it was to be covered with wooden boards and lifted on two–and-one–half–foot blocks. Peyroux declared that this rebuilding was worthless. A court hearing ruled that the contractor

Milon had to reimburse Peyroux. The mud and moss was replaced with bricks and the board covering incorrectly removed. When the house was on Bayou Road a gallery surrounded the building, covered by a hip roof, and it was raised off the ground on brick piers or columns.

933, 935, and 939 Burgundy Street

Marie Gabrielle Eugenie Peyroux, widow of Louis Lanoix and daughter of the one-time owners of this entire square, had these three once-identical row houses built about 1830 as investment rental property. Simple flat fronts, each with discreet balcony rails and segmental openings in one pedimented, front dormer at each house, are clues to the creole taste. Gable ends, delicate proportions, and the second–level casement openings with extravagant transoms indicate the Transitional period date. *Orleans Parish Landmark.*

1218 Burgundy Street

The José Antonio La Rionda house, a typical double creole cottage built in 1810 of plastered brick, soon after the property was purchased from Louis Dufilho, exhibits how Spanish colonial simplicity extended into the post-Purchase period. Batten shutters, *abat vent,* and position low on the banquette remained constant. Until you see the rear of the lot with pitched roof and two-story service buildings, it is hard to imagine how small, four-room houses such as this could take double occupancy. Some were used as single houses, although identical in outward appearance. HABS drawings show the peg frame roof, sidewalk overhang, or *abat vent* with its horizontal iron supports. When La Rionda sold the house to Jeanne Berquin Rousset in 1812, it was described as "a new brick house of four rooms, rear gallery with two *cabinets* and cellar, roofed in tile."

Chartres Street

400 Chartres Street at Conti Street

D'Estrehan–Perrilliat house. The first floor arches and the second–level wrought iron balcony with the owner's monogram are typical of the creole house built well into the Transitional period until at least 1835. This two-family house was erected in 1811 for Jean Noel d'Estrehan by William Brand, American architect-builder. D'Estrehan had bought the lot from Pierre Dulcide Barran in March 1802. In the creole fashion the dwelling features a rear–arcaded *loggia* off the courtyard containing two fine stairways. D'Estrehan's widow, Mme. Celeste Robin de Logny, sold the house to François Marie Perrilliat in 1825 for $24,000. Perrilliat added the wrought iron balcony with its initials.

440 Chartres Street

Maspero's Exchange, an *entresol* house, typifies the Spanish colonial style of the 1790s. The first–floor–high arches have fanlights covered by the usual iron grills. Jean Paillet bought the lot and the ruins of a house from Narciso Alva in June 1788 soon after the citywide fire and had this storehouse and the narrow building adjoining it on Chartres Street built. The buildings remained in his family until 1878. The building is known, however, as La Bourse de Maspero or "Maspero's Exchange," after the coffeehouse and exchange of the Maspero family, Paillet's tenants.

500 Chartres Street at St. Louis Street

Mayor Nicholas Girod House (Napoleon House). Frenchman Jean Hyacinthe Laclotte of Bordeaux probably designed this storehouse soon after 1814, when Mayor Nicholas Girod inherited the property and the two-story house facing St. Louis built in 1798 from his brother Claude. The three-story corner house with its belvedere, where Girod lived for about 30 years, is one of the best extant examples of the continuing French influ-

Portrait of Emma and Olivia Olivier and Zulime Maspero. By J.-B. Ange Tessier, 1851. Courtesy of the Historic New Orleans Collection. This portrait of three young creole women in their mid-Victorian afternoon gowns sitting in front of a backdrop of lush greenery romanticizes the new American city in its most affluent decade, before the Civil War. Zulime Maspero is a member of the family who owned Maspero's Exchange on Chartres Street, where slave trading took place.

ence in the architecture of post-Purchase New Orleans. Hyacinthe Laclotte, active in New Orleans from 1806 to 1815 had studied at the School of Fine Arts in Paris. The design, with its rounded corner where the corner pilasters don't quite meet, is a sophisticated touch. The dormers continue French tradition in their style, but the neat projecting plastered brick outlines of the windows and doors and the matching bands outlining the facades are a Spanish colonial custom. The cathedral–pattern wrought iron balcony and the scroll supports are the usual delicate work of the period. Walk through to the courtyard to see the curving stair and *loggia*.

514 Chartres Street

Louis J. Dufilho's pharmacy was built in 1837 by architect and occasional builder J. N. B. DePouilly across from the St. Louis Hotel he also designed. The four arched openings across the front of the three-story *porte cochère* storehouse are strongly outlined with handsome moldings, giving an arcade effect; they recall Parisian buildings along the Rue de Rivoli. The building's French character suited Dufilho, who, though his name is Portuguese, was thoroughly creole. Dufilho is credited with being the first licensed pharmacist in the United States.

617 Chartres Street

Bartolomeo Bosque's Spanish colonial urban residence, built in 1795, is the third building on the site. He lived here with his wife, Felicité Fanguy, a French creole of New Orleans whom he had married in 1792. Their daughter Suzette became the third wife of Governor W. C. C. Claiborne. Governor Bernardo Galvez and his creole bride, Feliciana de St. Maxent d'Estrehan, had owned a house on the property between 1781, when the British surrendered Pensacola to Galvez, and 1784, when Galvez was sent as viceroy to Mexico, where he died at 39. The Galvez house, along with 850 other buildings, burned in the fire of 1788 when Vincent Nuñez, army treasurer, lived there. The house burned again in 1794 during its reconstruction. Subsequent owner Joseph Xavier Delfau de Pontalba, a creole, sold a partly reconstructed, fire-damaged house to Bartolomeo Bosque, who again rebuilt the house in 1795 along the old colonial lines. Some attribute the design to Barthélémy Lafon, city surveyor and architect at the time.

The main building with its *porte cochère* measures 36 by 52 feet. The Spanish colonial wrought iron balcony, the curved wrought iron balcony sup-

Born in 1804 in Chatel-Censoir Sur Yonne, Jacques Nicholas Bussière DePouilly studied at l'Ecole des Beaux-Arts in Paris, bringing a solid architectural and engineering education with him to New Orleans when he arrived in 1833 with his wife, Laurant Drigny, and infant daughter. His brother, Joseph Isidore, joined him and the two worked together.

DePouilly's chief work in the French Quarter, the St. Louis Hotel, was demolished in the early twentieth century, as was the Citizen's Bank. St. Augustin's Church (1841–1842), Notre Dame Des Victoires, adjacent to the Ursuline Convent on Chartres, and his alterations to St. Louis Cathedral testify to his talent, as does the 1837 master design for Exchange Passage. He also designed a number of notable tombs in St. Louis Cemetery No. 2 for private families and for Benevolent Societies, such as the Plauché, Peniston-Duplantier, Bouligny, and Caballero family tombs and that of the Iberia Society. Over 200 drawings by DePouilly of New Orleans buildings have been preserved in the New Orleans Notarial Archives, where they were filed after sheriff's sales of the depicted property. In fact, he taught drawing "as applied to buildings, machinery, surveying with landscape and perspective" at his son-in-law's Audubon College on the corner of Dumaine and Burgundy Streets. He died in 1875 and is buried with his wife and brother in a small wall vault in St. Louis Cemetery No. 2.

ports, and the transoms with diamond–pattern muntins are notable. The carriageway molding is a Greek Revival addition. To the rear is a double *loggia* with an elliptical second–level opening above the *porte cochère*. A two-story wing extends along the property line on one side and housed servants, laundry facilities, and the kitchen.

Cabildo, St. Louis Cathedral, and Presbytère at Jackson Square

"Cabildo" signifies the Spanish governing body, and the Spanish Cabildo is their Municipal Hall; the Presbytère is the French version of a Casa Curial, offices and residence for Roman Catholic clergy. The first public buildings of a monumental character in the entire Louisiana Purchase region, this architectural ensemble was conceived by architect Gilberto Guillemard for patron Andrés Almonester y Roxas (see p. 11).

The group suggests Spanish colonial inspiration, if not because of the architect, perhaps at the insistence of Almonester, who paid for them. As architectural historian Talbot Hamlin has noted, the fronts of the Cabildo and Presbytère recall the facade of the second Government House in Oaxaca, Mexico, built around 1780. The covered arcade is common to any number of late-baroque–inspired Spanish colonial schemes for public buildings. Guillemard's cathedral, altered by Henry S. Boneval Latrobe's central tower and in the 1840s by DePouilly's extensive renovation, still recalls colonial churches of Mexico and South America, with its superimposed coupled columns and the original low, wide proportions.

The Presbytère, begun first, was not completed until 1813. The three buildings, as originally built, illustrate the introduction to New Orleans of classical forms, such as engaged columns and pilasters, that begin to appear on private houses of the period, such as the original two-story part of the Girod house on St. Louis Street near the corner of Chartres and St. Louis Streets.

The Cabildo incorporates some of the 1750 Corps de Garde designed by French architect Bernard de Verges, but Guillemard's aesthetic is the monumental double arcade system, with the central pediment breaking a deep parapet. A subsequent 1848 deep mansard roof replacing the flat tile terrace roof with its parapet vies for attention with this original design. The Presbytère has received the same treatment. Guillemard's Spanish colonial Cabildo, ironically, was finished just in time for the historic Louisiana Transfer in 1803, and it became the American City Hall.

Mayor Denis Prieur paid the wardens of the Cathedral $10,500 in 1831 for the land behind the Presbytère, a plot 40 by 122 feet for Ruelle d'Orleans Nord. At that time the Cathedral Garden was established. In 1853 Mayor A. D. Crossman paid the wardens of St. Louis Cathedral $55,000 for the Presbytère. Today, both the Cabildo and the Presbytère are part of the Louisiana State Museum complex, along with the Arsenal, Jackson House, the Lower Pontalba, Madame John's Legacy, and the U.S. Mint, a National Landmark complex.

Pontalba Buildings on Jackson Square

By the mid-nineteenth century, the old houses and shops, built after 1768, that Micaela Almonester, Baroness Pontalba, had inherited from her Spanish colonial father along each side of the Place d'Armes were in shoddy condition. She razed them to pursue her scheme for improving the French Quarter after DePouilly had re-worked Guillemard's Cathedral, which her father had financed.

In 1849 she contacted James Gallier Sr., who designed 16 row houses on each side of the Place d'Armes, the name to which it had reverted after the departure of the Spanish. In traditional creole fashion each row house was to have a store on the ground floor with a dwelling above, and a rear service wing bordering a small courtyard.

Historian Talbot Hamlin insisted on attributing the impressive columned galleried houses designed or built by Dakin and his contemporaries to the ego of the slave owners who lived in them. To the contrary, memoirs, building contracts, and observation combine to suggest that non-slave–holding architects and builders trying to make money catapulted the Greek Revival craze onto the owners, who had neither education nor aesthetics to select for themselves. When owners imposed their will, it was usually to copy a building down the street or to build a house like that of a neighbor.

The imposing plantation houses and urban mansions of the Golden Age of Louisiana, 1840–1855, paralleled the height in the numbers of slaves in Louisiana and New Orleans. They also paralleled the height in numbers of ships at the docks as well as steamboat convenience and speed. However, the house plans and their grandiose facades with columns and galleries and full entablatures were most often gleaned from books that were ordered from the north by architects and builders. The residents who supplied the money made it from sugar or cotton or from the numerous commercial enterprises that were by products of the agricultural system. The big Greek Revival mansions along the Esplanade behind the French Quarter illustrated the phenomenon.

Finally, decorative detail was the primary thrust for builders in the Greek Revival style. Front and rear galleries extended across elevations at both levels, enhanced by lavish use of columns and wide entablatures, with similar decoration in the double parlors, with their classically inspired window and door cornices, moldings and plaster or cast iron ceiling medallions and high–relief baseboards. From 1850, decorative cast iron galleries, colonettes, and crestings were applied to earlier buildings to provide a decorative surface, classically inspired.

The building site, and its relation to outbuildings, and the house plan, its numbers of rooms and their proportions, were similar whether built before slaves were available or after by both non-slave owners and by slave holders.

Hers constitute the last of the great row houses for investment purposes to go up in the French Quarter. The Baroness was difficult to work for and Henry Howard replaced James Gallier as architect, but she herself came from Paris to oversee the work and to make on–site alterations. Cast iron galleries were incorporated, probably for the first time in New Orleans, in place of the simpler wrought iron balconies of earlier Greek Revival buildings. Following the American Greek Revival style, she selected heavy granite columns to support the first level and hard Philadelphia bricks as building material.

In her sweeping style, the heiress determined to rework the old square, which she redesigned in its present pattern with the cast iron fence erected around it. In 1856 she ordered Clark Mill's equestrian statue of the hero of the Battle of New Orleans, Andrew Jackson, to adorn its center.

1021 Chartres Street

Major General Pierre Denis de la Ronde had this creole–style *porte cochère* house built around 1807.The openings and edges to the facade have Spanish colonial–style banding of plastered brick.

Subsequently, his St. Bernard Parish plantation became the site of an engagement of the Battle of New Orleans against the British on January 8, 1815. He maintained this townhouse until his death in 1825, leaving it to his daughter and son-in-law, Gabriel Villere. *Orleans Parish Landmark.*

1113 Chartres Street

Beauregard-Keyes House and Gardens. Carpenter-builder James Lam-bert built the center–hall house that architect François Correjolles (d. 1864) designed in 1826 for the Joseph Le Charpentier family in the Transitional style with both creole and American traditions. Le Charpentier, an auctioneer, purchased the lot from the Ursuline nuns in 1825, when they abandoned their old convent and sold their adjoining property to finance a new convent downriver (now covered over by the Industrial Canal). The American-style entrance with sidelights and overlight is flanked on each side by a pair of transomed casement openings that once had batten shutters panelled on the inside. The front gallery does not run across the facade but projects to cover three bays, having a classic pedimented Tuscan portico of four columns. An exterior stairway, originally planned with a wood railing, features iron railings and granite gate posts. The traditional creole raised basement lends itself to the Palladian motifs here.

The Le Charpentiers were grandparents to chess player Paul Morphy, who grew up nearby at **417 Royal Street** (Brennan's; see p. 34). Frances Parkinson Keyes set several of her historical novels in the French Quarter, and Richard Koch and Samuel Wilson Jr., architects, restored this house for her in 1945 and 1953. She called it the Beauregard house after General Pierre Gustave Toutant Beauregard, who rented rooms here as a widower after the Civil War. Her bequest launched the house as a museum.

Architect James Gallier, Sr. came to New Orleans in 1832 in the company of Charles Dakin after working as carpenter on Mountjoy Square in Dublin; on the Grosvenor estate in London, where he rose to the position of architect; and for the Town and Davis firm in New York. He spent a season in Mobile where he designed Barton Academy and worked with Charles Dakin, perhaps on Christ Episcopal Church. The two, oddly, were waiting out the yellow fever season in Mobile, where it ran as rampant as in New Orleans. He immediately associated himself in New Orleans with the leading Irish citizens, some of them Protestants, like Gallier, or Anglo-Irish who had come to the city early in the post-Louisiana-Purchase years. Gallier was a fine designer, and the drawings presented to his clients for consideration were outstanding (preserved in the Labrot Collection, Southeastern Architectural Archive, Tulane University Library and at the Historic New Orleans Collections).

Gallier learned, however, that the real money was in the building industry, so he set up a building yard in the American sector. He met great financial success in New Orleans, and after 1850 more or less retired from active practice to travel with his new wife throughout Europe. Before his death in 1866 in a steamboat accident Gallier had trained his only son to succeed him. Tragically, this son died two years later, leaving a widow and four young daughters.

1114 Chartres Street (see p. 9)

The Ursuline Convent, 1745–1750, designed by Ignace François Broutin and built by Claude Joseph Villars Dubreuil, responsible for the first levees in the city, is the only remaining French colonial building in New Orleans and the earliest in the Mississippi Valley. The second Ursulines convent on the site, this one incorporates the earlier stairway from a 1727 convent that collapsed due to structural problems.

The Ursuline nuns were the most affluent and influential force in the city after their arrival in 1727. Their monumental convent illustrates their acumen, as does the large amount of land they owned in the city, laid out in *par terre* gardens according to early plans.

The design of the convent as well as that of the nearby French barracks, now demolished, derives from Belidor's La Science des Ingenieurs (Paris, 1729). Restoration revealed original casement door, window and dormer details, shutters, transoms, and hardware to be of the same type used through the decades by both French and colonial craftsman even as late as the 1820s, almost a century later. Architectural traditions exemplified in Broutin's convent evolved as characterizing elements of the vernacular creole architecture.

In 1846 J. N. B. DePouilly designed Notre Dame des Victoires Church. The fine wood ceiling with its painting was discovered after a hurricane damaged a later replacement that covered the original.

1133 Chartres Street

Joseph Soniat DuFossat house. François Boisdoré, *personne de couleur libre*, designed this as a two–and– one–half-story creole townhouse with a central *porte cochère* in 1829 for sugar planter Joseph Soniat DuFossat, who had 13 children by two wives. The brick was exposed in the American style. The rear elevation once had a pair of winding stairs, like the one remaining. The post-1865 owner renovated, enclosing the *porte cochère*, changing the arched openings, and adding a cast iron gallery. Now a National Trust recommended hotel.

Soniat DuFossat, who died in 1852, was the second son of Guy Saunhac DuFossat, who came to Louisiana in 1751 under Louis XV, married creole Claudine Dreux, and stayed on during the Spanish colonial days as Alcalde at the Cabildo. The family plantation across the river was called Tchoupitoulas, acquired in 1808 from Bernard de Marigny. That 1820 plantation house was used as the Colonial Country Club until its recent demolition.

Conti Street

618 and 620 Conti Street

These are remnants of the kind of creole rows of storehouses planned by J. N. B. DePouilly in the 1830s for **Exchange Passage** (see p. 32) and the immediate area to complement his new St. Louis Exchange Hotel. Dueling masters had their studios alongside sugar factors' offices and coffee houses, which were also bars.

Dauphine Street

301 Dauphine Street

James Gallier, Sr. designed and built the three three-story side-hall townhouses in the Greek Revival style for merchant James Dick about 1847. The architect set the houses back from the street in an unusual French Quarter arrangement (now part of the Holiday Inn).

505 Dauphine Street

John James Audubon and his family rented this small creole cottage in 1821–1822 while he was working on *The Birds of America*. Lucy Bakewell, Audubon's wife, was sister to Mrs. Alexander Gordon, Anne Bakewell, whose husband was a cotton commission merchant with Gordon, Forstall and Co. The cottage is a detached part of the Maison de Ville Hotel.

521 Dauphine Street. Angel Xiques House. Drawing by James Gallier, Sr. Courtesy of the Southeastern Architectural Archive, Tulane University Library.

716 Dauphine Street. View of the back of St. Louis Cathedral from the grillwork of the Jean-Baptiste Le Prète House. Courtesy of the Historic New Orleans Collection.

521 Dauphine Street

Angel Xiques house. This raised-basement Greek Revival villa built in the 1830s embodies one of Irish architect James Gallier, Sr.'s most sophisticated achievements. Note the use of granite, the stepped gable ends, and the Spanish–style wrought iron.

716 Dauphine Street

Gardette–Le Prètre house. Frederic Roy, builder, erected this monumental house in 1836 for Joseph Coulon Gardette, a dentist who came here from Philadelphia during Spanish rule. Gardette married Zulime Carrière, mother of Daniel Clark's daughter, Myra Clark Gaines. Merchant-planter Jean Baptiste Le Prêtre bought the house in 1839 for $20,049 and owned it until 1870. He added the cast iron galleries to the 1836 Greek Revival, three-story house to create a covered walkway that wraps around the corner. The high basement level with its grilled openings is unusual with the recessed entrance cut through a string course.

1012–1014 Dauphine Street

This 1825 double creole cottage characterizes the Transitional period with its French-style arched openings, *abat vent,* and delicate proportions. The facade, outlined with the stucco band, a holdover Spanish colonial custom, makes a neat composition, and the fan transoms above the casement openings are exceptional.

1017 Dauphine Street

This post-Purchase creole cottage reflects the attenuation of form and proportion of the 1820s with its Federal –style influence. Note the narrow center service passage to the rear patio of the double house.

1012-1014 Dauphine Street. Photograph by Richard Koch, architect, ca. 1930. Courtesy of the Historic New Orleans Collection.

1017 Dauphine Street. Drawing by Edward Howard Suydam, 1930. Courtesy of the Historic New Orleans Collection. Suydam's illustrations made Lyle Saxon's Fabulous New Orleans a collectible.

Decatur Street

This first street facing the River was first named Rue du Quai, then Rue de la Levée. In 1870 it was renamed in honor of Stephen Decatur, the American naval hero famous for his exploits at Tripoli.

800 Decatur Street

Joseph Pilié, St. Domingue *émigré* who became an architect and surveyor after apprenticing with Barthélémy Lafon, designed the Vegetable Market in 1813. It was built originally as an open colonnade.

823 Decatur Street

Once popular as Begué's Restaurant, this 1830 building has been the home of Tujague's Restaurant (established in 1856) since 1929. While the interior has received unfortunate wood paneling, architectural details remain, such as the overlights with curvilinear muntins above the openings, the wrought iron balcony covering the sidewalk to make a corner arcade supported by iron columns, and the corner hip roof.

900 Decatur Street at North Peters Street.

Meat Market. Joseph Tanesse, architect and surveyor, with Gurlie and Guillot acting as builders in 1813, collaborated on the public Meat Market, then called Halle des Boucheries. The cupolas and the colonnade were added during a remodeling by the Works Progress Administration during the 1930s. Koch and Wilson were consulted by the French Market Corporation of the City of New Orleans for the extensive 1974 remodeling by Nolan, Norman, and Nolan, architects, and Cashio, Cochran, landscape architects for the entire French Market complex.

1103–1141 Decatur Street

Ursulines row houses. Even the Ursulines found a piece of their property to spare for speculative row houses, and they had the French architects Gurlie and Guillot design these in 1830 in the Transitional style. Typical arched openings with a wrought iron balcony in front of French doors emphasize the second level. A good view of the row is from inside the Ursuline Convent.

800 Decatur Street. Vegetable market, designed by Joseph Pilié, 1813. Etching by William Woodward, 1932. Courtesy of the Southeastern Architectural Archive, Tulane University Library

Dumaine Street

Dumaine Street, named after Le Duc Du Maine, one of Louis XIV's illegitimate sons, active in the Mississippi Company

632 Dumaine Street (see p. 9).

This 1788 Spanish colonial house illustrates the continuing French taste for colonettes, brick-between-post construction covered with weatherboards, segmental arch openings, exterior stairways, and double–pitch hip roofs. Don Mañuel Lanzos, a Spanish officer who assisted Governor Mañuel Gayoso y Lemos at Natchez and later in New Orleans, owned a house on this site in 1783, and his wife Señora Doña Gertrudis Guerro and their six daughters lived there. It burned in the 1788 fire and was immediately rebuilt by Robert Jones, an American builder, for Lanzos, who sold the house in 1813. After saving the house, which had been made famous by George Washington Cable's fiction, Mrs. I. I. Lemann donated it to the Louisiana State Museum in 1947. Monroe Labouisse, architect, restored it for the museum in the 1970s.

707–709 Dumaine Street

One of the few remaining tile-roofed cottages, this is the only one with a tile parapet made of red, half-round Spanish tiles. Part of a row of three built in 1800 by Majeur de Brigade de Garde Joachim de la Torre, it may have been built or designed by architect-surveyor Barthélémy Lafon, from whom de la Torre bought the lot. Such Spanish colonial houses which originally had flat roofs were described by Dr. John Sibley,

707-09 Dumaine Street. Watercolor showing a mid-nineteenth century presentation by Boyd Cruise, 1941. Courtesy of the Historic New Orleans Collection. Once, numerous such Spanish-colonial creole cottages lined the streets. Tall parapets with Spanish tiles hid flat roofs where the inhabitants relaxed with their brioche and *café au lait* in the morning and used the space as an outdoor living and workroom throughout the day. Architect Benjamin Latrobe commented on such roofs where he saw men jumping from roof to roof to visit friends.

a visitor from Natchitoches in 1802 just before the Louisiana Purchase. "The greatest number of the houses, particularly those newly built, are flat roofed. . . . A balustrade round ornamented with urns, balls, etc. The tops of the houses are as their back yards, and the women wash, iron, sit to work and the men walk on them and go from the top of one house to the top of another and visit their neighbors without having anything to do with the streets below. Many have shrubs and flowers growing on their houses—no wood shingles are used, either cement, slate or tile."

Exchange Passage

Conceived by J. N. B. DePouilly in 1837, this passage ran from Iberville to St. Louis to provide a suitable approach to the main entrance of the St. Louis Exchange Hotel. The arched first-floor openings of some of the remaining buildings indicate DePouilly's plan to bring to New Orleans the elegance of the Empire-style row houses in Paris, such as the Percier and Fontaine terraces in the Rue de Rivoli. Row upon row of such three–and–one-half-story buildings with arches below and iron balconies above, accessed through casement openings within, were designed or built by Claude Gurlie and his partner Joseph Guillot, and by DePouilly and his brother, who handled most of the firm's business.

111 Exchange Place

The Bank of America's commercial rental facility at the rear of the bank was designed by Gallier and Esterbrook, who, according to the building contract, based the Venetian Renaissance design of the cast iron facade on Cuthbert Slocumb's hardware store designed by William Freret on Canal Street (demolished). Freret, in turn, had derived his design from a Philadelphia cast iron store attributed to architect Stephen D. Button, dated 1857.

111 Exchange Place. Cast iron facade for the Bank of America by Gallier and Esterbrook, architects, 1866. Courtesy of the Southeastern Architectural Archive, Tulane University Library. The Itallanate building also housed the firm of C. Cavaroc and Company, Wine Merchants and Importers.

Governor Nicholls Street

Governor Nicholls Street was first Rue de l'Arsenal, then Rue de l'Hôpital, renamed in 1911 after the Civil War hero and twice governor of Louisiana.

721 Governor Nicholls Street.

The Jean Baptiste Thierry house dates from 1814, built for Thierry, editor of *Le Courrier de la Louisiane*, after designs by Henry S. Boneval Latrobe. The eldest son of America's foremost architect, Latrobe worked jointly with Arsène Lacarrière Latour on this project, which is the earliest example of Greek Revival in New Orleans, yet the most atypical; the design was never imitated. The shallow front yard was also perhaps unique at the time in the French Quarter.

Orleans Street

Orleans Street was intended to be the city's main thoroughfare. De Pauger's 1719 city plans made it 45 feet wide instead of the usual 38 feet. Named for the regent after whom the city was named, Orleans Street cut through the center of the Vieux Carré just behind the rear of the parish church.

700 Block Orleans Street

Creole–style row houses designed by French architects Gurlie and Guillot typify the Transitional period, with arched openings for commercial first floors, and casement openings and transoms above.

Royal Street

332 Royal Street

The Bank of Louisiana. The free-standing commercial building dates from 1826, when Tobias Bickle and Philip Hamblet contracted to build it after designs of Benjamin Fowler Fox for $80,000. After a fire in 1863, James Gallier, Jr. and his partner Richard Esterbrook reworked the building to present a monumental Greek Revival edifice. Engaged columns supporting a projecting entablature give the structure a strong American Greek Revival look. Few such iron fences set on masonry bases have survived.

700 block of Orleans Street at Royal Street. Photograph by Charles L. Franck, ca. 1922, printed by Nancy Ewing Miner, 1979. Courtesy of the Historic New Orleans Collection. This commercial architecture with residences above in the French style shows French architects Gurlie and Guillot at their best. Segmental arched dormers, the cornice featuring the classic swag, the signature lintels above the square-headed openings, and the rhythmical progression of arches at the first level are characteristic of their pre-Civil War work. This is commercial creole architecture at its most typical.

339 Royal Street

Vincent Rillieux house (Waldhorn's Antiques). French *émigré* architect Barthélémy Lafon designed this storehouse about 1800 for Vincent Rillieux, who sold it to the Planters Bank in 1811. Between 1820 and 1836 the Bank of the United States had offices here. After the banking panic of 1837 the building was sold to Dr. Paul Lacroix for $75,000. The delicate wrought iron corner balcony has Spanish-style S-curved support brackets. The projecting bands at the second level articulate the building with subtlety, providing shallow relief to the flat fronts.

401 Royal Street

Louisiana State Bank (Manheim's). This is the last work of Benjamin Henry Boneval Latrobe, an English-born architect who came to New Orleans from Baltimore. He died of yellow fever soon after completing the design in 1820. Benjamin Fowler Fox was the builder. The curved wall facing the rear courtyard enclosed the directors' room on the ground floor and the dining room of the cashier's apartment on the second floor. The interior dome and vaulted ceiling

are brick. A hip roof covers the original flat roof. Restrained and elegant, this Transitional period building fit perfectly into the French vocabulary of the period in New Orleans: The building recalls Latrobe's 1796 Bank of Pennsylvania in Philadelphia.

413 Royal Street

One of the earliest post-Purchase houses documented, this house was built in 1804 by Jean Marie Godefroy Dujarreau for himself. The architect-builder first rented to New England entrepreneurs Richard Relf and Beverly Chew, then in 1809 lost the building to his creditors.

417 Royal Street

Banque de la Louisiane (Brennan's Restaurant). Vincent Rillieux, great-grandfather of the artist Edgar Degas, purchased the site a month after the great fire of December 8, 1794. Either he or Señor José Faurie, a wealthy merchant during the Spanish colonial regime, commissioned this storehouse with *porte cochère* by 1802. Faurie bought the property from the widow Rillieux's daughter and son-in-law Santiago (James) Freret. The newly organized Banque de la

417 Royal Street. Rillieux-Faurie storehouse. Etching by William Woodward, 1934. Courtesy of the Southeastern Architectural Archive, Tulane University Library.

520 Royal Street. Courtyard of François Seignouret house. Photograph by Charles L. Franck ca. 1922. Courtesy of the Historic New Orleans Collection. Also known as the Brulatour Courtyard because of wine importer Pierre Brulatour's 1870-1887 ownership. Philanthropist William Ratliff Irby restored the courtyard in 1918 for use by the Arts and Crafts Club. WDSU-TV, New Orleans first television station, opened its offices here in 1949.

Louisiane bought it in 1805 for $25,000. In 1841 Judge Alonzo Morphy, father of Paul Charles Morphy, the internationally famous chess player, bought the property and the chess player lived in this house where he died at 41. William Ratliff Irby, a benefactor of both the French Quarter and Tulane University, donated the property to Tulane in 1920. Since 1955, the Brennan family has run a festive restaurant here, and they bought the building about 10 years ago. *Orleans Parish Landmark.*

509–511 Royal Street

Antoine Louis Boimaré, bookseller and Louisiana historiographer, had this wide creole storehouse built in 1832. Louis Barthélémy Macarty bought the unfinished building in 1835. The three-story creole building has a granite arcade with five lead-ornamented transoms and granite cornices above the second- and third–level windows. Note the iron tie rods that hold the building tight at the third level. *Orleans Parish Landmark.*

520 Royal Street

The François Seignouret house was built in 1816–1817 for the Bordeaux native, a noted furniture maker and importer who was also in the wine business. A central *porte cochère* has a wrought iron grill between two pillars. The original curved iron consoles support the wrought iron balcony with its fancy *garde de frise*. The courtyard, open under the ownership of station WDSU, illustrates the elliptical arched openings common to such courtyards, along with an exterior stair beneath a second–level balcony or loggia. *Orleans Parish Landmark.*

527–533 Royal Street

Jean François Merieult house. General and Mrs. Kemper Williams established the Historic New Orleans Collection in the Jean François Merieult house, one of the earliest Spanish colonial houses remaining, built in 1792 for the merchant-trader, with living quarters above the shop. Constructed on one of the original city lots, the house, which

527-533 Royal Street. Jean François Merieult house, built 1792. Watercolor by Boyd Cruise, 1939. Courtesy of the Historic New Orleans Collection. The artist made a composite presentation showing the building when it housed Albert Lieutaud's Print Store and Casey and Casey Antiques. Cruise imposed mid-nineteenth century costumes, carriages, and other period "restorations" on the scene.

incorporates part of the 1750s Guinalt house, was remodeled extensively for Lizardi Frères in the 1830s. Merieult married Catherine McNamara, daughter of an Irishman who was an entrepreneur and trader during the Spanish colonial period. McNamara père had married a creole and lived at **1027 Royal Street.**

The complex includes the John B. Trapolin house, an unusual example of early infill built in 1889 and remodeled in 1944–1946 by the architect Richard Koch for General and Mrs. Williams. Decorated by Leila Moore Williams with the aid of Koch and Marc Antony, then one of the few decorators in the city, the residence, eclectic in design and furnishings, reflects Mrs. Williams' interest in fine English antiques and the couple's knowledge of Louisiana art. (Antony painted murals at the Gumbo Shop at **630 St. Peter** (see p. 43).

534 Royal Street

The Jean Baptiste Cottin *entresol* storehouse dating from between 1813, when he bought the lot, and 1818, when his estate sold the property with the buildings at Maspero's Exchange by court order to architects Gurlie and Guillot.

534-36 Royal Street. Jean Baptiste Cottin storehouse,1815. Photograph by architect Richard Koch, ca. 1925. Courtesy of the Historic New Orleans Collection.

The architects probably designed and built the house, and Cottin died before paying for it. Notice the Ionic pilasters and plaster cornices with some Empire detail. Author Lyle Saxon lived in the house from 1920 to 1924.

541 Royal Street

Vincent Nolte storehouse. According to Samuel Wilson, Jr., the architect Benjamin Latrobe designed this house in 1819 for his friend, the German-born commission merchant and author Vincent Nolte. The delicate pilaster treatment is typical of the post-Purchase period. In 1829 it became the Planters Bank.

611 Royal Street

The home of Governor André Bienvenue Roman, who wrote a history of the Civil War, dates from 1831, when French architects Gurlie and Guillot built it in the lingering creole tradition. Segmental arches open below a wrought iron balcony. The Court of the Two Sisters at **613 Royal Street,** built at the same time by the same architects, houses one of the largest service complexes in the quarter. The latter building has a *porte cochère* and original architectural details such as the curving stairway behind the parlor and the woodwork around the arches.

624 Royal Street

This, one of two once-identical houses built in 1831 for Dr. Isadore Labatut and his wife Caroline Urquhart, suggests that the *porte cochère* style maintained its popularity toward the end of the Transitional Period (1820–1835). After Labatut's daughter, Angèle Caroline, married Magin Puig y Ferrer of Catalonia, Spain, the couple lived in the house. Their handsome Mallard rosewood and lemonwood furniture is now used in the 1850 museum house in the Lower Pontalba buildings.

640 Royal Street at St. Peter Street

Spanish colonial notary Pierre Pedesclaux began this house in 1795 after designs by the French architect Barthélémy Lafon, who set up office in the building in 1805. Pedesclaux lost the unfinished building at public auction; the physician Yves LeMonnier and apothecary François Grandchamps purchased it and finished the three-story house in 1811, following designs by architects LaCarrière Latour and Hyacinth Laclotte. In 1821 LeMonnier purchased the entire house and it remained his family's home for 50 years. LeMonnier's initials remain within a medallion on the wrought iron balcony.

French Empire motifs such as the two-story pilasters and the corner orientation give the house a sophistication not found in the local creole vernacular. An elegant oval salon on the third floor features a domed ceiling.

700–712 Royal Street at St. Peter Street

The row of 11 houses that wrap around the corner to **622–624 Pirates Alley** were built in 1840 for Malasie Trepagnier, widow of Jean–Baptiste LaBranche, a wealthy sugar planter in St. Charles Parish. LaBranche had lived in his own townhouse around the corner at **730 St. Peter Street** (see p. 44). from 1829 to 1831, when he died. By the time these were built, row houses had evolved into the mature Greek Revival style. The wide covered galleries with cast iron decoration replaced earlier wrought iron balconies after 1850. However, along the Pirates Alley elevation, the original 1840 wrought iron balconies remain. Other aspects of the creole tradition are also retained, such as the arched ground-floor openings for commercial occupancy and the narrow, side passageway to the courtyard. Notice the flagged street with its central gutters along Pirates Alley.

729–733 Royal Street

The Spanish colonial Montegut house dates from soon after the fire of 1794. The projecting bands of plaster, the flush opening without frames, and the delicate wrought iron balcony reveal the

700 block of Royal Street returning along St. Peter Street to Pirates Alley. Jean-Baptiste LaBranche row houses, 1840. Photograph by Clarence John Laughlin, ca. 1945. Courtesy of the Historic New Orleans Collection. The 11 three-story brick row houses had cast iron galleries added after 1850.

729-733 Royal Street. Dr. Joseph Montegut house, ca. 1795. Drawing by Alfred R. Waud, 1871. Courtesy of the Historic New Orleans Collection.

Spanish character of the building. Round-headed lights beneath pediments in the dormers complement the arched openings at the first level and the unusual wide central openings at the first and second levels. A sophisticated one-story wing for one of Montegut's daughters was built for the house in 1796 after Guilberto Guillemard's 1790 designs.

823 Royal Street

Daniel Clark, an Eton-educated Anglo–Irishman, arrived in New Orleans at 20 in 1786 and went to work in Governor Miró's office. Appointed U.S. Consul to Spanish colonial Louisiana in the 1790s, he amassed great wealth in New Orleans. Clark lived in this creole townhouse, after he bought the property

Portrait of Dr. Joseph Montegut, his wife, Françoise de Lisle Dupart, her mother Françoise de Lisle the Widow A. P. de Marigny de Mandeville, with Montegut's daughters Aimée, Feliciana, Maria and Catalina and sons Joseph and Raymond in their house at 729-731 Royal Street. By José Francisco de Salazar, ca. 1798. Courtesy of the Louisiana State Museum. The artist is New Orleans' foremost Spanish colonial artist and came to the city from Yucatan.

from Gilberto Andry on November 11, 1803, nine days before the Louisiana Purchase. In 1806 Clark sold the house to Baron Boisfontaine when he was elected to represent the Louisiana Territory in Congress, the same year that he shot Governor Claiborne in the leg in a duel.

934 Royal Street

General P. G. T. Beauregard lived here with his son, René, and a widowed older sister from 1867 to 1875, after leaving the house he had rented at **1113 Chartres Street** (see p. 26). Beauregard's first wife, Marie Villere, died at their daughter's birth. His second wife, Caroline Deslondes, sister of Mrs. John Slidell, died during the Civil War at their home on Esplanade Avenue while he was directing the Florida campaign. Jean Gleises, a Frenchman and wheelwright in New Orleans, owned the property for

decades and in 1853 left it to his daughter Athalie Gleises Maignan, who lived in France. She rented the house until 1885. The house appears Italianate, probably renovated by the post-1853 heir, with its monumental recessed entrance having paneled reveals and its segmental arched windows.

1132 Royal Street

James Gallier, Jr. designed this Greek Revival side-hall townhouse with a *porte cochère* for his own residence in 1857. He and his wife, Aglae Villavasso, lived here with their four daughters until his death in 1868 at 41, after which his widow and the children lived here until 1917.

1140 Royal Street

Lalaurie house. Built as a two-story house for Edmond Soniat DuFossat in

1132 Royal Street. Gallier House Museum, designed as his own home by architect James Gallier, Jr. Front and rear elevations; back parlor as it would have appeared ca. 1857. Interior photograph by Jerry Ward, 1990. Restoration architects, Koch and Wilson; project architect, Henry Krotzer. Courtesy of Tulane University.

1831, the unfinished house was sold to Mme. Delphine Macarty de Lopez Blanque Lalaurie, thrice married creole and then wife of Dr. Louis Nicholas Lalaurie, a native of Villeneuse-Sur-Lot and prominent physician in New Orleans. Madame Lalaurie allegedly tortured her slaves here, and after an enraged mob set fire to the house in April 1834 and discovered her manacled slaves, she and Dr. Lalaurie fled to France. The property was turned over to her son-in-law, Placide Forstall, married to Borqueta Lopez y Angulo, Madame Lalaurie's daughter, born after the death of her first husband, Ramón Lopez y Angulo, Spanish intendant. Research indicates that the 1837 purchaser, Pierre Edouard Trastour, redesigned the house, adding a third floor and the elegant French Empire detailing, then selling it to Charles Caffin. The widow of Horace Cammack bought the house in 1862; drawings by the architects Gallier and Esterbrook indicate that they may have renovated the house too, in 1865–1866. Unfortunate times followed and philanthropist William J. Warrenton set up a refuge for indigent men here during the Great Depression. Koch and Wilson, Architects, designed renovations for Dr. Russell Albright in 1976 and 1980.

St. Ann Street

917 St. Ann Street

Raimond Gaillard, free man of color and veteran of the Battle of New Orleans, had this cottage built in 1824. A prosperous businessman, Gaillard owned several other pieces of property in this square until 1861. Behind the cottage in the courtyard are a pair of two-story buildings, kitchens, and servants quarters, all restored by the artist Boyd Cruise, who painted the murals in the Royal Orleans Hotel. The bricks should be plastered.

1009 St. Ann Street

An 1840 building contract between Etiènne Courcelle, builder, and Bernard de Santos indicates that Courcelle built this as one of two houses of "two stories plus attic for $13,500" with an additional $1000 for the kitchens for the two houses. Courcelle, a second-generation builder in the city, worked mainly in the creole suburbs where he grew up. By 1853, then Keeper of St. Louis Cemetery No 1, he advertised that he built tombs and vaults and installed inscriptions and railings. Santos had bought the lot in 1840 from the widow of Vincent Ternant, and he sold the new house the next year.

Uninhabited for 50 years in the twentieth century, the house needed extensive repair, and the new owner stumbled upon one of the last *porte cochère* houses to be built in New Orleans. The house today is a full three stories, as are the extensive service wings. Outside fenestration has been altered, and the brick was once plastered, but the interior retains its creole appearance. Entrance to the first-level rooms is from the *porte cochère*, and behind them is a loggia with a winding stair lit by the traditional creole elliptical windows with wide fanlights.

St. Louis Street

720 St. Louis Street

This home of Pierre Soulé was built by Gurlie and Guillot between 1830 and 1835 in the Transitional style. The building features the architects' signature garlanded cornice.

820 St. Louis Street

Samuel Hermann, a German–Jewish immigrant and successful commission merchant, and his creole bride had the American architect William Brand design this American–style, center-hall complex with imported red brick laid in Flemish bond around double–hung windows. Even so, creole characteristics crept into the design at the rear elevation. These include the rear cabinet gallery and a galleried, three-story, detached brick service building and a

820 St. Louis Street. Hermann-Grima house, front elevation and kitchen, designed and built by William Brand, 1831. Restoration architects, Koch and Wilson; project architect, Henry Krotzer. Courtesy of Hermann-Grima house.

separate kitchen. The creole family of notary and Malta native Felix Grima acquired it in 1844, and five generations lived there until 1921. Judge Grima built the adjacent stable in 1850; now used as a museum shop, it is the finest private stable building remaining in the French Quarter. The Christian Woman's Exchange purchased the house and stable in 1924. After use as a shop and rooming house for decades, it opened as a museum house in 1965.

920 St. Louis Street

After a near bankruptcy in 1843, attorney Placide Forstall, member of a prominent military family in Spanish colonial Louisiana, recovered to have James Gallier design this elegant house for him in 1854, but he did not have the firm of Gallier and Esterbrook build it until 1859. The three-story house of plastered brick is articulated by colossal pilasters extending the full height of the house above a rusticated basement. These features, besides the arched windows and cast iron trim, suggest a French baroque treatment.

St. Peter Street

616 St. Peter Street

Orué–Pontalba house. This house, begun in 1789 for Spanish official Don José de Orué y Barbea, sustained damage in the 1794 fire and Orué sold it in 1795 to Joseph Xavier de Pontalba. He had architect Hilaire Boutet complete it for his aunt, Celeste Macarty, widow of Spanish colonial Governor Estebán Miró. Canary Islander Marcelino Hernandez fashioned the wrought iron balconies. Architect Richard Koch reconstructed the building in 1962 for Le Petit Théâtre du Vieux Carré, using some old parts, such as the ironwork. This is the only modern reconstruction among the landmarks of the French Quarter. Sophisticated quoins, the window treatment and the elegant balustraded parapet recall Gilberto Guillemard's one-story addition to the Montegut house at Royal and St. Ann Streets, designed in 1790, built by 1796 (**731 Royal Street**; (see p. 37).

620 St. Peter Street

Victor David house (Le Petit Salon). Samuel Stewart built this American-style house in the Greek Revival style in 1838 for the native of Gascony and his creole wife Anne Carmelite Rabassa. Side-hall houses above a full basement with outside steps are rare, even in the American sectors. This one has the brick exposed and a wood entablature pierced with grilled openings in the preferred Greek Revival style. Notice the handsome entrance designed after Minard Lafever's pattern book. Each balcony railing is a different design. Le Petit Salon purchased it in 1922, an early effort to preserve New Orleans culture and architecture.

630 St. Peter Street

Commagère–Mercier house (Gumbo Shop). Pedro Commagère had this two-story creole townhouse built about 1795, after the earlier house on the site was burned in the great fire of 1794. Segmental openings at the commercial level and the balcony in front of a short second level are identifying characteristics of the early period. Commagère sold it in 1806. The Gumbo Shop has opened the property to the public since 1945, with Marc Antony's murals showing the Presbytère and Cabildo before the mansard roofs were added in 1846. *Orleans Parish Landmark.*

632 St. Peter Street

Madame Augustine Eugenie de Lassize, the widow of Louis Avart, whose upriver

plantation was subdivided as part of Uptown, had this creole storehouse built in 1842 after J. N. B. DePouilly's designs, with Ernest Godchaux as builder. The cast iron gallery replaced a wrought iron balcony and the third story was added for a studio by Achille Peretti, a noted artist who lived here from 1906 to 1923. In 1946–1947 Tennessee Williams wrote *A Streetcar Named Desire* here.

600 Block St. Peter Street

Look behind the Cabildo for American architect James H. Dakin's Greek Revival facade of the State Arsenal. The building contract for $19,500, with $500 of it for drawings and preliminary work with Dakin and Dakin, was signed July 1, 1839 by James Harrison Dakin for himself and the "late Charles B. Dakin." His brother had just died in Iberville Parish, near Baton Rouge, of yellow fever and is buried in the Protestant, back section of St. Gabrielle Catholic churchyard along the river.

Bold and vigorous are the adjectives employed to describe the arsenal. Its architect, Dakin, trained in the office of Town and Davis in New York and was subsequently a partner in the firm and a founder of the forerunner of the American Institute of Architects. He first specialized in the temple style for public buildings, especially with columns in antis, but the capitol at Baton Rouge was his Gothic design. Most of the Dakin's massive work in New Orleans has been destroyed.

714 St. Peter Street

Coffee Pot Restaurant. Felix Pinson, architect, built this two-story creole storehouse in 1829 with a carriageway that leads past a tightly curving stairway to a small courtyard with a two-story service building. The original French doors with transoms remain.

718 St. Peter Street

Pat O'Brien's. Planter, commission merchant, and owner of a brick kiln, John

Garnier had this house built in 1817. It exemplifies the post-Purchase style that continued colonial forms in a more delicate fashion, with classical and attenuated detail, such as the pilasters that articulate the facade. You can see the fine courtyard beyond a rear elevation with elliptical openings and twin winding stairways. For years the house was thought to have been built by Etiènne Marie de Fléchier who lived in an earlier house here in 1792. Measured drawings of architectural details are available in Nathaniel Courtland Curtis' book.

726 St. Peter Street

Preservation Hall. Antoine Faisendieu bought a lot here from Guillermo Gros in 1803 and built a tavern, selling it in 1809 to Pierre and Barthélémy Jourdain. A subsequent 1812 sale advertises a "house lately belonging to M. Faisendieu, $4000 cash and two years of notes." In 1816, when the Orleans Ballroom burned, this building also burned, and according to an act of sale,

936 St. Peter Street. 1830s-style creole cottage. Watercolor by Boyd Cruise, 1941. Courtesy of the Historic New Orleans Collection.

the architects Gurlie and Guillot bought the lot and rubble for $5000 in 1816, selling the property to Agathe Fanchon, *femme de couleur libre*, for $13,500 in November 1817. Madame Fanchon owned the property until 1866. The service wing and patio were home and office to the photographer "Pop" Whitesell in the first half of the twentieth century. The *porte cochère* house appears to be Spanish colonial in style, simple and chaste in its anonymous facade, with a wrought iron balcony and the remnant of a terrace roof with tiles peeking out beyond the newer pitched roof. The facade even has the Spanish style banding bordering it. Like Madame John's Legacy (see 632 Dumaine Street, (see p. 31), this building seems to have been rebuilt or renovated after the fire in the same manner it was originally built.

730 St. Peter Street

The architects and builders Jean Felix Pinson and Maurice Pizetta designed and built this *porte cochère* house in 1825 as an investment, and they sold it to Giraud M. Plique in 1827. Jean Baptiste LaBranche, St. Charles Parish planter, bought it as a townhouse in 1829, keeping it until his death in 1837. Here a French-style *porte cochère* house must have been renovated in the conservative Greek Revival style after 1837, as suggested by the tasteful attic frieze with windows, the molded lintels, and the *porte cochère* entrance frame, all typical of the 1840s. The delicate wrought iron balcony in the entwined arrow design with its iron bearers is original from the 1820s. Note the *garde de frise* that protects the balcony. *Orleans Parish Landmark.*

936 St. Peter Street

This tiny, single creole cottage facade is ornamented by one dormer having a pilastered pediment. Notice the granite step and the two Corinthian pilasters framing the front elevation. The cottage as it appears today has 1870s trim applied.

722. Toulouse Street. Watercolor by Boyd Cruise executed in 1955 from the original drawing in the New Orleans Notarial Archives, plan book 44A, folio 76. Courtesy of the Historic New Orleans Collection.

Toulouse Street

722 Toulouse Street

Built about 1800 for Louis Adam, this two-story colonial storehouse has recently been restored to its late Spanish colonial appearance by the Historic New Orleans Collection to house their archives. The house originally had a tile roof with typical small dormers and a wood balcony supported by S–curve iron brackets below and turned colonettes of wood. The first level featured batten shutters with panels having a diagonal design.

723 Toulouse Street

Valery Nicolas house. Hilaire Boutet, a designer–builder, built this two-story, four-bay creole post-Purchase house in 1808 during the Territorial period after his wife, Mlle. Boisdoré, inherited the property from Jeanne Touton Lemelle, *femme de couleur libre*, who had bought it in 1802 from banker Gerôme Flinard or Hinard. The wrought iron balcony, the exterior back stairway off the court-yard, and the interior apron mantels with their overmantels and channeled pilasters are fine examples of the style. An 1834 auction advertises "a brick house with upper story, a fine store, corridor and *porte cochère*. Upstairs consists of four large rooms, two cabinets, rear gallery and French balcony. A kitchen with an upper story of five rooms. Yard paved with bricks and a cistern." Previously it was thought that the banker Gerôme Flinard or Hinard had built the building after buying the lot from Pierre Dulcide Barran. This property displays the interaction in real estate among French and Spanish creoles and creoles of color.

828 Toulouse Street (see p. 195)

Jacques N. B. DePouilly, architect (1804–1875) designed the Olivier house in 1836. As built, this house varied from New Orleans prototypes, having a central window with an arched carriage drive on each side. DePouilly eventually redesigned the first floor to this typical New Orleans design.

Portrait of Antoine Jacques Philippe de Marigny de Mandeville (1811-1890.) By Jean Joseph Vaudechamp, 1833. Courtesy of the Louisiana State Museum. Marigny, whose father, Bernard, developed Faubourg Marigny, is the paradigm for a creole. His father descended from early French colonials and his mother, Anna Mathilda Morales, was a daughter of Juan Ventura Morales, Spanish Intendant of West Florida. In repayment of a debt owed his father by Louis Philippe, King of France, Mandeville was enrolled in St. Cyr Military Academy in France in 1830. He married Sophronie Louise Claiborne, daughter of Governor William C. C. Claiborne and his Spanish colonial wife Suzette Bosque. Marigny wears the uniform of a captain in the First Squadron of Cavalry, Orleans Lancers of the Louisiana Militia. Later he was a colonel in the Confederate Army, Tenth Louisiana Regiment. The French artist, Vaudechamp, wintered in Louisiana where he received numerous commissions in the 1830s from creole families.

The
Creole
Suburbs

A rchitect Benjamin Latrobe sailed to New Orleans early in the post-Purchase years and was in town by 1807 to design a customhouse. By the time Latrobe returned again in July 1819, his son, architect Henry B. Latrobe, had died of yellow fever in New Orleans, where he had been supervising construction of the waterworks. Latrobe bought a house facing the river on Rue Clouet, in one of the six small faubourgs downriver from Faubourg Marigny, the recently divided subdivision across Esplanade from the French Quarter. He brought his family from Baltimore to live near the old French plantation home of Brognier de Clouet, with a rum distillery or *guildive* in the next square. The area, like all the neighborhoods below the city, was thoroughly French, or creole as it was called by 1820.

Latrobe expressed appreciation for the creole mode of living and architecture when he wrote: "The sort of house built by the French is not the best specimen of French arrangement, yet it is infinitely superior to what we have inherited from the English." He understood that creole culture was ephemeral, as, indeed, was his own life among them, for he died suddenly of yellow fever on September 3, 1820, the time that his customhouse, just 13 years old, was demolished.

He had spent some time recording his impressions of New Orleans, observing at one point how the "merchant from the old United States, . . . daily gaining ground on the manners, the habits, the opinions and the domestic arrangements of the French, has already begun to introduce the detestable lop-sided London house, in which a common passage and stair acts as a common sewer to all the necessities of the dwelling and renders it impossible to preserve a temperature within the house." All his neighbors and the inhabitants of Faubourg Marigny must have agreed heartily, since they avoided such houses that were filling Faubourg St. Mary. Indeed, Faubourg Marigny and the six small faubourgs downriver, now called Bywater, developed as retreats for the creoles and the new French immigrants from St. Domingue and from France. Life there went on much as it did before the Louisiana Purchase.

In the 1803 Treaty of Paris between France and the United States, the inhabitants of the colony had been granted all the rights and privileges of U.S. citizens. These, however, did not impress the creole New Orleanians. They found trials by jury vile, they detested the lack of manners of the hordes of "Kaintucks" who descended the river on flatboats and keelboats, and they believed that American buildings wasted space and materials.

Americans even dared to try to suppress the popular custom of dueling, but their repressive laws were to no avail, and the creoles taught the Anglos a custom or two in that field. Even the new Governor Claiborne was shot in the leg in a duel with Anglo-Irish Daniel Clark, the American Consul before the Purchase. Bernard de Marigny fought 27 duels, introducing the custom to Americans, to their disadvantage.

The pious Presbyterians, who had outnumbered the Episcopalians for years, disapproved of gambling, cards, and the age-old custom of the "quadroon balls" on St. Philip Street. No one, however, could keep the mothers of the creole *demoiselles de couleur* from launching their daughters into relationships with creole gentlemen.

In Faubourgs Marigny and Tremé, mixed-race persons predominated. By 1840 *femmes de couleur libre* owned about 40 percent of the property there. Much of this was the result of *inter vivos* donations from white men who wanted security for these *femmes de couleur*, whom the law did not permit to inherit real property. A double creole cottage, for example, pro-

Plan Book 21, folio 23, New Orleans Notarial Archives. Watercolor by Benjamin Buisson, surveyor 1842. Courtesy of the Historic New Orleans Collection. This French colonial style raised house with double-pitched hip roof (demolished) is the kind of establishment, with outbuildings, that first went up in small faubourgs such as that of d'Aunoy, downriver from Faubourg Marigny.

vided both a home and a means of support from the rented side.

The French and Spanish creoles found Anglo-American attitudes toward these women and other well-to-do *personnes de couleur libres* atrocious. Americans even had the nerve to disapprove of the long-established custom of *plaçage*. While the Code Noir of 1724 and subsequent Spanish law, enforced by post-1803 American regulations, prohibited marriage between whites and blacks, slave or free, custom permitted white men to set up housekeeping, a *plaçage*, with *femmes de couleur libre*, called their *placées*. The children of these arrangements were, when acknowledged by

Portrait of Madame Gabriel Boyer (1800-1846) By Charles-Achille d'Hardiviller, ca 1820. Executed in France. Courtesy of the Louisiana State Museum. Among the waves of French émigrés to New Orleans after the French Revolution and Terror, Napoleon's defeat, and the reestablishment of the monarchy came Madame Boyer, Pauline. She taught music while her husband was a "professor of languages."

their white father before a notary, natural children, not illegitimate, and these children inherited an equal share of their father's estate.

Such was the case in the family of Narcisse Broutin, a notary and distinguished French creole, descendant of the king's engineer who designed the Ursuline Convent. In his will of 1819, Broutin declared that he had never been married and had "no legitimate descendants." He acknowledged his children Rosalie, Augustine, and Frumence, born of Mathilde Gaillau, a free woman of color, who lived with him in his dwelling in Faubourg Marigny. Broutin left these children one-half of his property, all the common law allowed for legitimate children.

Another important resident of the creole suburbs was Thomy Lafon, *homme de couleur libre* and prominent businessman, philanthropist, and benefactor to the community of *personnes de couleur*. He retreated into the creole Faubourg Tremé to avoid the new Americans. His father was the French architect and surveyor Barthélémy Lafon.

These are just a few examples of the hundreds of men and women, black and white, who moved to the creole suburbs to preserve their culture and to take advantage of Bernard de Marigny's inexpensive lots on streets he gave esoteric names, such as "Craps," the popular card game, or "Bons Enfants." Lot prices started at about $108, suitable for the small investor.

1809–1811 Dauphine Street. Creole cottage (see p. 58). Photograph by Betsy Swanson. Courtesy of the Historic New Orleans Collection. Brick creole cottages, gable ended and dormered, lined the streets of Faubourg Marigny from the 1820s. Essential to such establishments were detached, two-story kitchen buildings beyond a rear patio or par terre garden.

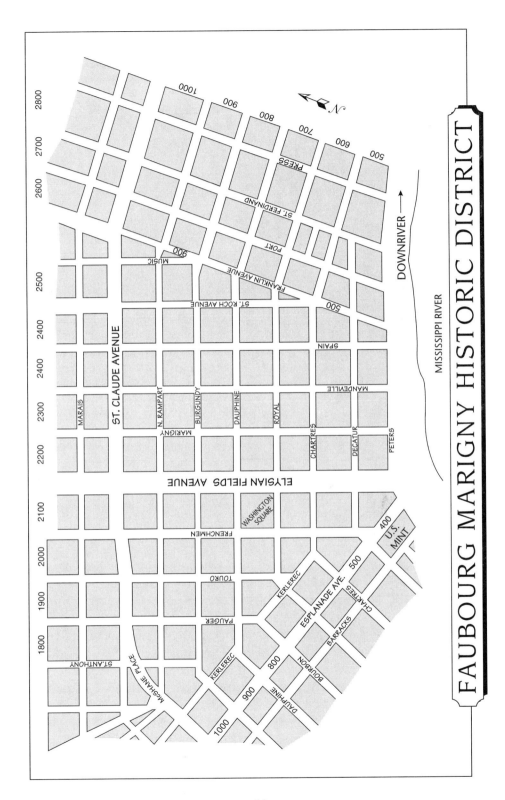

FAUBOURG MARIGNY HISTORIC DISTRICT

2701–2707 Chartres Street at Port Street. Plan book 40, folio 8, New Orleans Notarial Archives. Watercolor by J. A. Pueyo and Cosnier, 1854. Courtesy of the Historic New Orleans Collection. Ten three- and- one- half story creole-style row houses were built on the block in 1836. Only two remain.

The area developed as a series of architectural types and styles, small in scale and repetitive in decorative details, with the four-bay creole cottage of the 1840s **(1809-1811 Dauphine Street; see p. 58)**, predominating amid creole townhouses **(2701-2707 Chartres Street)**, storehouses **(704 Marigny Street)**, and *porte cochère* houses **(1424-1428 Royal Street)**. The resulting look is creole, where French and Spanish traditions in architecture, although subtle and restrained, overcome the imported American materials and traditions of scale, floor plan, and decoration.

The later, American-style late Victorian shotguns of the 1880s and 1890s that replaced earlier creole cottages fit well into the scale of the creole sector. Most shotguns share with creole housing the commonality of a four-bay system, frame construction, a front gallery or porch, and lack of hallways. Like creole cottages, they sometimes appear in tiny two-bay versions like the row at **5327, 5329 and 5331 Dauphine Street.** These late shotguns are either built at the *banquette*, raised up to 3 feet on brick piers, like many creole cottages, or they are set back only slightly, up to 10 feet. One of the earliest shotgun-type houses in the city, dating from before 1846, is at **920 Spain Street,** the J. B. Bordenave house. This Greek Revival example is built on the front property line in the manner of creole cottages but has the American recessed entrance and rusticated wood facade. Another is **1431 Bourbon Street**, built in 1869 in the Classic style. The same house type, 40 years later, is the row of 1880s galleried shotguns in the **800 block of Kerlerec Street.** Their frame construction, narrow galleries, small pediments, segmental-arched opening, and their height from the ground fit well into the neighborhood developed heavily in the 1840s.

1431 Bourbon Street. Three-bay frame cottage in the Classic style. Photograph by Betsy Swanson, 1969. Courtesy of the Historic New Orleans Collection. Through the mid-nineteenth century, new houses continued in scale and material the patterns established in Faubourg Marigny in the 1820s.

800 block of Kerlerec Street. Victorian shotgun cottages. Photograph by Eugene D. Cizek. Toward the end of the nineteenth century Victorian shotgun houses flourished: two- bay, three-bay and four-bay, with full galleries, sometimes slightly set back on the lot with a fence at the property line. Often these filled sideyards or replaced earlier creole cottages, but they did not disturb the scale of the neighborhood nor alter its overall appearance.

Faubourg Marigny

Clustered near the French Quarter and Esplanade are the earliest houses and commercial buildings in Faubourg Marigny. These reveal a variety of types and styles, giving the building watcher, whether walking or driving, an idea of the creole suburbs. One creole manor house remains at **3933 Chartres Street** near the river where the Lombard plantation was established for Joseph Lombard, Jr. in 1826 by his father. This four-room, galleried creole residence with its slate hip roof must represent for the visitor the dozens of eighteenth- and early nineteenth-century French and Spanish colonial plantation complexes that once lined the river.

The creole faubourgs exhibit a Federal style or post-Purchase version of the creole cottage that features a narrow center-hall (**1445 Pauger Street**) or even a service passage like a "dog trot" [**2016-2020 Burgundy Street** (see p. 57) open to the public since it serves as headquarters for the Education Through Historic Preservation Program].

The creole *porte cochère* house at **1428 Royal Street**, a three-story example, illustrates continued use of a Spanish colonial building type. The double American side-hall townhouse of frame construction that penetrated the area by the mid-nineteenth century can take on a creole aspect such as the one at **1416-1418 Bourbon Street** (see p. 56), between Esplanade and Kerlerec. Faubourgs Marigny and Tremé were largely rental areas, and such double houses on the English plan became useful to imitate. Houses at **1809 Dauphine Street** (see p. 58) and **905 Kerlerec Street** around the corner from each other share a pair of common-wall kitchen-service buildings that epitomize service building traditions.

3933 Chartres Street. Lombard Plantation house. Photograph by Betsy Swanson, 1969. Courtesy of the Historic New Orleans Collection. The lone survivor of the plantation houses that faced the Mississippi River downriver from the French Quarter, the house has been restored, since this photograph was taken.

Portrait of Brigadier General Carlos Favré d'Aunoy and Son. Artist unknown, probably executed in Spain by Spanish academician, ca. 1812. Courtesy of the Louisiana State Museum. Despite his French name, d'Aunoy was a Spanish colonial officer in Louisiana, but after the Louisiana Purchase he sailed to defend Spain against the invading army of Napoleon. After his leadership at the 1808 siege of Madrid and other battles, he was declared a national hero of Spain. Captured by the French, he was executed. This portrait of the man who owned a small plantation beyond the holdings of Marigny was sent to his family in Louisiana probably after his young son in cadet uniform had been added to the painting. Faubourg d'Aunoy below the Marigny tract is named after his small river plantation.

The creoles initiated their own version of the townhouse they carried over from the French Quarter to the creole suburbs: a four-bay double, gable-sided hall-less two-story house with four French doors at each level and a balcony above, such as **2340 Chartres Street** (see p. 59). Variants at **2401 and 2405 Chartres Street** with their hip roofs and second-level balconies illustrate the grace and subtlety of this creole building type.

The building-watcher tour can be combined with breakfast at La Peniche, **1940 Dauphine Street**, a corner commercial creole cottage. Snug Harbor at **626 Frenchman Street** features live music and is currently home to the city's best burger. Feelings-Cafe d'Aunoy is farther down in Bywater at **2600 Chartres Street,** but it's the perfect resting spot for lunch or dinner to get the feel of the creole neighborhood where architect Benjamin Latrobe's family lived. Mrs. Latrobe wrote that their house was "a very excellent and convenient dwelling, buried in Orange, Pomegranate, Oleander, and Althea trees."

Bourbon Street

1416-1418 Bourbon Street

Louis Clairain built this pair of frame Greek Revival semidetached townhouses in 1859 for $9500 for Neville Bienvenu. Note the similar double townhouses at 1427 Bourbon. The building contract specifies 17- by-20-foot double parlors, separated by columns. A wing with a 15- by-18-foot dining room is separated from the parlors by an 8-foot-wide gallery. Paneled doors were to have 17-inch surrounds and baseboards had 14-inch molded plinths.

1428 Bourbon Street

Laurent Ursain Guesnon, a free man of color and carpenter, bought the lot in 1807 and built the brick-between-post creole cottage soon after his marriage in 1811 to Mathilde Zolla, free woman of color. He then lived in the house until his death in 1842 with at least one daughter, Helôise Guesnon. His widow sold the house in 1854.

The beautiful arched openings with their fanlights and the arched dormers, under round-heads beside fluted pilasters with casement openings, intimate the early date and the endurance of creole building traditions. The gabled ends, the delicate overhang supported by iron bearers, and the position of the house on the banquette, set low to the ground, constitute creole urban traditions. Alterations have not spoiled the proportions of this early house.

Pauger Street

A continuation of Bourbon Street. Named after French surveyor Adrien Pauger who died in service at New Orleans.

1436 Pauger Street

Dolliole-Clapp house. Pauger Street was first named Bagatelle by Marigny, and this small house is an ironic little trifle for the visitor to enjoy. The house and its owner-builder typify Faubourg Marigny's inhabitants and their homes. Jean Louis Dolliole, a free man of color, entre-preneur, and leader in his social community, bought the lot in 1820. The plastered brick-between-post five-sided house he built fits the curve in the street, resulting in a double-pitch hip roof covered in its original flat pan-tiles. Although buildings with tile roofs became the law for the Vieux Carré after the fires of 1788 and 1794, few examples remain.

In the 1940s and 1950s a talented architect, illustrator, and man of letters, Lewis Clapp, owned the cottage; he shortened the spires of French casement openings. Superdome architect Arthur Davis subsequently renovated it in the 1960's.

1445 Pauger Street

The delicate, arched center opening with fluted surrounds and a fanlight of this 1825 house, built for commission merchant Antoine Boutin, is a clue to the center-hall plan and the Federal period of its construction. The house, despite its center-hall, continues the creole tradition of double cabinets to the rear flanking a recessed gallery, now enclosed. Boutin, a partner with Hyppolyte Gally in a real estate and commodity investment partnership, lost the house in 1845 in a forced liquidation.

1455-57 Pauger Street

A modest cypress weatherboard-covered brick-between-post creole cottage with a double-pitch hip roof, once slate, was built by Joseph Prieto, free man of color, soon after 1810. Prieto died in the house after writing a will in 1836, arranging that the ultimate sale of the house in 1841 for $5000 finance the purchase of his nephew's freedom and the purchase for emancipation of certain of Bernard de Marigny's slaves, the children of Marie Jeanne, free woman of color, and wife of Joseph Mandeville. Testamentary executor for the deceased 71-year-old Prieto was his neighbor, Jean-Louis Dolliole. The will directed Dolliole to free seven of Prieto's slaves, who probably lived in the service building behind the house.

1613 Pauger Street

This is an unusual three-bay cottage with a Greek Revival entrance leading to a side hall: the Greek Revival door surround and the hall reveal Anglo-American influence in construction. Lucien Mansion, a free man of color and a prominent tobacco manufacturer, built the house after his purchase of the lot in 1848.

1624 Pauger Street

This is is an ashlar-fronted creole cottage of wood cut to resemble stone. The regular gable ends incorporate the overhang, and the large pilastered and pedimented pair of dormers date the house to the 1850s.

Burgundy Street

2016-2020 Burgundy Street

In 1836 Jean Asher Moses Nathan, a Dutch-Jewish immigrant, rebuilt an 1806 brick-between-posts cottage erected for free woman of color Constance Bouligny. Nathan established his *placée* and two children in the unusual Greek Revival house with three dormers, eight Doric box columns supporting a deep overhang and a rusticated wood facade. The house is open by appointment and contains a bed and breakfast.

Dauphine Street

1801 Dauphine Street

Charles Laveaux storehouse. The plastered-brick first floor of this two-story corner storehouse was built before 1833 for free man of color, Charles Laveaux, father of the Voodoo Queen, Marie Laveau [sic]. Laveaux bought the property directly from Bernard de Marigny in 1817. C. Erne, the 1869 purchaser, added the frame second story and the cast iron gallery that turns around the corner, like the building, to follow the bend in the road.

2016-2020 Burgundy Street. Sun Oak, built about 1807 and renovated by 1836. Headquarters for the Education Through Historic Preservation Program. Photograph by Eugene D. Cizek, Restoration architect Cizek presented the triple house as it appeared during the Greek Revival period, preserving, however, what remained of the older part of the complex in his 1976 restoration.

1809-1811 Dauphine Street (see p. 50)

Built between 1833 and 1840 for Frenchman, Joseph Sauvinet, as rental property, this creole cottage retains its outbuildings and all the character-istics that make it one of the best examples in Marigny. Outstanding, common-wall brick kitchens serve both 1809 Dauphine Street and 905 Kerlerec Street around the corner, which Sauvinet also built.

An attorney, Sauvinet, native of Bayonne, France, lived at 831 Governor Nicholls Street in the French Quarter from 1822. His 1843 will assigned the house at 905 Kerlerec to Rose Dazema, *femme de couleur libre*. Dazema, the unmarried Frenchman's *placée*, left the house to Sauvinet's brother.

1903 Dauphine Street

Built for Joseph Drouet, this center-hall Greek Revival villa dates from soon after 1864. Only the recessed central entrance with its attendant hall shows American influence even at this late date.

2014-2016, 2018-2020, and 2022-2024 Dauphine Street

William Kincaide, a free man of color, drew the plans and built this row of three creole cottages for Pierre and Albert Hoa in 1841 for $6250. The narrow alleys between the houses are bricked and once were guarded by narrow batten gates. All have lost the second-level dormers.

2111 Dauphine Street on Washington Square

Governor Claiborne's son W. C. C. Claiborne, Jr. and his Parisian wife, Louise de Balathier, and their 10 children moved into their new home in 1859. This Greek Revival center-hall two-story house built on a lot acquired in 1850 cost them $14,000. A large, two-story brick kitchen extends along one side of the lot, connected to the main house at the second level by a gallery extension. The Claiborne house interior continues the Greek Revival exterior motifs; often, restrained Greek Revival exteriors turn inward to exuberant interiors that match the furniture, not the architecture.

1809-1811 Dauphine Street. Photograph by Betsy Swanson.

2100 Dauphine Street. Claiborne-Burglass house from Washington Square. Photograph by Eugene D. Cizek.

Chartres Street

A drive downriver through the Marigny district along Chartres Street is delightfully instructive. The back of the Marigny has interesting creole storehouses and townhouses developed by the Architects Company, mixed among 1840s creole cottages and frame late Victorian shotguns, such as those from the 1890s at **2311-2313 Chartres Street**.

2340 Chartres Street

This house was designed and built in 1828 by Nelson Fouché, a free man of color and architect-builder who came from St. Domingue via Cuba. His sale of the new house to Richard Lambert the year it was built, along with two slaves for $8500, reveals the custom, usual in New Orleans, for free persons of color to own slaves. Chattel property was often sold along with the houses or buildings where the slaves resided with their owners. Arched openings with fanlights below, the hip roof, and the arched dormers give creole character to the building.

2718 Chartres Street

This house was built in the 1830s for Louis Charles Faurie, a brass founder and blacksmith with a shop in the French quarter. The four-bay two-story creole townhouse has its original two-story brick kitchen with pan-tile roof and a double cooking fireplace. The complex is another asset to a fine square with good buildings in the **500 block of St. Ferdinand Street** and in the **2700 block of Decatur Street**.

2800 Block Chartres Street at Press Street

Press Street was named for the cotton press established there, followed by a number of sugar storage warehouses. A set of 1830s warehouses remain on this square along with later, decorative brick warehouses in the style of the 1880s.

Notice the tie rods, the patterns made by recessed and projecting bricks, and imagine such buildings rehabilitated for residential use, containing popular loft-type spaces.

Downriver past Marigny is Bywater, a National Historic District on the way to St. Bernard and Plaquemines Parishes. The character of Bayou Terre Aux Boeufs and the rural marsh environment settled by the French in the early eighteenth century and by Canary Islanders in the last half of the eighteenth century can be sensed by a drive to Jackson Barracks to see the Louisiana State Military Museum. Visit the Chalmette National Park (504-589-4430) 6 miles southeast of downtown with the plantation home of Judge René Beauregard, following St. Claude Avenue to Louisiana Route 46 (St. Bernard Highway). Go next to the Isleño Center of the Jean Lafitte National Park on La. Route 46, St. Bernard Highway, about 9 miles south of the Chalmette Battlefield site (504-682-0862).

Delery Street at the Mississippi River

Jackson Barracks, with its group of brick, double-galleried plantation-type buildings, was designed by Lt. Frederick Wilkinson between 1825 and 1835 and completed for $182,000. This quadrangle of Greek Revival officers' quarters and soldiers' barracks served as an embarkation point for troops bound for Mexico in the War of 1848, and was a hospital for those returning. The post's exciting military history matches the architecture.

Reynes Street at the Levee

Holy Cross College was established in 1849 by five brothers of the Holy Cross and three nuns from France as an orphanage for children of yellow fever victims. Reynes, the street name, commemorates the family who had owned the plantation and the house where the orphans lived until its demolition in 1895 to be replaced by the present building by architect James Freret, unfortunately mutilated by additions in 1912. A wood gazebo at the levee end of the campus was once a waiting station for streetcar-riding students.

400 and 504 Egania Streets

This curious pair of houses beneath the levee at the Orleans Parish line were built for Captain Paul Doullut and his son in 1905. They have achieved international fame, as they have captured the imagination of photographers across the world. Few New Orleanians are familiar with these out-of-the-way houses that the steamboat captain built after seeing the Japanese exhibit building at the St. Louis World's Fair in 1904. The Doullut family were early benefactors of nearby St. Maurice's Church and the houses have never left the family. One is open to the public.

Judge René Beauregard House

At the Chalmette National Historical Park. This country house, one room deep with three-over-three room plan without halls, having a hipped roof pierced by dormers on each elevation, was remodeled in 1856 and again in 1865, reportedly by James Gallier, Jr. A raised basement country house in the colonial manner was given a Greek Revival gallery and decoration. The full-length columns front and rear provide a monumental appearance to a modest-sized house. Architect Samuel Wilson, Jr. rehabilitated it in 1957-1958 as a visitors' center for the National Park Service.

Chalmette Battlefield Judge René Beauregard house, now the Service Center for the National Park Service. Photograph by Betsy Swanson.

St. Philip Street between Marais and Tremé Streets seen from the edge of Louis Armstrong Park with St. Augustin's Church steeple in the background. Photograph by Betsy Swanson. Faubourg Tremé was the neighborhood of many musicians in New Orleans throughout the nineteenth and twentieth centuries, creoles of color and blacks, such as Buddy Bolden and Jelly Roll Morton. From community of the creoles of color came poets, like Rodolphe Desdunes, prominent businessmen, such as Thomy Lafon, and political activists, such as Homère Plessy.

Faubourg Treme and the Bayou Road

Claude Tremé, after whom the creole suburb behind the city ramparts is named, has a history as amazing as Bernard de Marigny's is colorful. A French immigrant from Sauvigny, France, a hat seller by trade, Tremé became well acquainted with most of the important landowners in the city after his arrival in the 1780s. Nonetheless, he was sentenced to five years' imprisonment in the garrison by Governor Miró in 1788 after shooting and killing an alleged thief on his own property, a black slave belonging to François Bernoudy, who had a plantation across the river. Out of prison by 1791, Tremé was once again a member of the local militia, and in March 1793 he petitioned for permission to marry Julie Moreau. They married the same year, after he proved his purity of blood according to Spanish regulations, in a notarized document.

His bride's grandmother, Julie Prevost Moreau, died the same year, and the former prisoner found himself owner of one of the great plantations of French colonial Louisiana. The newlyweds moved into the French colonial plantation house, which stood near the city ramparts from about 1739 until after World War I.

Tremé began selling off a few lots of his property behind the city before the Louisiana Purchase, and in 1810 he sold the entire plantation, minus the few lots, for $40,000 to the city for a subdivision. Jacques Tanesse, city surveyor, laid out the new Faubourg Tremé in 1812. Between that date and the Civil War the land from the city ramparts to the Bayou St. John developed from smaller habitations and suburban country seats to city blocks with urban homes in the creole tradition much like Faubourg Marigny. The continuing cut-through of Esplanade Avenue across Bayou St. John helped the development of Faubourg Tremé. The Meilleur-Lansford House at 1418 Govenor Nicholls (see p. 63) and the nearby St. Augustin's Church by J. N. B. DePouilly, dating from 1841, anchor the area.

Plan book 74, folio 16, New Orleans Notarial Archives. Watercolor by E. Surgi and A. Persac, 1860. Courtesy of the Historic New Orleans Collection. This little group of buildings drawn for a sheriff's sale in 1860 typify the one-time appearance of Faubourg Tremé prior to the 1956 urban renewal program. These once stood on Conti at the corner of North Villere Street backed by St. Louis and Marais Streets.

1114-1116 and 1122 Barracks Street at North Rampart Street. Photograph by Betsy Swanson, 1969.

1114-1416 Barracks Street

Creole cottages were still being built in the Classic style in the late 1860s when 1114-1416 appeared on its containing lot. The three-room two-story brick kitchen pre-dates the house on the lot and served an early house on South Rampart Street.

1122 Barracks Street

Built by creole builders Jacques Michel St. Martin and Nicholas Duru in 1846, this is an unusual, Greek Revival- style, three-bay cottage with the entrance leading to a side gallery in the piazza style of Charleston, rare in New Orleans. Like many creole houses it has a masonry front with wood sides.

1301-1313 Bayou Road

Monrose Row, three masonry two-and-one-half-story Greek Revival row houses, was begun in 1839.

1418 Govenor Nicholls (old Bayou Road)

Simon Meilleur, once Keeper of the City Jail, had this *maison de maître* built in 1829. The dormer was added to a center hall raised villa that retains outbuildings, its original interior, and much of its large lot.

2100 Block of Conti Street

Shotgun doubles line the street, these examples dating from the 1890s. Shiplap board fronts, also called dropsiding, weatherboard sides, and deep

1418 Governor Nicholls Street (Old Bayou Road). Simon Meilleur house. Photograph by Betsy Swanson. The finest remaining maison de maître in the historic neighborhood was the home of prominent bookseller Franklin Goldthwaite, then of Alonzo Lansford, painting conservator and director of the Delgado Museum. John C. Williams and Arthur Q. Davis are restoration architects for the villa's use as the center for the Tremé Historical Education Network.

2100 block of Conti Street. Street scene featuring shotgun houses.
Photograph by Betsy Swanson.

bracketed overhangs characterize these, built at the *banquette* in the urban manner. They form a pleasing rhythm of roof lines, brackets, segmental windows, and doors with molded cornices. The property once belonged to the Baroness de Pontalba, the indomitable Micaela, inherited from her father, Andrés Almonester y Roxas.

1717 Kerlerec Street

Charles Martinez, a well-to-do free man of color, entered into a contract in 1842 with his brother-in-law, builder Pierre Theodule Olivier, and entrepreneur François Muro, for *a maison principale*

and kitchen to cost $1106. According to the contract, the creole house is brick-between-posts, 28 feet by 32 feet, divided into two rooms with a front gallery and a rear cabinet gallery and two gables on the front. The house was to be raised 24 inches on brick piers. The kitchen was to be made of barge planks, covered with wood staves, divided into three rooms, whitewashed in and out.

411 North Rampart Street

Our Lady of Guadeloupe Church was built in 1826-27 as a mortuary chapel for the new cemetery St. Louis No. 1 after

1717 Kerlerec Street. Martinez-Abadie cottage, 1842. Photograph by Betsy Swanson. Galleried creole cottage in its semitropical setting, built for free man of color Charles Martinez by his brother-in-law, builder Pierre Olivier.

designs by Gurlie and Guillot. The commission was awarded after a competition, although William Brand had impressed the church wardens, too. The triple-arched facade with the covered walkway recalls the first story of the Cabildo.

Rampart Street at Ursulines Street

Louis Armstrong Park and Congo-Beauregard Square. The development of a memorial to Louis Armstrong, the great jazz musician, on a 32-acre site that was cleared of the homes and bars where he and other developers of jazz lived and played their music is irony indeed. Adjacent is Congo-Beauregard Square, the site of slave dances on Sundays in the pre-Civil War period. Plans from 1974 for the redevelopment as a park of the section of Faubourg Tremé razed in the final years of 1950s urban renewal included preservation of four historic buildings that remained in the compound after the urban renewal clearance.

Perseverance Hall was built in 1820 by architect-builder Bernard Thibaud for the *Loge La Perseverance* and is one of the oldest Masonic buildings in Louisiana. Membership was primarily refugees from St. Domingue. The separate, two-story *maison a étage* was designed and built in 1830 by architects François Correjolles and Jean Chaigneau for the Masonic Lodge.

Rabassa-DePouilly House in Louis Armstrong Park was built for Louis Rabassa soon after 1825. The plan is creole, with four square rooms and two *cabinets* flanking a recessed back gallery. Original to the house are the sloped gable ends with a canted roof in the rear to extend out over the rear gallery and *cabinets*. The house is raised in the rural tradition. In 1875, the elderly J. N. B. DePouilly, New Orleans' notable French architect of the early American period, lived in the house.

1433 North Rampart Street

Etoile Polaire Masonic Lodge No. 1. This Greek Revival building probably dates from 1832 when the lodge, chartered by the state legislature in 1816, received a $7500 loan from the Grand Lodge of Louisiana.

Esplanade Ridge
and Bayou St. John

E splanade Avenue was the creole equivalent of the elegant St. Charles Avenue in American New Orleans. Spanish colonial Fort San Carlos had to be demolished during the decade after the Louisiana Purchase to begin the Esplanade. Not until 1850 did the Esplanade reach Bayou St. John because lawsuits and settlements had to be negotiated as the city cut through numerous plantations.

Anchored at the river by William Strickland's 1836 U.S. Mint, one of the major Federal period buildings in North America, the Esplanade follows a high ridge between the River and Bayou St. John. It cuts through creole Faubourg Tremé to meet and pierce the colonial plantations established by French Canadians as early as 1699.

Esplanade evolved as the mid-nineteenth-century creole answer to the Garden District. Between 1850 and the end of Reconstruction in 1877, it far surpassed St. Charles Avenue in grandeur. By the time Esplanade Avenue had been extended to the bayou, philanthropist John McDonogh had bequeathed his large plantation there to the cities of New Orleans and Baltimore, and a city park had been initiated at the juncture of bayou and avenue.

In 1850, too, Esplanade Avenue was in its prime. The men who commissioned houses here were mostly creole, in business with Americans. A few well–known American men resided on Esplanade, but invariably they had creole wives or connections; Aristide Hopkins of **730 Esplanade Avenue,** agent to the Baroness Pontalba of Paris, was one such American. Another was John Slidell, of **1020 Esplanade Avenue**. Slidell's 1835 mansion was designed by architect James Gallier and is now enveloped in the *Unione Italiana* building; Slidell had married creole Mathilde Deslonde in 1835 and went on to resign his senate seat to become Commissioner to France for the Confederacy, where he and his family remained after the Civil War.

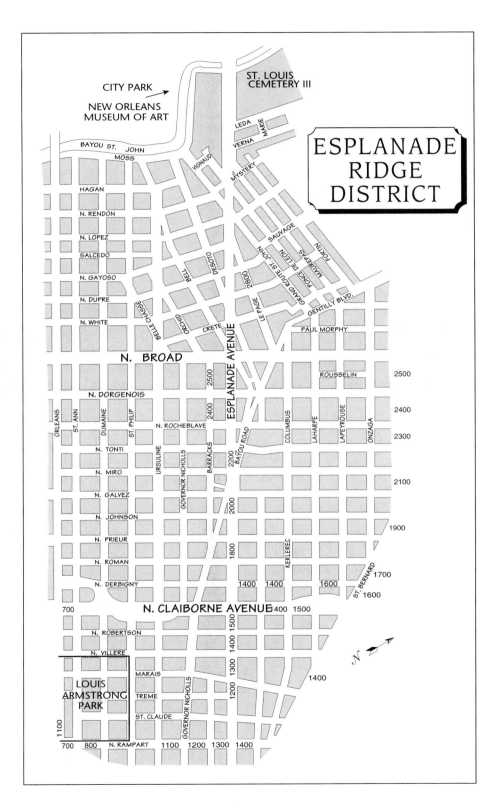

CITY PARK

NEW ORLEANS
MUSEUM OF ART

ST. LOUIS
CEMETERY III

LEDA

MARIE

VERNA

BAYOU ST. JOHN

MOSS

VIGNAUD

MYSTERY

HAGAN

N. RENDON

N. LOPEZ

SALCEDO

N. GAYOSO

N. DUPRE

N. WHITE

SAUVAGE

DESOTO

BELL

PONCE DE LEON

MAUREPAS

GRAND ROUTE ST. JOHN

FOXTIN

2800

ORCHID

BELLE CHASSE

CRETE

LE PAGE

GENTILLY BLVD.

PAUL MORPHY

N. BROAD

ESPLANADE AVENUE

2500

ROUSSELIN

2500

N. DORGENOIS

ORLEANS

ST. ANN

DUMAINE

ST. PHILIP

2400

COLUMBUS

LAHARPE

LAPEYROUSE

ONZAGA

2400

2300

N. ROCHEBLAVE

N. TONTI

URSULINE

GOVERNOR NICHOLLS

BARRACKS

2200

BAYOU ROAD

2300

N. MIRO

2100

N. GALVEZ

2000

N. JOHNSON

1900

N. PRIEUR

1800

KERLEREC

N. ROMAN

N. DERBIGNY

1400

1400

1600

ST. BERNARD

1700

1600

700

N. CLAIBORNE AVENUE

400

1500

N. ROBERTSON

1500

1400

N. VILLERE

1300

MARAIS

1200

1400

LOUIS
ARMSTRONG
PARK

TREME

GOVERNOR NICHOLLS

ST. CLAUDE

1100

700

800

N. RAMPART

1100

1200

1300

1400

N

ESPLANADE
RIDGE
DISTRICT

67

    The buildings along Esplanade Avenue exhibit American influence at the front elevations, reflecting their usually mid-nineteenth–century construction dates. After about 1835 most of the well–known French architects, such as J. N. B. de Pouilly, Gurlie and Guillot, Pinson and Pizetta, and François Correjolles, had quit design.

U.S. Mint, anchor of the Esplanade Ridge at the Mississippi River, designed by William Strickland, 1835. Pencil and white wash by Alfred Rodolph Waud, 1866. Used for wood engraving in *Harper's Weekly*, March 9, 1867. Courtesy of the Historic New Orleans Collection.

504 Esplanade Avenue. Plan book 71, folio 43, New Orleans Notarial Archives. Watercolor by M. Harrison, civil engineer, 1845. Courtesy of the Historic New Orleans Collection.

Esplanade Ridge

400 Block of Esplanade Avenue

The U.S. Mint, designed in 1836 by William Strickland, reflects the architects's clear, structural interpretation of a restrained Greek Revival style and relates to his work in Nashville, Charleston, and Washington. Even so, the building also relates to its French Quarter setting, with galleries running across the rear elevation. The Mint is now part of the Louisiana State Museum and houses the Jazz and Mardi Gras collections. *National Historic Landmark.*

504 Esplanade Avenue

In 1840 the Citizens' Bank hired builder E. W. Sewell to build a bank with three stores here. The 1840s contract stipulated that the cornice was to be like that of the "Fabric Store at Royal and Orleans." That store had been designed by French architects Gurlie and Guillot and had the familiar garland. The millwork was "to follow that of Mr. Soniat's on Hospital [Governor Nicholls Street] between Levee and Conde [Chartres Street]." Building by analogy was common then, and it gives coherence and a frame of reference if not uniformity to New Orleans's constructed environment.

524 Esplanade Avenue

One of the earlier remaining houses on the Esplanade, built in 1845, the John Wesham house, looks quite American with its solid Greek Key surround at the American-style central entrance. The projecting central element with its wide pediment relates the house to the Beauregard house **(1113 Chartres Street, see p. 26)** and the Xiques House **(1519 Dauphine Street, see p. 28)** in type and style.

524 Esplanade Avenue John Wesham-Maud O'Bryan house. Photograph by Betsy Swanson. Courtesy of the Historic New Orleans Collection.

606 Esplanade Avenue

Michel Doradou Bringier of l'Hermitage Plantation on the river bought this townhouse, one of three once-identical Greek Revival houses, in 1837. It had been built in 1834 for attorney Henry R. Denis. Bringier and his wife, Aglae DuBourg of Jamaica, used it when they were in the city until 1850. Edward Barnett, notary, an 1850 purchaser of the house, had Elijah Cox, architect-builder, enlarge it in 1859.

704 Esplanade Avenue

John Gauche was a rich crockery merchant who tore down an earlier house to build this one in the creole taste in 1856. The *Daily Crescent* reported in 1856 that the $11,000 house was built under Gauche's "own superintendence." The chaste granite portico is unusual for New Orleans. The simplicity of the large masonry cube with its even articulation transfers emphasis to the iron balcony with its bracketed cresting and to the cast iron fence. Richard Koch restored

704 Esplanade Avenue. John Gauche house. Photograph by Betsy Swanson.

the house for Matilda Geddings Gray after her 1937 purchase, and her niece, Mrs. Harold Stream, had Koch and Wilson architects do further work in 1969.

905 Esplanade Avenue

This plantation-style brick raised house with a Greek Revival floor plan was built soon after 1831 for Frenchman and sugar planter François Gardère. The front elevation was altered for Judge Charles Claiborne after 1894, but the sides and the rear have not been changed and exhibit the original creole detail. The segmentally arched dormer windows with pediments and pilasters are also typically creole. Like Louisiana plantation houses and villas, this house, unusual for Esplanade Avenue, was designed to be seen from all elevations, and as is the custom in creole houses, numerous architectural amenities enhance the rear elevation.

917 Esplanade Avenue. Service wing of Gardére house. Photograph by Betsy Swanson. Courtesy of the Historic New Orleans Collection.

1037 Esplanade Avenue. Petronille Monsignac house. With a small creole cottage to the right, 1029 Esplanade Avenue. Plan book 104, folio 8, New Orleans Notarial Archives. Watercolor by J. A. Guerard, Jr., surveyor, 1839. Courtesy of the Historic New Orleans Collection. This archival drawing made for an 1839 sheriff's sale of an 1833 house reveals the house as it was built.

917 Esplanade Avenue

François Gardère also had this town-house built soon after 1831, selling it in 1836 for $20,000. A recessed entrance, three openings, and double-hung windows suggest anomalous American influence for a Frenchman's house; the brick was originally painted and penciled. However, the chaste iron balcony and the small single dormer at the front and rear along with a handsome curving stairway in a rear semi-enclosed gallery are creole characteristics.

1037 Esplanade Avenue

This double creole townhouse reveals Spanish colonial tradition, although it was built in 1833–1836 for Petronille Bordrier Monsignac, a *femme de couleur libre* from St. Domingue. She left to it attorney Charles Kosselius, for whose estate sale the drawing was made. Once it had a full third–story setback behind a roof garden protected by a wrought iron railing. Notice the ornate series of dentil and sawtooth rows and molded string-

courses that define the location of the original roofline.

1308 Esplanade Avenue

Only one of this row of four creole cottages remains, but it indicates how the area of Esplanade within Faubourg Tremé continued to have creole cottages, the primary building vocabulary for the creole suburb. Each had separate outbuildings, according to the colonial tradition.

1519 Esplanade Avenue

The Marsoudet villa is a victim of the elevated expressway splitting Esplanade at Claiborne. In 1846 Mme. Eliza Ducros Marsoudet, acting in a separate capacity from her marital community, entered into a contract with creole builders Nicholas Duru and Jacques Michel St. Martin, to build this villa for $5800. The nine-page document describes in every detail the interior embellishments of the 54– by 60-foot house with its recessed

1308 Esplanade Avenue. Plan book 21, folio 25, New Orleans Notarial Archives. Passebon Row. Watercolor by E. Surgi, 1844. Courtesy of the Historic New Orleans Collection. The artist-surveyor Eugene Surgi, has made a genre painting of the elevations hinting of the lifestyle in this area of Esplanade Avenue not so long after the cut-through. Two-story service wings are perceptible behind the corner house. Fencing is of the seven board variety, still seen in the old neighborhoods today. Service pass-through gates connect the detached cottages, all identical investment housing, having batten shutters with strap hinges, casement openings, and two chimneys between gable ends. Each house has a delicate *abat vent* (overhang) with iron bearers above a chaste brick dentil. The houses seem to have plastered brick fronts and weatherboard sides, customary to the area. Note the street light fixtures and newly planted trees with their protective surrounds. The militia is marching on a grassy neutral ground, and a plank walkway crosses the neutral ground from Marais street.

Mourning portrait of Marie Basilice Pedesclaux, Madame Bernard Duchamp with her children and a portrait of her deceased husband, native of Bordeaux. Anonymous oil on canvas, ca. 1832. Daughter of Pierre Pedesclaux, a Spanish colonial notary in New Orleans, Basilice Pedesclaux Duchamp ran the plantation her father had established on part of the old Company of the Indies property from 1827 until 1839 when it was subdivided. She also owned Duchamp townhouses on Toulouse street in the French Quarter. Such mourning portraits were quite stylish among the Roman Catholic creoles of New Orleans. Soon after this mourning portrait was finished the young child in her lap, Henry, died, as did Louise Thomeguez, a daughter from her first marriage.

central entrance having seven steps. The front elevation was to be painted in red with "white lines designating the bricks." "All shutters to be a beautiful green," stipulated the contract in French. All walls except the ceilings were to be prepared for wallpaper. The detached timber kitchen, measuring 46 by 12 feet, was divided into eight rooms with a middle stairway to the second level.

1707 Esplanade Avenue

The Cyprien Dufour house was designed by Henry Howard and Albert Diettel in 1859 on a lot costing $12,000. Wing and Muir built the $40,000 house, one of the most expensive in the city at the time. A side–hall house with double galleries, it is translated into an exuberant late classic decorative project. Paired columns and paired brackets abound to complement the prerequisite wing with bays and segmental arched openings. This is not just facade architecture, though; the entablature with its bracketed cornice returns around the house along an undulating rear elevation to encompass an interior curved stairwell. The house has recently become an inn.

2023 and 2033 Esplanade Avenue

Esplanade Avenue, after it cut through original farms and plantations, provided home sites for descendants of the earliest settlers. In 1860 A. B. Charpentier hired Alexander Castaing to design his villa at 2023 that Hubert Gerard built for $11,000. 2033 may possibly be an 1890s enlargement of the old Spanish colonial Rodriguez–Castanedo plantation house, moved to this site when Esplanade Avenue was cut through. The old house would have stood in the middle of the new avenue; Mme. Castanedo lost her battle with the city to prevent the prolongment of the Esplanade. So she just moved her house out of the thoroughfare to border the new, wide boulevard.

1707 Esplanade Avenue. Dufour-Baldwin house, rear elevation. Photograph by Betsy Swanson, 1969. Courtesy of the Historic New Orleans Collection.

2306 Esplanade Avenue. Plan book 5, folio 18, New Orleans Notarial Archives. Watercolor by E. Surgi and A. Persac, civil engineers, 1860. Courtesy of the Historic New Orleans Collection. This house is notable as the place where French painter Edgar Degas visited his uncle, Michel Musson, his brother, René and his wife, Estelle, and their children in 1872-1873. The archival drawing illustrates the amenities that the municipality installed along Esplanade Avenue on the eve of the Civil War: street trees, gutters, and curbing. Notice the detached two-story service wing behind the carriage entrance way.

2306 Esplanade Avenue

The Musson house, built in 1854 by builder William Belly for $5595, has been sliced in two and redecorated in the Italianate style. The archival drawing shows the house as it appeared in 1860 when the extended family of Michel Musson, prominent cotton factor, rented it. Musson's daughter, Estelle, had married René Degas of France, her first cousin, and brother of Edgar Degas, the painter. Edgar Degas visited his brother and cousins for about three months in 1872–1873, a trip represented in a number of his paintings.

Degas painted a scene from the back door of the Musson house, showing the home of Judge Olivier out beyond the garden. Little did he know that René was looking out that way, too, for he abandoned the blind Estelle and their children, running off to France with the young creole wife of the older Judge Olivier. The family gave up the name Degas, and René's descendants are known today as Mussons.

2337, 2341 Esplanade Avenue. Photograph by Betsy Swanson. Courtesy of the Historic New Orleans Collection. A second story has been added to one of these Classic-style side-hall shotgun houses with plastered brick fronts and frame sides, dating from about 1862, built to rent to creoles or plantation owners who needed a townhouse.

2337–2341 Esplanade Avenue

It's hard to imagine that these two houses were once identical plaster-front weatherboard-side one-story shotguns in the classic style. John Budd Slawson had them built in 1862 soon after he bought the Bayou Road Omnibus Line for $36,000. Slawson saw opportunity for the development of Esplanade once he owned the horse-drawn coaches that ran along Bayou Road. The recessed entry leading to a wide hall behind a classic set of pilasters with their deep dentiled entablature signifies American influence, as do the double–hung windows. The ironwork banding the overhang on the two houses is unusual.

2447 Esplanade Avenue

To find Second Empire–style houses in New Orleans that are not simply traditional villas or side–hall houses with appended mansard roofs is unusual. This was one of two well-designed Second Empire houses dating from soon after 1874 when George Washington Dunbar, a local manufacturer, had them built for his family and their children.

2623 Esplanade Avenue. DeSoto Park. The Art Nouveau-style fence around this tiny park encloses much of the agricultural and romantic history of Bayou St. John. The land for the park was donated to the city by the Louis A. Jung family in 1896. The Jungs are an old Spanish colonial family owning land that had belonged through the preceding two centuries to New Orleans most historic figures, Andrés Almonester, Nicolas Maria Vidal, last Spanish Intendant, and Daniel Clark, an Irish entrepreneur who fought a duel with Governor Claiborne. As the history of the land unfolds, French colonial characters appear: Brasilier Tourangeau, Vincent le Sénéchal d'Auberville, Louis Césaire LeBreton, Elizabeth Desruisseaux and others.

2447 Esplanade Avenue. George Dunbar House, built about 1874 in the Second Empire style. Photograph by Betsy Swanson, 1969. Courtesy of the Historic New Orleans Collection.

One has been demolished and this one has lost its front porch and railing, a side gallery, and the second–level balcony. The interior is impressive in its exuberance and the house exhibits the progression of architectural styles that marched toward the bayou along Esplanade Avenue.

2623 Esplanade Avenue

About 1896 or soon after, Hinderer's Ironworks fashioned this art nouveau fence with its two delicate gates supported by contrasting heavy posts.

3400 Block of Esplanade Avenue at 1438 Leda Street

Florence Luling, a native Alsatian, appeared in New Orleans before 1848, married into the Hermann family (*see*

Portrait of the Musson Sisters of New Orleans: Marie Célestine, Mme Auguste de Gas, mother of the French artist, and her sister Anne Eugénie, La Duchesse de Rochefort. Oil painting by Catherine Longchamps, 1835. Courtesy of the Historic New Orleans Collection. Daughters of Jean-Baptiste Germain Musson, a native of St. Domingue, and Marie Célestine Désirée Rillieux of New Orleans, these ladies and their brother, Michel Musson, were raised by their widowed father in Paris. Germain Musson's fortune was made in New Orleans, in cotton and in Mexican silver. Family homes were in the French Quarter, with a business on Canal and Royal Streets in the granite buildings at 633-637 Canal Street. His son Michel built a house at Coliseum and Third Streets in the Garden District about 1859, living there until 1869. He had a cotton factoring business in the 800 block of Perdido Street at Carondelet Street, where Edgar Degas painted his famous painting of the Musson family and employees in 1873, now at the Municipal Museum at Pau, France. After 1869 Michel Musson rented a house at 2305 Esplanade Avenue, then 372, where his wife, Odile Longer, died in 1872, but where he raised his grandchildren by his daughter, Estelle, and his nephew and son-in-law, René de Gas, brother of the artist.

3400 block Esplanade Avenue, facing Leda Street. Elevation of the Florence Luling Mansion by James Gallier, Jr., 1865. Florence Luling had the architectural firm of Gallier and Esterbrook design and build this important mansion, The plan recalls the Philadelphia work of John Notman rather than local Italianate prototypes such as the Dufour house nearby. The elevation shows the flanking pavilions, now demolished, connected to the magnificent three-story main house by a pair of arcaded and balustered bridges above a dry moat. The concept recalls Thomas Jefferson's Monticello, also northern Italian in inspiration.

820 St. Louis Street, p. 41) and moved into the Garden District at **1433 Philip Street.** He made a fortune during the Union occupation of New Orleans sending turpentine to New York. After the war, he contracted with the firm of Gallier and Esterbrook to design and build this lavish residence.

The Luling Mansion is a major departure from the traditional New Orleans reflection of the Italianate style to an Italian Renaissance palazzo mode, with bows to Palladian vocabulary and the interpretation of Town and Davis in New York. It shows Gallier, Jr. reworking the plans by Richard Morris Smith for the Garden District palazzo of James Robb, now demolished. The pair of two–story flanking pavilions connected to the main house with bridges have been destroyed, and there have been other mutilations.

The neighborhood brought tragedy to the Lulings, whose two young sons drowned in nearby Bayou St. John. This, combined with reverses in cotton factoring during Reconstruction, caused Luling to sell his new house in 1871. The appropriate purchaser was the Louisiana Jockey Club. Luling moved to England, then returned to Mobile, Alabama where he renovated the Dawson house in Springhill in the Italianate style.

Only three other houses on Esplanade Avenue may have equaled the Luling mansion in scale and concept, and they have been destroyed. In the Garden District, only the Buckner–Soulé mansion on Jackson Avenue approaches it in scale since the Washington Avenue Robb mansion (once Newcomb College) was demolished in the 1950s.

Bayou St. John

Bayou Road led to Bayou St. John, the site of the earliest settlement in the Mississippi Valley. Canadians came downriver in the late 1600s before the founding of New Orleans to establish plantations there.

Branching off Esplanade Avenue in the 2200 block of Bayou Road is a remnant of the old Bayou Road where two landmarks appear, one showing how the Esplanade cut-through disturbed the bucolic rural farmland and the other, an 1859 center–hall house, showing the height of development of the Esplanade Ridge style of architecture.

2257 Bayou Road

The Benachi–Torre house is an outstanding center–hall house built in 1859 for Nicholas Benachi and his second wife Anna Marie Bidault for $18,000. The house and detached two-story service building are enclosed on the spacious grounds by a high cast iron fence with a Gothic-style gate. The complex was donated to the Louisiana Landmarks Society in 1978 by Peter Torre and later sold for use as a private residence.

2275 Bayou Road

The Fleitas–Chauffe house, a *maison principal,* was built for Domingo Fleitas about 1802 and moved here and remodeled on a lowered base in 1836 by his son, Jean Mañuel Fleitas, when Esplanade Avenue was extended, cutting through his property. The son enclosed a rear *cabinet* gallery and added another gallery, appending the dining room and kitchen to the rear. In 1901 Henry S. Chauffe brought his bride to this house, altering and renovating it as he enlarged it.

This important early architectural document was, when built, raised on high brick piers or thick columns with *colombage* construction above. It is plastered over on the front beneath the gallery and weatherboarded on the sides. Pedimented dormers have round headed lights. These characteristics, along with the casement openings, shutters, hardware, and interior proportions, reflect a Purchase-era building date.

1342 Moss Street, Bayou Saint John. Evariste Blanc house. Pen-and-ink drawing by Samuel Wilson, Jr., 1930. Courtesy of the Southeastern Architectural Archive, Tulane University Library. Wraparound galleries and high hip roofs with dormers appear to be endemic to the tropics of the West Indies and the semi-tropical climate of the Gulf south. Ironically, French Canadians brought the type and style with them by 1700 from along the St. Laurence River, where steep-pitched roofs did not collect snow, and the galleries provided covered storage area for wood and equipment during the long, frozen winters.

924 Moss Street

The Louis Blanc house, built between 1816 and 1822 on land acquired by Louis Antoine Blanc in the 1790s, recalls Spanish and French colonial plantations such as Parlange at Point Coupé Parish and the old Fortier Homeplace (Keller House) on the River Road. *New Orleans Historic District Landmark*

1300 Moss Street

The Spanish colonial plantation house was probably built about 1784 for Don Santiago Lloreins, who owned it between 1771 and 1807. It was remodeled or rebuilt after 1807 for Captain Elie Beauregard by Robert Alexander, who built the first U.S. Custom House in 1807–1809. Like the Pitot house, it continues French colonial traditions. *Orleans Parish Landmark.*

1342 Moss Street

The Evariste Blanc house, now Our Lady of the Rosary Rectory, is typical of the smaller plantations of the colonial period but has alterations or was rebuilt about 1834 for Evariste Blanc with classic–style details at the doors and elsewhere. His family retained the property until 1905, when it was donated to the Roman Catholic Church. *New Orleans Historic District Landmark.*

1347 Moss Street

This raised villa–style house in the Greek Revival style was built for Cristobal Morel in the 1840s. The exterior stair piercing the gallery is a holdover from the French colonial traditions. Drop siding and turned balusters are Victorian changes. *New Orleans Historic District Landmark.*

1440 Moss Street

The Pitot house. In its setting on the bayou, this eighteenth century French–style house provides the perfect metaphor for creole Louisiana, encapsulating the French, Spanish, and early American heritage of the area. Dating from the late Spanish colonial period, it continues the traditions established as early as 1708 by Canadian settlers such as Juchereau de St. Denis and Rivard Lavigne. Bartolomeo Bosque, a native of Palma, Majorca, and a local merchant and ship owner, built the house around 1799.

Three rooms across the front with casement doors open onto a broad gallery. Stairways penetrate the gallery floor to the second level, and the traditional small *cabinets* to the rear originally flanked a recessed gallery. Raised above plastered brick columns with a plastered brick raised basement, the main level was built of brick-between-posts, plastered where protected by galleries and covered with wide shiplap siding on the sides.

French doors have transoms with muntins set in a diamond pattern, a motif repeated in the gallery railing. The French traveler C. C. Robin commented upon the handsome house in 1803, "built of wood, surrounded by galleries, in the Chinese fashion." Such detailing unifies the house design.

This was Bosque's country home, his primary home being **619 Chartres Street,** and it, like his townhouse, was probably built by Hilaire Boutét, a prominent builder in New Orleans in the last years of the Spanish colonial period and the post–Louisiana Purchase years. By 1810, when the widow Vincent Rillieux, who lived in the French Quarter where Waldhorn's is today, sold the house to James Pitot for $8400, it looked much like it does today. Pitot, an *émigré* from St. Domingue, arrived in New Orleans in 1796 when he was 35 years old, to become mayor of the city. Madame Pitot, Marie Jeanne Marty, died in the bayou house in 1815 after giving birth to twin girls who died a few weeks later.

The house had to be moved to save it from demolition by the Missionary Sisters of the Sacred Heart and was restored under the direction Samuel Wilson, Jr. for Louisiana Landmarks, which runs it as a museum house today.

1440 Moss Street, Bayou Saint John. The Pitot House. Courtesy of the Louisiana Landmarks Society. Bayou Saint John was settled prior to the founding of New Orleans by French Canadians from Montreal, Quebec and Isle St. Jean on the St. Laurence River. The style of architecture they first built continued to be popular as a building type and style until the 1840s.

City Park

Like Audubon Park, City Park was a French colonial concession or land grant. Ground was broken, however, earlier at the Bayou St. John plantation where François Hery (Duplanty) took title to the land by 1723 and built a "habitation." One of New Orleans's first builders, he was contractor for the first Cabildo, built under Governor O'Reilly in the late 1760s. An 1829 $27,500 mortgage of the same plantation by the Allard family resulted in a sheriff's sale, and John McDonogh bought 654 acres with 19 slaves, 10 horses and mules, and 140 head of cattle for $40,500.

John McDonogh left this and other acreage throughout the city to the cities of Baltimore and New Orleans at his death in 1850. In 1854 the Fourth District Court pronounced the property a public park. Prior to this sudden interest in public parks, New Orleans had a number of privately owned "Pleasure Gardens" financed by subscription. One of the first, Le Jardin du Rocher de Ste Hélène, was developed in the 1830s on land that had been part of the old Leper Hospital that Andrés Almonester y Roxas had built at the "bend in the Bayou Road" (Miro Street) by 1785 when he donated it to the city. In such parks subscribers were expected to bring their families on certain Sundays, and special times were set aside for "subscribers and *femmes de couleur libres,*" according to newspaper advertisements in 1812.

The new City Park languished, except that a French immigrant Jean Marie Saux established a coffeehouse with residence above at present **902 City Park Avenue**, to serve the projected visitors, who would take all-day mule-carriage rides to the acreage across the road. Subsequently, he was appointed caretaker for the park, which was throughout the Civil War and Reconstruction little more than a cow pasture.

In May 1872 John Bogart of Bogart and Culyer, park designers, received a letter in New York asking him to hurry to New Orleans before the beginning of the "sickly season" to consult on park improvements. Bogart was paid $2500 of a $5000 contract and sent a simple plan of City Park, afterward receiving neither correspondence nor the rest of his money.

Finally, in 1891 creoles along Esplanade Avenue and Bayou St. John formed the City Park Improvement Association. In 1899 a local firm, Daney and Wadill made a "Plan of Existing and Proposed Improvements in the New Orleans City Park," inaugurating the concept of the City Beautiful planning vision that captured the imagination of numerous donors to the park.

In 1903 Andry and Bendernagel, local architects, designed the Anseman Bridge according to the Neoclassic preference, setting the taste for the common amenities and embellishments financed by donations from New Orleanians. In 1906 the same firm designed a dancing pavilion; this $15,330 Neoclassic Peristyle has grown old gracefully, although it has lost an ornate parapet. Lumberman John F. Popp preferred the Classic taste in 1917 when he donated $7500 for New Orleans's architect Emile Weil to design a bandstand as a replica of the Temple of Love at the Trianon at Versailles. William Harding McFadden, a Ft. Worth, Texas, oil man, donated the stone bridge leading from the Museum Circle to his own house and the stone Girl Scout cabin built before World War II near Grandjean Bridge (rebuilt 1938), still used by scouting troops. McFadden's 1920s mansion and indoor swimming pool with extensive oriental gardens was eventually sold to the park and the Christian Brothers, who run a school there.

Other buildings and projects have come and gone at City Park. Steamboat Captain Salvatore Pizatti contributed an impressive gateway for Alexander Street in 1910, reflecting Gilded Age taste with ornamental ironwork. Delgado Trade School was built in the early 1910s on the west side of the Orleans Canal with a donation by Isaac Delgado of a working sugar plantation and refinery, Albania, near Jeannerette, in St. Mary Parish, Louisiana.

In 1929 the Chicago firm Bennett, Parsons and Frost produced the blueprint for the extensive WPA work in the 1930s in City Park. At the same time, art deco touched City Park, influenced by the Paris Exposition des Arts Decoratifs in 1925. Mexican sculptor Enrique Alferez, chief of WPA artists who completed the Popp Memorial Fountain in 1936, designed the fountain's central waterspout using lotuslike waves and stylized dolphins, perpetually suspended. Alferez's dolphins were smashed by vandals after 1975.

Alferez, working with architect and park board member F. Julius Dreyfous and architect Richard Koch, began to use cement, an essential material for the art deco aesthetic, for replacement and new bridges in the park. Alferez also designed the sculptures that ornament the geometric walkways in the Rose Garden, the garden's two marble buttresses, and the slender nude figure on Schreiver Fountain.

Louisiana colonial revival architecture also came to the park, under Richard Koch's influence and with the support of local regionalists such as the Woodward brothers, artists who favored exhibiting local art at the new Delgado Museum. The style is preserved in the golf headquarters and the Corral building. Ironically, these *faux* colonial buildings went up even as volunteers wrested the French Quarter from the mauls of demolishers.

Today, City Park, the fourth largest in the United States spreads out over 1500 acres for about 2 miles along Bayou St. John almost to Lake Pontchartrain. Its clusters and rows of live oaks recall the earliest French inhabitants and their agricultural endeavors in the area. The Allard plantation oaks became the site of choice for duels throughout the nineteenth century until the activity was finally outlawed in 1892.

It took the organization Friends of City Park in 1978 for City Park to become the revitalized attraction it is today. "Celebration in the Oaks," begun in 1984 by Friends of City Park, symbolizes the importance of the live oak tree to Louisiana's fertile landscape. Massed planting, as in the Rose Garden and the Montreuil Camellia Garden, as well as the groves of cypress, magnolias, and palms, restored by Friends of City Park, reflect the gardenesque attitude for urban landscapes.

New Orleans Museum of Art.

Isaac Delgado's 1910 surprise gift to City Park of $150,000 for a museum resulted in an Esplanade Avenue focus to the park, and Lelong Avenue was laid out as a tree-lined axis visually extending Esplanade Avenue into the park. A competition for the museum circulated instructions to submit plans "in keeping with the architectural style of a subtropical country." The Chicago firm of Lebenbaum and Marx was selected. While the prevailing taste for tile, terra–cotta, and subtropical notes may have won the assign-ment for the architects, the traditionally classic use of limestone and the recessed porticos with ionic columns supporting a full entablature set a stylized, classic tone that complements the architecture of Esplanade Avenue, the cut-through of which had reached the bayou in 1855 with houses continuing to go up primarily in the Classic style.

Park Commissioner Anthony Monteleone in 1913 donated the entrance to the museum at Lelong Avenue. Giant pylons with engaged Ionic columns frame the park entrance just beyond Beauregard Circle.

Beauregard Monument Association dedicated Alexander Doyle's equestrian stature of Civil War hero and superintendent of West Point, Pierre Gustave Toutant Beauregard, on May 26, 1915, the ninety–seventh anniversary of the creole general's birth in St. Bernard Parish.

The Delgado Museum board, under director James Byrnes, determined the future course of the one-time regional museum by changing the name to the New Orleans Museum of Art, thrusting it into the national scene. Byrnes instigated the first expansion program for the building. August Perez and Associates designed three wings for the museum, completed in 1971 with funds from the Edward Wisner Foundation.

John Bullard who came as director in 1973 directed a second expan-sion of the museum. Clark and Menefee, architects, won a national com-petition for a 1980s extension of the museum. Eskew and Filson of New Orleans executed the final design plans that were built. The addition has preserved the restrained integrity of the Delgado building. Windows from the addition throw open views of the original Beaux Arts rooftop with its green tile and acroteria. The new addition also reveals and displays as an interior wall much of the original rear elevation of the old Delgado building.

AMERICAN
NEW
ORLEANS

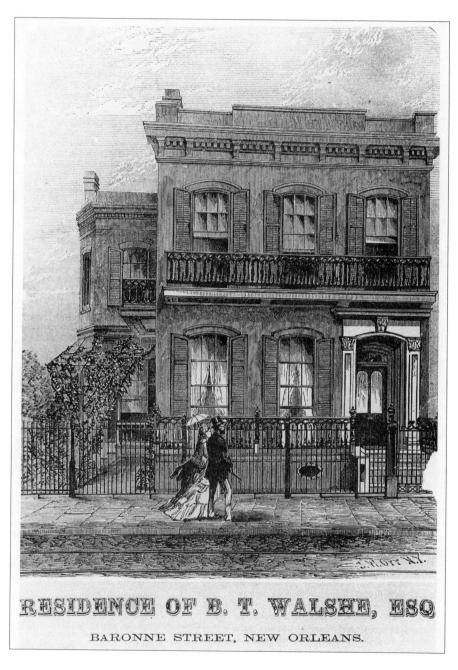

RESIDENCE OF B. T. WALSHE, ESQ

BARONNE STREET, NEW ORLEANS.

Street scene in Faubourg St. Mary, 1873. Wood engraving by J. W. Orr. Photograph courtesy of the Historic New Orleans Collection.

Faubourg St. Mary:
Central Business District.
Old Algiers and Gretna

The problem with the French-speaking creoles is that they just didn't get the picture. That, at least, was the opinion of the American merchants, brokers, factors, and real estate developers who rushed to fill up the new Faubourg St. Mary after the Louisiana Purchase. Just look at what French Governor LaMothe Cadillac wrote Louis XIV from Dauphin Island, Alabama, in 1714, before Bienville and John Law had established New Orleans: "What! Is it expected that for any commercial or profitable purpose boats will ever be able to run up the Mississippi, into the Wabash, Missouri, or Red River? One might as well try to bite a slice off the moon."

The Americans, mostly Whigs, knew what to do with the Mississippi River and the port near its foot and the Gulf of Mexico, and they did it. They turned the port into the busiest in the Western world much to the chagrin of the Democrat Frenchmen, *Locofocos,* as the Americans called them. These newcomers even managed to divest themselves of the French Quarter and the creole suburbs in 1836, dividing the city into three municipalities. Faubourg St. Mary across Canal Street from the French Quarter became a new "American" municipality. A Municipal Hall designed by Irish architect James Gallier, Sr. at Lafayette Square in the middle of Faubourg St. Mary served the Americans. When it went up in 1848 the monumental Greek Revival U.S. Custom House on Canal Street faced the new American sector. English Gothic–style St. Patrick's Church rose on Camp Street to serve the Irish Catholics thronging into New Orleans. These Irish were an anomaly: Catholic, but they spoke English. They threw in with the English-speaking Protestants and Ulster Irish to make money, but in religion and politics they stuck with the creoles.

**500 Block of Canal Street, northside, 600 and 800 blocks of Canal Street, southside (see p.
97).** Ink and wash on pasteboard by Adrien Persac, 1873. Courtesy of the Historic New Orleans
Collection. 507 Canal Street at Decatur Street is the oldest building on Canal Street, built in 1821.
The building remains, now disguised behind a newer front today. The 600 block of Canal Street
is the best remaining block of the famous street today. Shown at 622 is a cast iron front designed between 1853 and 1859 by W. A. Freret, Jr. Left, at the corner of Canal and Camp Streets,
is one remaining of five 1833 stores designed by architect William Brand for himself. The 800
block of Canal Street includes the Boston Club at 824 Canal Street, designed in 1844 by James
Gallier, Sr. for Dr. William Newton Mercer, who financed St.Anna's Asylum in the Lower Garden
District and St. Elizabeth's uptown. The Jesuit Church of the Immaculate Conception appears in
the background.

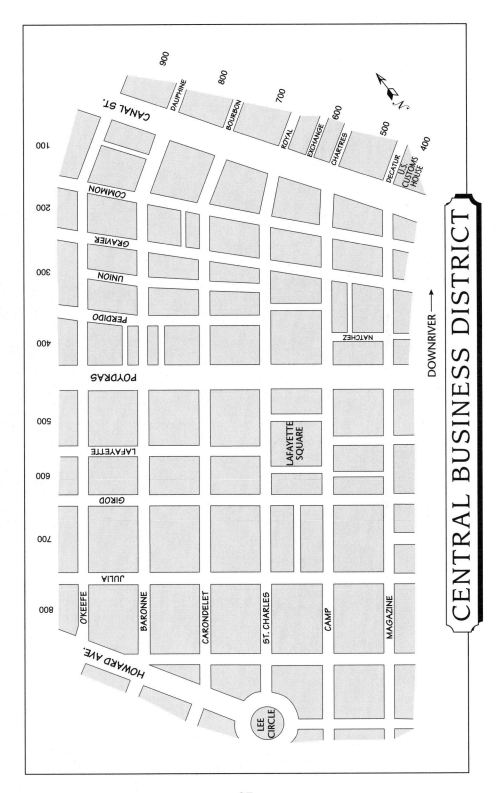

CENTRAL BUSINESS DISTRICT

DOWNRIVER →

N

545 St. Charles Avenue (see p. 103) Municipal Hall at Lafayette Square, now Gallier Hall. Courtesy of the Southeastern Architectural Archive, Tulane University Library.

Column cap of the U.S. Custom House on Canal Street. Photograph by Betsy Swanson.

By 1850 Anglo-American Faubourg St. Mary controlled New Orleans. Only a few old street names recall that New Orleans' central business district was a late–eighteenth–century Spanish colonial suburb, laid out by Spanish Royal Surveyor Carlos Laveau Trudeau, a French creole.

The plantation that formed Faubourg St. Mary had been purchased by Andrés Reynard in 1773 as a part of the old Bienville–Jesuit land grant. Reynard died in 1785, and within three years his widow, Marie Josephe Deslondes, a creole of the German coast toward Baton Rouge, was remarried and her property was being developed by her new husband, Beltran Gravier. Gravier lost no time in having Trudeau subdivide it in a plan of April 1, 1788. His was just one marriage that proved a convenient way for creole men to acquire plantations that they subdivided after the Louisiana Purchase. Claude Tremé did the same thing.

In the middle of the new suburb Trudeau placed a plaza to be called Gravier, renamed Lafayette Square after the French hero's visit in 1825. Gravier, the developer and plantation owner's name, was preserved on Gravier Street. Carondelet was Louisiana's Spanish colonial governor in 1791, transferred as viceroy to Quito, Ecuador, in 1796. His wife, *la Baronne,* was memorialized in the naming of the parallel street. Julien Poydras of Point Coupée parish had encouraged Gravier to subdivide, buying the first lot at the corner of the Camino Real and the street named after him. Nicolas Girod was a prominent mayor and supporter of Napoleon. The faubourg, slated to be called Gravier, was renamed as early as 1798 Sta. Maria in memory of the deceased Madame Gravier, who, after all, was the owner before Gravier through her first husband Andrés Reynard.

As often happens in economically feasible commercial districts, architecture goes up just in time to be demolished. So went the early works of Benjamin Henry Latrobe, appointed through his friend, President Jefferson, as Surveyor of the Public Buildings of the United States. He designed a customhouse and his son, Henry S. Latrobe, designed the first Protestant church in New Orleans, Christ Church, built in the Gothic style in 1815 for $3000, and Charity Hospital, all demolished by 1850.

600-632 Julia Street. Photograph by Roulhac d'Arby Toledano.

In the 1830s and 1840s, residences of the Americans, mostly new arrivals from the east, intermingled with the commercial buildings, warehouses, commission houses, and banks built after designs by the English-speaking architects. Benjamin Latrobe remarked, somewhat condescendingly, as early as 1819 that "in the Faubourg St. Mary and wherever Americans build, they exhibit their flat brick fronts with sufficient number of holes for light and entrance. The old English side-hall passage house with the stairs at the end is also gaining ground."

Faubourg St. Mary thronged with human activity as New Orleans became the busiest port in the Western world, fulfilling Jefferson's prophecy. In the European urban manner, residential mixed with commercial, rich lived not far from poor, and all the buildings extended flat and straight to the property line. A few colonial raised master houses, or *maisons de maître,* with overgrown gardens stood adjacent to sprawling cotton presses and warehouses near the river.

Irish immigrants, indentures, and slaves swarmed about the neighborhood. Many lived in service wings or stables behind commercial buildings or in garrets above them and in warehouse yards, where they worked as clerks, janitors, errand boys, and stevedores. Among them was a 14-year-old English boy who arrived in the winter of 1855, having worked his way as a cabin boy from Liverpool to most of the major ports of the world. The young Welsh orphan was called John Rowlands. Much later he was known as Sir Henry Morton Stanley, recognized by his query "Dr. Livingston, I presume," during his explorations in Africa. Yet it was in New Orleans' Faubourg St. Mary that he found opportunity.

In fact, the faubourg brought Henry Morton Stanley a name, a set of parents, and an education. The young boy had found a job at Speake and McCreary, commission merchants, 109 Tchoupitoulas, where he worked with the slaves. Henry Hope Stanley, a well-to-do merchant, then living in a nearby townhouse in the 600 block of Carondelet, noticed the boy at work, and after Mr. Speake died of yellow fever, he and Mrs. Stanley, childless, adopted him.

Stanley remembered Faubourg St. Mary years later in his autobiography, and his commentary shows that he understood American New Orleans of the 1850s even as a child:

> We reached the top of Tchapitoulas Street *[sic]*, the main commercial artery of the city. The people were thronging home from the business quarters, to the more residential part. . . . The soft, balmy air, with its strange scents of fermenting molasses, semi-baked sugar, green coffee, pitch, Stockholm tar, brine of mess-beef, rum, and whiskey drippings, contributed a great deal towards imparting the charm of romance to everything I saw. In the vicinity of Poydras we halted before a boarding house where we sat down to okra soup, grits, sweet potatoes, brinjalls, corn scones, mush-pudding, and fixings—every article but the bread was strange and toothsome . . . .

527-39 Tchoupitoulas Street. Benedict Simon, lithographer, 1869. Courtesy of the Historic New Orleans Collection. This harmonious block is filled with mid-nineteenth-century four-story stores costing about $6000 each. Granite lintels and cast iron or granite pillars unify them, as does the overhang. The building contract specifies brick plastered with "hydraulic cement" and sharp sand, then "colored and blocked off to represent sandstone." Some of the iron scroll brackets that support the overhang remain.

423 Canal Street (see p. 97). U.S. Custom House. Courtesy of the Historic New Orleans Collection.

Portrait of Pierre Gustave Toutant Beauregard. Oil on canvas by T.C. Healy after G. P. A. Healy, 1861. Courtesy of the Louisiana State Museum. Beauregard, as an engineer in the U.S. Army and West Point graduate, supervised the construction of and alterations to the U.S. Custom House on Canal Street. He is a native of the New Orleans area, descended from a French creole family of St. Bernard Parish. The painting shows him at Fort Sumter, Charleston, South Carolina, where he commanded Confederate troops that fired on federal troops to launch the Civil War.

[The] stores were . . . massive and uniform and over the doors were the inscriptions, "Produce and Commission Merchants," etc. [Inside] Negroes commenced to sweep the long alleys between the goods piles and to propel the dust and rubbish of the previous day's traffic towards the open gutter. Then flour, whiskey and rum barrels, marked and branded, were rolled out, and arranged near the curbstone. Hogsheads and tierces were set on end, cases were built, sacks were laid out in orderly layers, awaiting removal by drays, which at a later hour, would convey them to the river-steamers.

I shared in the citizens' pride in their splendid port, the length and stability of their levee, their unparalleled lines of shipping, their magnificent array of steamers and their majestic river. I believed with them, that their Custom House, when completed, would be a matchless edifice, that Canal Street was unequalled for its breadth, that Tchapitoulas [sic] Street was, beyond compare, the busiest street in the world, that no markets equalled those of New Orleans for their variety of produce, and that no city, not even Liverpool, could exhibit such mercantile enterprise or such a smart go-ahead spirit as old and young manifested in the chief city of the world.

Stanley recorded the richest and most exuberant days in the history of the Faubourg St. Mary. Now we have only the buildings as symbols of that youthful spirit and time. These low-scale Greek Revival brick rows with marble or granite bases, the English-style side-hall townhouses in Faubourg St. Mary, stand as sentinels to the taste of the first English-speaking architects in New Orleans. They give human scale and retain a unified aesthetic set among the 1950s skyscrapers, Harrah's oversized, derivative, and unfinished casino at the foot of Canal, and Curtis and Davis' postmodern technodream, the Superdome.

Central Business District

With leadership from the Preservation Resource Center and the Historic Faubourg St. Mary Corporation, the New Orleans Historic District Landmarks Commission has established four historic districts in Faubourg St. Mary. Each has its own distinguishing characteristics. The Warehouse District was reinvigorated by the 1984 Louisiana World Exposition and is bound by South Front Street and the Riverwalk, Howard Avenue, Magazine Street, and Poydras Street. The Canal Street Historic District commemorates one of the most exciting commercial strips in the country. The Picayune Place Historic District is noted for an unparalleled collection of nineteenth–century commercial buildings, bounded by Camp, Common, Tchoupitoulas, and Poydras Streets. The Lafayette Square Historic District bounded by Magazine, Lafayette, Baronne, and St. Joseph Streets, encompasses the major residential section of nineteenth–century Faubourg St. Mary.

Period lithographs and archival drawings made by engineers, architects, and surveyors for sheriff's sales illustrate how the buildings looked in the nineteenth century when Stanley wandered the streets of Faubourg St. Mary. It would also have been the neighborhood future architect Henry Hobson Richardson last saw before the Civil War, sailing north to leave the family plantation and the townhouse on Julia Street forever. Richardson went to Harvard, remaining in Boston for his architectural career.

132 Baronne Street

The Jesuit Church of the Immaculate Conception is a replica with some changes of a church built between 1851 and 1857 after designs of the Reverend John Cambiaso working with architect T. E. Giraud. When built, the newspapers described it as "Saracenic or Arabian style." One of the first churches in the world to be dedicated to the Immaculate Conception, after Pope Pius IX promulgated the doctrine in 1854, it was demolished for reconstruction in 1926. Architects Wogan, Bernard, and Toledano used much of the old material and the iron pews and columns on the interior.

Camp Street

700 Block Camp Street

St. Patrick's Church. Ironically, the Roman Catholics emerged as the only active congregation in the American sector, the first Protestant neighborhood of the city. The Irish Catholics contracted in 1838 for Charles B. and James H. Dakin, just arrived from New York, where James was a partner with Town and Davis, to design and build St. Patrick's for $115,000. The specifications called for the "Pointed Style of the Second Period of Ecclesiastical Architecture. . . principally imitated from that unrivalled example of splendor and majesty, York Minster Cathedral." The Dakins were fired, and Charles died of yellow fever in June 1839. The trustees signed a new contract with Irish Protestant James Gallier, Sr., born Gallagher, in County Louth, Ireland, to "make all the necessary drawings for completing the design for $1000 and to direct its construction for an additional fee of five percent of the cost." Gallier retained all of the Dakin design that had been built, but he simplified the overall appearance of the church. Three enormous 1840 oil paintings by Leon Pomarede have been preserved.

Establishment of the parish at the site between Girod and Julia was the impetus for nearby residential construction in the 1830s. The earliest houses still remaining are the four of an original five row houses at **630–640 Carondelet Street** (see p. 98), at the corner of Girod. The **700 and 800 blocks of Camp Street** offer architectural examples dating from Faubourg St. Mary's finest years, as does Girod Street around the corner. The building watcher must look around the mutilations and upward to see the original fenestration in some buildings. Those that have been renovated, usually as law offices, can serve as models for restorations of the others.

724 Camp Street.

St. Patrick's Rectory was designed in the Italianate style by architect Henry Howard and built by Thomas Mulligan for $22,000 in 1874. The parapets and balconies have been removed and the recessed portion of the facade enclosed.

717 Camp Street.

Henry Palfrey had the side-hall townhouse put up soon after he bought the property in 1838, selling it in 1840, Marble molded lintels, paneled inside shutters, the arrow pattern iron railing and the wooden architrave applied to the brick facade typify the period.

132 Baronne Street.
Immaculate Conception
Church, front elevation and
interior. Photographs by
Charles L. Franck, 1935.
Courtesy of the Historic
New Orleans Collection

734 Camp Street. St. Patrick's Church. Front-elevation photograph by Robert S. Brantley. Interior photograph by Jan Brantley. The American sector was the bailiwick of rich and rising-rich Protestants, but the Irish Catholics who worked for them prevailed in numbers. The result is this Catholic church, the premier landmark in the most Protestant section of nineteenth-century New Orleans.

727 Camp Street

The three-bay Italianate building, articulated by paneled pilasters running from the dentiled lintel course at the first level to the frieze below the cornice recalls the Placide Forstall house by James Gallier at **920 St. Louis Street** (see p. 42) in the French Quarter. John Barnett, architect, designed it, and Little and Middlemiss built it for the Southwestern Bible Society for $9940, but what you see now is a reworking by T. K. Wharton in 1858, according to his diary.

822 Camp Street

This is a townhouse built for W. P. Converse in 1851 for $15,250 after architect Henry Howard's designs, complete with triple, lacy cast iron galleries by Samuel Stewart. Front walls were specified to be Baltimore pressed brick with white marble steps, plinths, landing, and lintels. The entrance was designed with square antae and entablature with "Venetian blinds," the door grained in imitation of oak.

842 Camp Street

Joseph Lenes, president of the New Orleans and Carrollton Railroad Company, remodeled this 1845 townhouse in 1870. The result is a sophisticated three-story masonry townhouse, with a rusticated first story and quoins at the ends of the upper levels. The fancy second-story cast iron gallery, high style parapet, and the bracketed entablature are from the 1870 work.

Canal Street

423 Canal Street

The U.S. Custom House at Canal and Decatur is one of the most important Federal buildings in the South. Designed in 1848, the fourth customhouse on the site, it went through a number of architects before it was finished. A. T. Wood, who came to New Orleans in the 1830s from New York, submitted the original design, a monumental translation of the Greek Revival, and work began in 1848 after Wood had traveled to Washington to secure funds for its construction.

Wood had been convicted in 1835 of manslaughter in the murder of his partner, George Clarkson, in a fight, and he was sent to the penitentiary at Baton Rouge until 1841. Yet he won the commission over James Dakin. When Wood died in 1854, architect Thomas Kelah Wharton wrote that the architect had no professional equal in this city. Subsequent architects included Pierre G. Toutant Beauregard. Assignment as Commander at West Point and subsequent appointment as general for the Confederacy in the Civil War interrupted his work on the Custom House. T. K. Wharton continued it. Today, the great marble interior and the exhibition about the Custom House are well worth seeing.

500, 600, 800 Blocks of Canal Street (see p. 86)

Canal Street, running from the Custom House to the Mississippi River, dividing the French and American cities, has long been considered one of the most exciting thoroughfares in America. **600–640 Canal Street** is the best preserved block along the street.

507 Canal Street at Decatur Street

This is the oldest building on Canal Street, built in 1821 by architect Felix Pinson and Maurice Pizetta for Joseph Mary for $11,500. Mary left his many properties to his son, Aristide Mary, a prominent free man of color. The corner storehouse originally exhibited fine creole style with arched openings below a dentiled cornice with small dormers above. One side of the building had a gable end with chimneys while the corner was hipped, typical to the corner storehouse. The fabric of the building remains behind various alterations.

98   American New Orleans

622 Canal Street

This is one of two fine surviving cast iron-front buildings in the city. Designed between 1853 and 1859 by W. A. Freret, Jr. and built by C. Crozier, it exhibits ascending columns of different styles at each level. The spiral columns and the bull's-eye windows are dramatic elements of a facade full of relief sculpture in cast iron.

633–637 Canal Street

The Musson Building at Canal and Royal is one of the oldest buildings remaining in the American sector. Maurice Pizetta and Felix Pinson built the row of six stores in granite of four stories in 1825 for creole cotton broker Germain Musson. They were to be used as "house, stores and buildings" and cost $11,000. As early as 1839 they were appraised at $142,000. This single appraisal indicates the amazing commercial success of the new American sector.

633-637 Canal Street at Royal Street. Germain Musson Buildings, 1825. Photograph by Charles Franck, 1918. Courtesy of the Historic New Orleans Collection.

824 Canal Street

This is one of the few remaining residences among many that lined Canal Street. James Gallier, Sr. designed the side-hall townhouse in 1844 for Dr. William Newton Mercer, army surgeon who settled in New Orleans after the War of 1812. Gallier used marble for the lintels, sills, entrance pillars, and entablature. The front elevation was scored and painted *faux marbre.* It has been restored by the Boston Club. Notice the Jesuit Church of the Immaculate Conception on Baronne behind the house. (see p. 86)

Carondelet Street

630–640 Carondelet Street

Four row houses built for John Prendergast by John Fitz Miller in 1832. Prendergast lost the buildings immediately to his builder for a $5900 debt. With their delicacy of proportion, the houses reflect the Regency style; note the discrete second–story wrought iron balcony and the single dormers with pilasters and arched lights. While the first level had a transomed entrance beside two double–hung windows, the second level revealed an unusual arrangement for New Orleans, with a full-length central opening with one window on each side. An 1839 notarial drawing shows that the plaster was painted yellow, the shutters light green, and the doors had a *faux bois* finish of two-tone brown. The shutters below were batten, while those above were louvered. When I Drove the late English architectural historian, Sir Nicholas Pevsner through New Orleans, he told me these were his favorite buildings, reminding him of London and home. The Custom House was of interest as the city's only truly monumental structure.

700–716 Carondelet Street

This half-block of mid-nineteenth–century residences has been restored as law offices. **700 Carondelet Street.** Designed by James Gallier, Sr. in 1845 for the Gas Light and Banking Company, the storehouse has been restored after decades of mutilation. A residential entrance for the second level faced Girod Street. A wrought iron gallery once returned around the side of the building. **704 Carondelet Street.** This house was designed about 1847 by architect William Freret for his brother's home. **714-16 Carondelet Street.** This house dates from the late 1860s, and was built with an Italianate entrance surround.

500, 600 and 800 Blocks
of Fulton Street

These streets are filled with rows of brick warehouses built between 1845 and 1855. Iron shutters, wide overhangs supported by huge S-curve brackets, and restrained Classic-style details are signs to look for. Spurred by the 1984 Louisiana World Exposition, some long-time owners of the empty buildings sold, which allowed creative redevelopment for hotels, apartments, galleries and restaurants. The fair, then, caused an exciting revitalization of a long-dormant area.

723–727 Girod Street

This is an early double house, built about 1838 for Andrew Hodge, president of the Bank of New Orleans. The unusual raised-basement Greek Revival building has a wide opening leading to a courtyard with two service buildings attached. A wood entablature, typical of the 1830s, has an attic frieze with windows beneath a dentiled cornice.

512 Gravier Street

Architect James Dakin designed a row of three-story granite-front stores in 1843 as part of a project for the Canal Bank. The bank is at the corner of the row at Magazine and Gravier Streets at **301–307 Magazine Street** (see p. 101).

822–828 Gravier Street

Gravier Row, attributed to Lewis E. Reynolds, was built in 1865 for Jackson and Manson, cotton factors, and John Thornhill, also a cotton factor. The facades of this row of three–story Italianate masonry commercial buildings feature cast iron pillars with Egyptian motif capitals and low arches with paneled spandrels. The cast iron balcony has been removed.

Howard at Camp Street

Howard Library is a posthumous work of Henry Hobson Richardson, with the characteristic rugged textures, rock-faced stone, and a cavernous arched opening. Polygonal and round turrets, Romanesque-style engaged, coupled columns, and the fortress-like slits evoke the medieval theme. Ironically, the building is near his own childhood home in Faubourg St. Mary in the Julia Street Row. It is slated to open as the Ogden Museum of Southern art in 1998.

Julia Street

420 Julia Street

Great Western Warehouse, built in 1887 for the Loubat family, replaced an 1861 warehouse for the same family. Brick belt courses, corbelled cornice, and the band courses that connect doors and windows create a rhythmic pattern along the block.

535–545 Julia Street at Camp Street

These three-story brick store–houses are among the earlier remaining buildings in Faubourg St. Mary. Samuel Peters bought them nearly finished from John Green, who built them in 1832. The absence of Greek detail and the narrow cornice are clues to the early date.

600–632 Julia Street

Julia Street Row, 13 red brick row houses, was designed for the New

630-632 Julia Street. Service wings of rows of three-bay side-hall townhouses on Camp Street. Photograph by Clarence John Laughlin. Courtesy of the Historic New Orleans Collection. Two- and three-story service wings behind commercial and residential buildings teemed with activity in the mid-nineteenth century. Slaves, Irish immigrants and indentured servants lived in the narrow rooms with the patios and carriageways their outdoor living rooms.

Orleans Building Company in 1833. Long attributed to A. T. Wood, James Dakin's son and daughter have stated that their father was the architect, having designed them in New York at the firm of Town, Davis, and Dakin, two years before he came to New Orleans. Wood, who knew Dakin in New York but had come to New Orleans earlier, probably supervised the construction work of Daniel Twogood.

The doors of this intact row are Georgian in style, with side lights and elliptical fanlights, unusual in New Orleans, and the fans match those of the Tredwell house in New York, built the same year, after Town, Davis, and Dakin designs. The use of red brick, the standard side-hall floor plan, three stories with attic faced by a pierced entablature providing windows, and the handsome gabled ends with chimneys epitomize the American taste of Faubourg St. Mary. The extension of the third-level window frames to include a panel below six–over–six windows became customary, too.

Lafayette Street

327 Lafayette Street

François Adolphe and François Bizoton d'Aquin had builder John Randolph Pikes build this row of brick three-story stores in 1844. Koch and Wilson, architects, restored them in 1981. Now the twofold doors between the granite pillars, the rows of lintels, and tie rods make the Greek Revival building an asset to the Warehouse District.

938 Lafayette Street

Turner's Hall was designed by Prussian refugee and architect William Thiel in 1868 for the Turner Society, composed largely of Germans. Thomas O'Neill built it for $39,758. The handsome Italianate building with its paneled pilaster theme is one of the few remaining institutional buildings built by New Orleans' many charitable organizations. Errol Barron and Michael Toups, architects, converted it into offices in 1980.

Magazine Street

301–307 Magazine Street

The Canal Bank was built in 1831 by J. Reynolds and J. M. Zacharie, but by 1843 it was rebuilt as you see it today after a simple design by architect James H. Dakin. The Quincy granite used in the earlier building was used again to provide a solid and sophisticated appearance. The building contract called for the door to be painted in imitation of bronze. The bank entrance was emphasized by a pair of fluted Doric columns and a frieze of triglyphs and metopes. The store doors were to have four folds, each with molded panel shutters, glazed sashes, and brass recessed shutter lifts and screws. They were to be grained in imitation of oak.

336 Magazine Street

The J. Aron Coffee Company restored one of the city's finest Classic-style rows at the corner of Natchez Street. Charles F. Zimpel, surveyor, designed them for Thomas Banks in 1833 in red brick with granite at the first of three levels. The double-level cast iron gallery and the balconies were added after the Civil War, when a high roof balustrade was removed. This row was to be a merchants' gathering place planned to serve the American sector much the way that Maspero's Exchange served the French Quarter. By June 1843 Banks was bankrupt, because of his financial support of the Texas Revolution.

401–405 Magazine Street

Mid–nineteenth–century cast iron pillars on this brick commercial building, now the Bon Ton restaurant, came from the once-nearby Julia Street Foundry.

400–408 Magazine Street

This row of four-level stores includes three "marble stores" as they were called in the building contract of 1865. Marble blocks, granite pillars, and lintel

401-405 Magazine Street. Mid-ninteenth-century commercial building with cast iron pillars. Benedict Simon, lithographer, 1869-1871.Courtesy of the Historic New Orleans Collection.

courses suggest a continual preference for the Greek style.

755 Magazine Street

La Belle Creole Cigar Factory, built in 1882, for Simon Hernsheim, who built 3711 St. Charles, now the Columns Hotel, as his home. He employed 1200 workers in the factory, and there he killed himself in 1898 after his wife died and his daughter married. The sandstone building, where geometric tie rods decorate the vertical pillars, has rhythmical progressions of arched and segmental arched openings. It has been renovated and converted into law offices.

802–822 Perdido Street

Lewis Reynolds designed Factors Row in 1858, and Samuel Jamison and James McIntosh, builders who owned the two corner segments, built the entire row.

Each floor has a different treatment of cast iron Italianate ornamentation, but a cast iron balcony has been removed. The building is famous as the setting for artist Edgar Degas' 1873 painting of the cotton office interior, now in the Municipal Museum of Pau, France. Degas' brother and his cousins and uncle were cotton factors here, and are depicted in the painting.

St. Charles Avenue

200 Block of St. Charles Avenue

Federal troops are seen marching down St. Charles Avenue during Reconstruction past **119 and 125 St. Charles Avenue** and the second St. Charles Hotel, built after Gallier's design. This one has also been demolished, as has a third designed by architect Thomas Sully.

200 block of St. Charles Avenue. James Gallier Sr.'s 1836 St. Charles Hotel (demolished) was one of the nation's grand lodgings. Alfred R. Waud, delineator: wood engraving dated August 18, 1866, when federal troops marched down St. Charles Avenue. Courtesy of the Historic New Orleans Collection.

119 St. Charles Avenue

With its three stories of cast iron galleries above iron colonettes, this building was probably designed by James Gallier, Sr. for John and Thomas Hagan soon after they bought the lot in 1842. Irishman Hagan often used his fellow countryman, Gallier, for his many building projects.

125 St. Charles Avenue

This home of Kolb's restaurant throughout the century until late 1994, housed New Orleans' first major art gallery soon after it was built in 1844. The Louisiana Jockey Club took over the gallery building in 1845, and in 1899 Conrad Kolb of Landau, Germany, started his restaurant here.

301–307 St. Charles Avenue at Gravier Street

Judah Touro, Jewish benefactor of Newport, Rhode Island and New Orleans, had Thomas Murray build this row of six stores in 1851 for $60,000. The second-level balcony is thronged with nighttime spectators of the Mystick Krewe of Comus in this 1858 wood engraving. The same thing occurred each year until 1991 at the culmination of the public Mardi Gras.

545 St. Charles Avenue (see p. 88).

Municipal Hall (1845–1851). James Gallier Sr.'s magnificent St. Charles Hotel (1835–1837) burned in 1851, but his City Hall stands, now named in his honor. At Lafayette Square, this is the best surviving example of monumental Greek Revival architecture in New Orleans. The stairs and tomblike parapet motives recall the Regency designs of Sir John Soane. Projecting the Hall to cost $120,000, Gallier managed to foist on the new municipality a building that cost $342,000 by the time it was dedicated in 1853.

301-307 St. Charles Avenue, at Gravier Street. Parade of the Mystick Krewe of Comus at night turning off St. Charles Avenue.Anonymous wood engraving, 1858. Courtesy of the Historic New Orleans Collection.

631–633 and 639–641 St. Charles Avenue

These are two remaining row houses built by James Gallier in 1836 for the speculator Samuel Moore. Study of the 1836 building contract reveals customs of the period. Each lot was 24 feet 6 inches by 101 feet. Fronts were to be "Baltimore or Philadelphia pressed bricks. The first story 13 feet high, the second story 12 feet and the attic story five feet five inches."

923 Tchoupitoulas Street. Gothic-style iron foundry elevation. Signed Gallier, Turpin and Co. Architects, 1850. Courtesy of the Southeastern Architectural Archives, Tulane University Library.

Tchoupitoulas Street

517–533 Tchoupitoulas Street

This row of 1854 stores were built by a variety of builders, but they present a fine Classic street scene with granite and iron pillars, granite sills and lintels, and molded cornices. The brick fronts were originally plastered, then "colored and blocked off to represent sandstone." Some of the scroll brackets supporting the overhang remain.

600 Block of Tchoupitoulas Street

This block has rows of Greek Revival–style warehouses, some with cast iron ground–floor columns.

701–703 Tchoupitoulas Street

This Nicolas Girod storehouse was built in 1831 by builder John Fitz Miller and was probably designed by him since he was the lessee. Fitz Miller also built **630–640 Carondelet Street** (see p. 98), and both these early buildings exhibit Regency details, such as the second level where a central door is flanked by one double-hung window on each side for each three-bay section. The Girod building with its corner hip roof had a wrought-iron balcony. The arched openings on the first floor recall a French Quarter tradition, very rare in this area.

923 Tchoupitoulas Street

Gallier, Turpin, Co. architects and builders designed and built this Gothic-style store and warehouse in 1852 for the Leeds Iron Foundry.

Old Algiers

One of the last great free rides in the country that doesn't lead to something dangerous is the free ferry from the foot of Canal to Old Algiers on the west bank of the Mississippi River. The ferry wasn't free in 1838, though, when the St. Mary's Market Steam Ferry Company received authorization to develop two small villages across from Faubourg St. Mary. These were eventually incorporated into Gretna. Philanthropist John McDonogh, who in 1813 had bought the Bernoudy plantation, which became McDonoghville and later part of Gretna, never took the ferry. One of the many slaves he freed rowed him over to New Orleans from his French colonial plantation, Monplaisir.

Monplaisir, built in 1750 by the Chevalier Jean de Pradel, was taken by the river in the last half of the nineteenth century. However, many of the old plantation houses are hidden here and there in the area, and are now used as clubs, offices, and private homes.

Gretna and Algiers grew into towns from the mid–nineteenth century when the Texas cattle trails ended there. Ship building, farming, and railroading offered livelihoods in both little towns.

Old Algiers, now known as Algiers Point, after the river pilots' lexicon, remains stubbornly colloquial, where Irish bars and baseball take up a lot of time, hardly the destiny that might have been expected from the site of the original Company of the Indies plantation, slave depot, and colonial *abattoir*, and the plantation of Barthélémy Duverje after 1805.

Duverje's home became the courthouse until it burned in 1869. Even its replacement burned in 1895 along with much of the town. A walk through Algiers Point will demonstrate that a good portion did not burn, and much of it is being restored. Walk along Olivier Street from Opelousas Street to the levee. Small-scale residences and storehouses set against the Delta sky with the Mississippi River and a view of New Orleans as foreground is a sight worth seeing.

John McDonogh typifies the American success story in the Faubourg St. Mary. He arrived in New Orleans in 1800 from Baltimore, where he had been an indentured apprentice and then commission merchant. By 1804 he was building warehouses in the American sector to store the vast amount of manufactured goods furnished by William Taylor of Baltimore. Shepherd Brown, New Orleans' Garden District resident, supplied the agricultural products. Profits from the commission merchant venture provided funds for land speculation. In Faubourg St. Mary McDonogh was landlord to the Citizens Bank, Union Bank, a ferry, Mansion House Hotel, and even tables in the Poydras and St. Mary's markets.

John McDonogh crossing the Mississippi River to New Orleans. Lithograph, 1850. Courtesy of the Historic New Orleans Collection.

405-407 De La Ronde Street, Algiers. Photograph by Betsy Swanson.

405–407 De la Ronde Street

This double townhouse was built about 1850 for Augustin Seger and Thomas Rees, partners in a shipbuilding business. Chaste in its Greek Revival style, it is the finest example of the style to survive the fire of 1895.

225 Morgan Street

Algiers Courthouse. Paired windows with arches articulate this Romanesque Revival 1896 building with its pair of crenelated turrets. Recently renovated by architects Lyons and Hudson for use as a courthouse and community center.

225 Morgan Street. Algiers courthouse, 1896. Photograph by Betsy Swanson.

2009 Patterson Street at Valette Street

The old Emporium, a two-story brick storehouse built about 1870 in the still-popular late Classic style, is complete with cast iron galleries with anthemion cresting that cover a colonnaded walkway.

Pelican Avenue at Olivier Street

Mount Olivet Episcopal Church, built in 1845 in the Florentine Gothic style is the oldest remaining church structure in Algiers. Later additions are unfortunate, but cannot disguise the charm of the tiny wood church.

705 Pelican Avenue

The 1850 plantation–style François Vallette house has a masonry basement below a frame level with box columns. The center-hall house is the most elaborate Greek Revival–style house in Algiers.

511 Seguin Street

The Converse creole cottage built about 1850 was used many years as a convent school. The gable roof is canted to incorporate the front gallery, with its box columns typical of the Classic style. The French doors continue the French colonial tradition.

232 Vallette Street

This is an unusual side-galleried version of the gable-sided creole cottage. The roof extends to cover a side gallery, cntered piazza style from a front door. Otherwise, the house is typical Algiers vernacular, in the 1850s Classic style.

348 Vallette Street

Susselin's Bakery, built about 1900, illustrates the typical hip-roof, owner-occupied storehouse. The curved corner gallery, half wood and half screen supported by bracketed columns, creates an arcade over the sidewalk.

Gretna

The prime feature of Gretna is the David Crockett Fire Company Engine House and Meeting Hall in the **2900 block of Lafayette Street.** Organized in 1841, they purchased the land here in 1859. The brigade is said to be the oldest continuously functioning volunteer fire company in the nation. The firehouse has been restored and the two cottages that flank it have been restored by the Gretna Historical Society to form a tiny complex that suggests the mid–nineteenth–century appearance of Gretna. Both creole cottages date from the 1840s. The dormered cottage on the right, **209 Lafayette Street,** the Lily White Ruppel house, was built soon after William White bought the lot in 1840, and has remained in the family ever since. **201 Lafayette Street,** the Kittie Strehle house, was built by Claudius Strehle for his family soon after he bought the lot from the St. Mary's Market Steam Ferry Company in 1840.

Berdou's, at **300 Monroe Street,** is the place to go for creole cooking, not for the building. It has the best pompano en papillote in town, and all the seafood is good and inexpensive (504-368-2401).

511 Seguin Street, Algiers. Photograph by Betsy Swanson.

Lower Garden District: Bartholemy Lafon's Classic Suburb

rmand Duplantier, New Orleans creole and former Revolutionary War aide to the Marquis de Lafayette, realized right after the Louisiana Purchase that New Orleans would fulfill Jefferson's prophecy and grow swiftly now that the river was open to free trade. He purchased the old Duplessis–Delord–Sarpy plantation in 1807 upriver from Faubourg St. Mary and asked French *émigré* surveyor Barthélémy Lafon to continue immediately with plans for a new faubourg.

Upriver plantation owners jumped in to take advantage of Lafon's services, so that he was able to plan a coordinated, Classic-style suburb, far more sophisticated than any conceived before or since, including the French Quarter. Lafon had come to New Orleans in 1790 from his birthplace in Villepinte, France (1769). He became city engineer and a chief consulting engineer for the U.S. Army. Although untrained as an architect, he was an active designer for French Quarter houses **(339 and 640 Royal Street, see p. 37)** Architect Benjamin Henry Latrobe was just one of his close associates, implying in Washington that Lafon was "no fool." He was, however, a business partner of the notorious pirates, brothers Jean and Pierre Lafitte, and through this association he became a millionaire before his death in about 1820. Lafon had a *plaçage* relationship with Modeste Foucher, a third–generation African-American and one-time slave, as a child, of a Monsieur René Brion. Their son, Thomy Lafon, became a wealthy entrepreneur in his own right and benefactor to institutions for African-American New Orleanians.

The surveyor included in his subdivision plan not only Duplantier's *arpentage* but the upriver tracts of the Saulet family, who had owned their plantation from 1763, and the holdings of the recently deceased Jean Baptiste de Marigny. Robin de Logny, son-in-law of Jean Beaupré d'Estrehan, had just bought seven arpents or half of the Marigny plantation for $70,000 in 1807 from Marigny's heir, his sister, Céleste, Madame Jacques François Enoul Livaudais II. Lafon called this new section Faubourg de la Course (Racetrack). The remainder of the Marigny holdings there were subdivided by Monsieur and Madame Livaudais as Faubourg de l'Annonciation up to what is now Felicity Street.

The next tract upriver belonged to the Ursuline nuns, and Lafon added this five–arpent plantation to his subdivision in 1810. He called the bounding street Chemin de la Felicité, and parallel streets St. Mary and St. Andrew, to commemorate the three nuns who signed the acts of sale.

By 1818 the widow Panis's daughter by her first marriage, Catiche Milhet, widow of Pierre George Rousseau, sold her mother's entire undeveloped subdivision contiguous to the nuns for $100,000, along with a subdivision plan widow Panis had commissioned in 1813. The Faubourg Panis, including Josephine and Philip Streets and Cours Panis, now Jackson Avenue, developed with ease and acquired instant cachet, so that by the 1850s it had become part of the newly fashionable Garden District. Cours Panís, renamed in honor of the hero of the Battle of New Orleans, Andrew Jackson, filled with fashionable houses in the style of the Garden District. Trinity Episcopal Church was built there to serve Lafon's suburb and Garden District Protestants.

Like all the surveyors in New Orleans, Lafon preserved a large quadrangle for each of the extant plantation houses and their immediate grounds. The streets and squares had shapes predicated on the size and location of such complexes. All the new squares were shaped to fit into the curve in the river, another prerequisite. An opportunity emerged for some creative planning, with triangles and polygons necessary to follow the river. Architect Henry Krotzer suggests that Lafon may have used as guidelines extant drainage ditches from the cultivated fields and old clusters of habitations with their village-like dependencies and slave quarters.

Whatever his inspiration, Lafon's plan followed the latest classical taste, and he went further, organizing the new suburb into a classic campus with planned fountains, basins, schools, public squares, and churches. He named streets after the Greek gods Apollo, Bacchus, and Hercules and Naiades and Dryades Streets after wood nymphs. Above the Cours des Tritons, the sea god's attendants, were streets named after the nine muses. For example, one might have lived on Naiades Street (St. Charles Avenue) between Clio and Erato Streets.

A double-sized block was conceived to hold a prytaneum, a classic school, and a space for a coliseum was devised, along with a church and a pleasure garden or public resort for subscribers. For his residential squares Lafon followed the old plan adopted by the French military engineers in the plan of 1721 for the Vieux Carré. Twelve lots, five facing the street parallel to the river and a key lot facing each of the two side streets, made each square. Thus Lafon continued the module of 60-foot lots that could be halved to 30-foot lots and halved again to lots with 15-foot frontages. Depths ranged between 120 and 150 feet.

Use and manipulation of water became an essential element of Lafon's vision, conceived for both beauty and drainage. He designed basins, ponds, and canals, all tree-lined, introducing a square tree-lined basin connected to the river by a canal. Market houses flanked the basin with a large park in front of one of the old plantation houses. Lafon used water as a design component in the center of many squares. A small central basin in the selected square was to have a canal extending to an adjacent wide street canal.

In the 1830s Classic-style buildings began to line the classically named streets. Individual structures were composed of symmetrical forms and had symmetrical decorative details, all based on classic prototypes. Invariable use of columned galleries, parterre gardens, and wood fences and balconies using stylized classic motifs augured for a neighborhood that would have filled Lafon with pleasure had he not died in 1820. First, villas and mansions appeared in farmlike settings. Outbuildings flanked them with parterre gardens and orchards between them and the inevitable *potager* or soup garden with its herbs and root vegetables. *Pigeonniers* and *garçonnières* appeared as part of such complexes.

A sale advertisement in 1833 for the summer residence of John Longpré characterizes the classical suburb. The summer house faced both on Coliseum Place and Prytania Street, between Euterpe and Polymnia Streets: "[The] improvements consist of two spacious and well-divided houses with galleries and their dependencies, two brick wells, two large cisterns, a well-cultivated garden enclosed with hedges of orange trees and planted with a variety of fruit trees, shrubs and flower plants. There are, moreover, beautiful rows of orange trees, most of them bearing fruit, pecan trees, peach, plum, fig and plantain trees, two orange groves, several nurseries of sweet orange trees, a fish pond."

The advertisement of the Longpré property (demolished and replaced by **1420 Euterpe Street**) foreshadows the change from rural and semi-rural, then semiurban, to a full urban pattern of life in the Lower Garden District, brought about by the great wave of Irish and German immigrants in the late 1840s, the Catholics settling on the riverfront back to Magazine Street. Eventually, the strip of blocks between Magazine and Tchoupitoulas Streets became known as the Irish Channel, and the channel spread uptown with Irish tenants as the American city developed.

For the first time in New Orleans, the urban-style houses were set back slightly from the street, not always, but often, with narrow front gardens as well as the usual side parterre and back garden. Most houses were frame construction, and even brick ones around the more expensive Coliseum Place exhibited their wood galleries, so that Lafon's suburb took on the look of a well-carved wood sculpture.

Exterior appearance and floor plans did not differ too much between a $5000 house and one costing $25,000, which represented the standard high price paid to build any house before 1900 in this first American suburb. Double parlors might be used as bedrooms for a poor Irish family, but there were always mantels with pilasters or trabeated surrounds to match the so-called Greek key doors frames. All ceilings were at least 12 feet high, and transoms were essential in even the most modest. Twelve-inch-high baseboards with appropriate moldings were common in houses for rich and poor alike. Cypress six-paneled doors and wide cypress frames prevailed as did full service wings.

A commercial strip developed first on Magazine Street and then on Dryades Street, where Greek Revival and Classic-style brick buildings proliferated, embellished with dentils, string courses, pilasters, and iron balconies. Like the houses, they had service wings because the upper levels were used for residences.

Institutional buildings, churches, and utilitarian brick warehouses for tobacco, sugar, and cotton, even industrial structures on the riverfront (cotton presses and sugar mills), exhibited a commonality of uniform Greek Revival decorative motifs and classic proportions that houses dis-

Magazine Street at Felicity Street looking downtown at the Redemptorist spires. Drawing by A. R. Waud, 1871. Courtesy of the Historic New Orleans Collection.

played. Many of these commercial buildings were designed by architects such as James Gallier after 1834, his partner John Turpin, or by Henry Howard at the same time their residential designs proliferated.

The growing population of non-French-speaking Catholics brought the Redemptorist order into the Lower Garden District in 1842 to serve the Irish and Germans. These priests provided a comprehensive way of life for

2000 block of Constance Street (see p. 120). Redemptorist Complex during St. Patrick's Day Parade. Photograph by Robert S. Brantley.

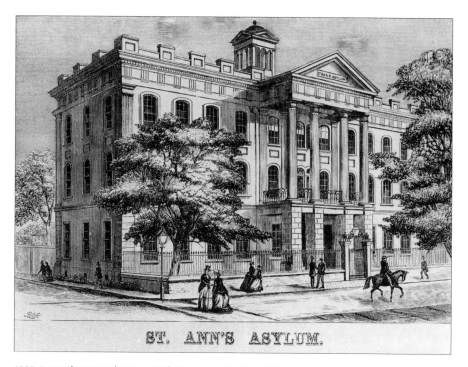

ST. ANN'S ASYLUM.

1823 Prytania Street (**see p. 127**). St. Anna's Asylum. Wood engraving, initialled R. N. R., 1874. Courtesy of the Historic New Orleans Collection. Built in 1853 for the Society for the Relief of Destitute Females and Their Helpless Children, financed by Dr William Newton Mercer of 824 Canal Street, now the Boston Club.

the area throughout the last half of the nineteenth century up to World War II. The red brick orphan homes, homes for widows, schools, and gymnasiums put up by the Redemptorists for the Germans and Irish characterize the area. These were followed by Protestant asylums, such as St. Annas Asylum at 1823 Prytania Street.

Another thing that the new immigrants had in common was disease. The Redemptorists' church rolls tell the story of fierce epidemics of Asiatic cholera and yellow fever. Parishioners numbered in the thousands, for example, at St. John the Baptist Church in 1852. After the yellow fever epidemic of 1853, only 800 survived. Lafon's suburb was the territory of choice for Margaret Haughery (1813–1888), who befriended the poor and the Irish, financing institutions for their relief and housing; her statue and a small park named for this heroic immigrant are near St. Theresa's Gothic–style church, at **1100 Prytania Street** and Camp Street.

Perhaps there were too many rental houses such as **1305–1307 St. Andrew Street** or too many poor people. Perhaps the suburb was too complete too soon because Lafon's dreams quickly collapsed into a transitional neighborhood. Greek Revival mansions became hospitals, schools, and orphan homes. Single-family owner-occupied houses became rental

1305-1307 St. Andrew Street. Photograph by Robert S. Brantley. Multiples of such double houses, replete with architectural and decorative detail, were conceived as speculative rental property by developers like Edward Conery, a second-generation Irish grocer.

units as the affluent moved uptown to the Garden District by the 1850s. Railroad yards and industry overturned the delicate balance. When the Mississippi River bridge set its entrance at the head of Coliseum Place in the 1950s, Lafon's plan was finally truncated. Now in 1995, too late, the entrance is being removed from this area where the houses are being restored.

Some enclaves of inhabitants held out, such as the people around Coliseum Square, and on Naiades (St. Charles Avenue), by 1850 a booming railroad thoroughfare. Author Grace King with her sister bought a beautiful house on Coliseum Square in the early 1900s because it was cheap and lived there graciously in the declining neighborhood until her death in 1932. John T. Moore not only stayed on in the family's house designed by Henry Howard at **1228 Race Street** facing Coliseum Square but gave his son-in-law, architect James Freret, property to build **1309 Felicity Street** (see p. 124) for his own family in 1880.

Henry Morton Stanley's adoptive parents moved out of their house on Annunciation Square where he had been raised. Writer George Washington Cable lived on Orange Street as a child, but he moved to the Garden District when he acquired wealth from writing about the creoles, who resented the German-American.

However, intrusions and mutilation could not suppress the vigor and rhythm of the street scene. The prevailing Greek Revival style offered details that were identical and appeared in multiples, and the multiples multiplied to present a cohesive Greek Revival neighborhood. Volume I of *New Orleans Architecture, The Lower Garden District* (1971) became a catalyst for restoring the neighborhood. Volunteers who had worked on the book for the Friends of the Cabildo bought homes in the area, and other young people followed, finding that access to the shops on Magazine Street, to their central business district offices, and to St. Charles Avenue as well as to uptown amenities was an asset.

For example, Camille and Duncan Strachan bought the house she had researched at **1717 Coliseum Street** (see p. 120). They named their daughter Felicity after the street, and Camille, an attorney, worked with Louise Martin to renovate the 1800 block of Magazine and Sophie Wright Place, where she has her offices. To save the childhood home of Sir Henry Morton Stanley and to recycle an empty lot the Strachan's and their neighbors moved the historic Henry Hope Stanley House to Coliseum Square. St. Vincent Infant Asylum at **1501 Magazine Street** has been transformed into a hotel by Peter and Sally Schreiber.

Operation Comeback, under the leadership of residents like Lydia and Howard Schmalz has established headquarters at the Bertucci building of 1870 at **1500–1504 Magazine Street.** This project of the Preservation Resource Center, is helping to stabilize the exterior of scores of houses in the area.

1228 Race Street. Samuel Moore House on Coliseum Square. Photograph by Robert S. Brantley. Focus on architectural detail rather than the whole make the house look like a stage set, appropriate for a suburb designed in the Grecian manner by Barthélémy Lafon.

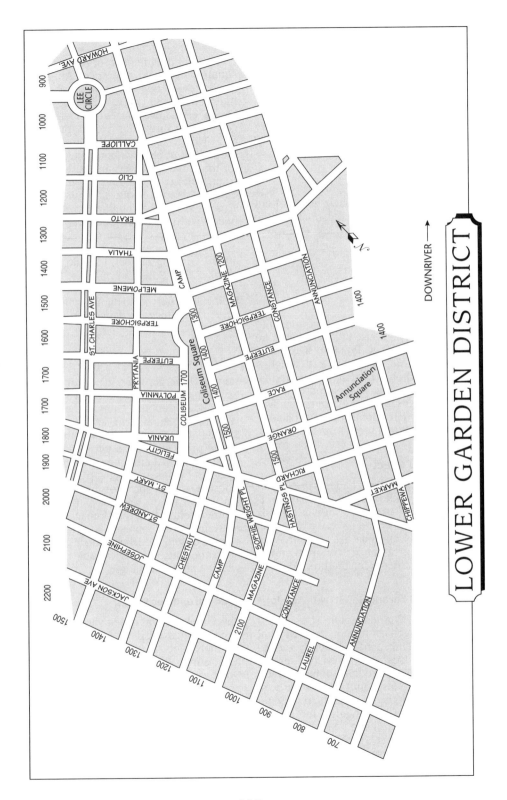

LOWER GARDEN DISTRICT

DOWNRIVER →

1061 Camp Street

This unusual Second Empire house has a *porte cochère* with a side carriageway extending back to the court, one of the latest examples of the carriageway house, a type that flourished only in the French Quarter.

1376 Camp Street

Coliseum Place Baptist Church. John Barnett designed the red brick Gothic Revival–style church in 1854. The tower failed and Thomas Kelah Wharton redesigned it. The steeple was destroyed in 1965 by Hurricane Betsy.

1456 Camp Street

E. T. Robinson had this large masonry Italianate-style house built soon after he purchased the site in 1857. It was the original home of Sophie Bell Wright's Home Institute—English and Classical School for Young Ladies and Children. The founder (1866–1912), an early advocate of women's rights, established adult night schools and social service agencies.

1531 Camp Street

Archibald Bouleware had this brick side-hall house with its stepped gabled ends built in 1854. Use of Corinthian capitals at both levels of the gallery is unusual. The arched iron trellis is a rare surviving example of a once common nine-teenth–century garden feature.

1316–1318 Carondelet Street (Apollo)

Maison St. Charles Hotel. This pair of brick townhouses in the Greek Revival style were flanked in the 1850s by a series of townhouses with extensive service wings that filled a square bound by Erato, Thalia, Naiades, and Apollo Streets. These townhouses and all the remaining Greek Revival buildings on the square were incorporated into a hotel project in 1980–1983, Peter Trapolin, restoration architect and design consultant, Allen Bacquet, project architect. Precast con-crete infill buildings reorganized the square, giving it coherence. An 1853 Greek Revival two-bay townhouse faces Erato Street and two Classic-style, double-gallery double houses that were once General Beauregard's rental property face Thalia as part of the hotel. The Carondelet Street townhouses were built for the Parlange family, and perhaps the sugar plantation family from Point Coupeé Parish used one as a townhouse. This massive rehabilitation project for a once lovely neighborhood, was spear-headed by Ben C. Toledano. As project manager and managing partner of this award winning project, I would like to thank Pierre Rossillon of Paris, France and Bob Wright of Lafayette Louisiana for their gallant nerve and humor, when they agreed to finance this daunting preservation project.

2027 Carondelet Street (see p. 119)

Henry Thiberge, working with Henry Howard, designed this house in 1859 for steamboat Captain Thomas Leathers. William Day built it in six months for $24,590. Leathers fussed about the price of the proposed house with Day, who, exasperated, said that he could build an Episcopal House or a cheap Methodist House. Leathers opted for the Presbyterian in-between, said Day. Even so, Leathers refused to pay his builder without a lawsuit. Carefully preserved by longtime owners despite a decline of the neighborhood, the house retains its stable building with its careful detailing.

2120 Carondelet Street.

This Greek Revival raised villa once had large grounds and dates from 1850. Built for merchant Alexander Philips, it has had distinguished owners and residents. Duncan Kenner of Ashland plantation bought it in 1877, and D. R. Carroll lived there.

1145 Coliseum Street

St. Theresa's Church at Camp and Erato Streets is a feature of the neighborhood,

2027 Carondelet Street. Leathers-Buck house, 1859. Front elevation (above) and carriage house (below). Photograph by Clarence John Laughlin, ca. 1943. Courtesy of the Historic New Orleans Collection.

built in 1848 after the Gothic Revival designs of architect T. E. Giraud.

1717 Coliseum Street

William Garrison had his side-hall house built about 1850 in the late Classic style. The bracketed column capitals on the front gallery are unusual and relate to the Robert C. Young house at 1524 Euterpe Street and Charles Wilson's house at 1205 Louisiana Avenue, suggesting that Wilson, an architect, built it. The bays are a later addition.

1721 Coliseum Street

Goodrich–Stanley house. Charles Goodrich, rector of St. Paul's Episcopal Church from 1838 to 1868, had this 1830s center–hall cottage built. Set low to the ground with triple dormers, the house is an atypical villa example. Henry Hope Stanley, cotton merchant, bought the house in 1858, leaving Faubourg St. Mary for Lafon's suburb to raise his adopted son, the future renowned explorer, Henry Morton Stanley. The house was moved here in 1981 from Annunciation Square.

1741 Coliseum Street (see p. 121)

Hugh Wilson of Bradley, Wilson and Company, commission merchants, had this plastered brick house built in 1847 to face Coliseum Square. Chaste compared to its neighbors, all double–galleried side-hall townhouses, the house shows the Greek Revival at its purest in the Lower Garden District. The service wing's side location is unusual.

1749 Coliseum Street (see p. 121)

The Frederick Rodewald house, built in 1849 for the successful banker and treasurer of Christ Church. The sophisticated Classic-style house has an unusual curvilinear projection of three windows on the front elevation on two levels. The deep cornices over the windows are notable, as is the decorative frame around the recessed front door.

1805 Coliseum Street

The Greek Revival style raised–frame villa dates from the mid–1850s, built for the Nalle family. Mayor Walter C. Flower and later Mayor de Lesseps Morrison lived here. The etched–glass double entrance doors postdate the house.

1365 Constance Street (see p. 122)

This early classic Greek Revival raised villa dates from the 1840s. The old photograph indicates how picket fences were used instead of latticework here to fill the space between the raised piers. The wide wood steps are also original and appropriate for the villa-style entrance. The front elevation of the frame house is plastered, with the front gallery treated like an interior room. Such galleries served as outdoor living rooms, much like the rear courtyards in the French Quarter. Mark Twain commented on the young ladies in white dresses adorning suburban galleries.

2000 Block Constance Street (see p. 113)

Redemptorist Complex. Among the German architects who fled after the failure of the 1848 Revolution was Albert Diettel of Dresden. He associated himself with the Redemptorists, who came here in 1840 from Baltimore and began commissioning institutions and churches for the Irish and German Catholics. The Redemptorist complex in the Lower Garden District was the anchor for the district for over a century. Most of the brick buildings were built between the 1850s and 1870s, and the exceptional brickwork of the German masons distinguishes them, like **2030 Constance Street**, the rectory, the old stable, and service building at the corner of St. Andrew Street, and the brick school from 1867 at **2118–2122 Constance Street.**

2052 Constance Street (see p. 122)

St. Mary's Assumption Church (1858), is the most unusual of the brick churches

1741 Coliseum Street. Wilson-Josephs house 1847. Photograph by Clarence John Laughlin. Courtesy of the Historic New Orleans Collection. Classic-style houses like these lined the streets of Lafon's suburb planned in the Classic style.

1749 Coliseum Street at Race Street. Rodewald-King house, 1849. Photograph by Robert S. Brantley. Author Grace King bought the house in 1904 after her stories began to be published and she lived here until her death in 1932

1365 Constance Street. Samuel Smith-John Kemp House, ca. 1843. Photograph by Clarence John Laughlin, ca. 1942. Courtesy of the Historic New Orleans Collection.

2052 Constance Street at Josephine Street. Architect Albert Diettel's St. Mary's Assumption Church Tower (1858-1860) illustrating the fine brickwork of German immigrant masons. Photograph by Betsy Swanson, 1969.

built for German congregations. The façade is an exuberant display of corbeling and molding in brick. Arches, crosses, and niches advance and recede to create a patterned surface. The tower rises to 142 feet, changing from a square to an octagon in plan, incorporating buttresslike elements. *1974 National Historic Landmark.*

2029 Constance Street (see p. 123)

St. Alphonsus Church across the street was built in 1855–1857 after designs of Louis L. Long, Baltimore architect, to serve the Irish Catholics. Italianate in style, arches and pilasters form a rhythmic surface on the outside and in the sumptuous interior.

1139 Dryades Street

St. John the Baptist Church. Dresden native Albert Diettel designed the church for Irish immigrants in 1869–1872. The fine brickwork was his signature. With its onion dome and baroque curves, the church recalls German churches, as it should.

2029 Constance Street. Architect Louis L. Long's St. Alphonsus Church interior, 1855-1957, part of the Redemptorist Complex. Photograph by Robert S. Brantley. This church was built for the newly arrived Irish immigrants.

Felicity Street

Felicity Street, still paved with bricks and granite block paving, has fared well through 150 years. From Magazine Street toward Prytania Street in the **1100, 1200, 1300, and 1400 blocks** are single and double Greek Revival houses punctuated by John McGinty's Italianate side–hall house dating from 1870 at **1322 Felicity Street.** James Freret designed a Victorian house with Italianate features in the home he built for his family in 1880 at **1309 Felicity Street.** The Felicity United Methodist church at the corner of **1226 Felicity Street** and Chestnut Street is a rebuilding in 1888 of an 1850 church designed by architect Thomas Kelah Wharton.

1322 Felicity Street

The use of the slender colonettes for the second level is unusual for the Lower Garden District and the Garden District, but look out for this distinguishing feature on a few Italianate side-hall London plan houses. The John McGinty house (1870) and enclosure makes a composition in cast iron. Note the anthemion cresting at the parapet and the Gothic-style pointed gate with the newest fencing of its period, woven wire.

1328 Felicity Street

The John Auguste Blaffer house, designed by Charles Lewis Hillger in 1869, built by Ferdinand Reusch for $11,000, is an unusual side-hall townhouse for the area. Its Italianate entrance projection effects a towerlike block. Instead of a full pair of galleries across the entire facade, balconies front two windows at each level.

1305 Jackson Avenue
at Chestnut Street

Built for Augustus J. Tardy soon after his 1869 purchase of the lot, the double–galleried house illustrates the Greek Revival style modified by Italianate motifs, including brackets, segmental arched entrance and windows, tripartite parapet, and an Italianate wing to the side.

1329 Jackson Avenue

Trinity Episcopal Church. The mid-nineteenth-century Gothic Revival church was designed by Scotsman George Purves, architect, in 1852–1853 to serve the Garden District and the Lower Garden District Protestants. The facade and tower were rebuilt in 1873 by Charles L. Hillger, architect, and P. R. Middlemiss, builder.

1411 Jackson Avenue

The William Martin Perkins house designed by American architect Lewis E. Reynolds in 1850 is one the area's most sophisticated and atypical designs in the Classic style. The two-story columns in antis, the pediment with recessed parapet, the heavy entablatures with pediments on the first-floor openings, the carefully conceived architectural masses, and the incorporation of service buildings into the design of the house result in an international version of the Classic style.

1435 Jackson Avenue

William Fitzner was the architect in 1883 for this late Italianate-style raised villa, built by Conrad Wundenburg for Mrs. Hattie Thorn. Large dormers, full arches, windows where muntins have all but disappeared, and an Italianate side bay that extends off the gable end characterize it.

1529 Jackson Avenue

James Gallier, Jr., designed this side-hall house in the Italianate style about 1860 for J. J. Warren. The architect continued the preferred New Orleans floor plan, adding the required Italianate bay to the dining room, but he specialized in Italianate details and beautifully paneled doors. Note the second–floor area above the dining room with its bay. Gallier provided a picturesque "boudoir" and sitting room backed by a gallery and an interior bathroom with a bathtub and water closet. Recent scholarship matched this house to the drawing, initiating efforts to restore the long-mutilated facade.

1117–1127 Josephine Street

Stewart and Hoffman, architects and surveyors, designed this one-story commercial building in 1888. A recent renovation of the group of buildings for Kelly and Gottshegen, two young women who design and manufacture furniture, augurs well for the vicinity. Parapets with a flare reveal the date of the conservative buildings.

1431 Josephine Street

This outstanding villa-style house with Greek Revival decoration has Italianate details in the cornice and a large double-windowed dormer in the style of the late 1870s, perhaps added to an 1850s house. It was the residence of Edward J. Bobet of Bobet Bros., importers of slaves.

1200 through 1500 Blocks of Magazine Street

These blocks illustrate the full spectrum of Greek Revival housing dating from the 1850s and 1860s. **1507 Magazine Street,** St. Vincent's Infant Asylum, designed and built by Thomas Mulligan in 1864, has a fine cast iron front gallery recessed between two projecting ends of the building.

1800 Block of Magazine Street

This block on both sides presents Greek Revival brick commercial buildings that originally had living quarters above. Prominent among the developers was Samuel Hastings, after whom Hastings Place is named. Recent renovations of the mid-nineteenth-century commercial buildings along Hastings and Sophie Wright Place have brought the buildings

back to their original usage, offices below with residences above.

2000 and 2100 Blocks of Magazine Street

These blocks offer over a dozen antique shops in fine mid-nineteenth-century brick commercial buildings.

443 Market Street

Tobacco Warehouse. Gallier and Turpin, architects, built this brick warehouse in 1854 for Armand and Michel Heine, for whom Gallier also designed a house (demolished). The wide entablature with string courses and the evenly spaced brick pilasters articulate this warehouse well.

623 Orange Street

John Donovan had this two-bay brick house built between 1845 and 1850. With its front gallery continuing along one side of the upper floor, and with its front garden, it is a rare survivor of an unusual house type.

1514 Prytania Street

This side-hall double-galleried Italianate house was built for Michael Gernon about 1860. Monroe Labouisse was the architect chosen to salvage the once disguised and mutilated double galleries and to reveal the fine interior.

1518 Prytania Street

The Fairchild House reveals its 1850 building date compared to the later building at **1514 Prytania Street.** The Greek Revival side-hall house has been restored recently as an inn.

1780 Prytania Street

Eagle Hall. Philip Meyer bought the narrow triangular site creating the boundary between Faubourgs Annunciation and Nuns in 1851 to build this three-bay brick storehouse, with its second-level

2000 block of Prytania Street. Front and side elevations: Peter Conery double house, designed by architect Henry Howard soon after the Civil War. Photograph by Robert S. Brantley.

gallery creating a sidewalk arcade. The German Lafayette Volkstheater opened here in 1862. *Orleans Parish Landmark.*

1823 Prytania Street (see p. 114)

St. Anna's Asylum was built in 1853 by Little and Middlemiss, builders, for $37,500. William Newton Mercer, who lived on Canal Street in what is now the Boston Club, donated the land to the Society for the Relief of Destitute Females and their Helpless Children. Architect Thomas Kelah Wharton, who lived nearby on Coliseum Square in the 1850s, referred to it as the most handsome building in the vicinity. It is one of the few New Orleans institutional buildings that has been preserved for its original use.

2000 Block of Prytania Street

Peter Conery lived at **1616 Carondelet Street** in an 1836 mansion demolished in the 1920s for Beth Israel Synagogue. A partner in the firm of Gasquet, Parish and Co. on Canal Street, he also owned a number of rental properties in the Lower Garden District, such as this double Greek Revival house built soon after the Civil War after Henry Howard's designs. Tower of the Wind columns below Corinthian on front galleries was a Henry Howard signature. The side elevation reveals an unusual example of service wing galleries facing the outside rather than the inner court. Notice the progres-

sion of three service sections of different heights. Usually, the rear elevation of the house had a gallery and elevation similar to the front with simpler detailing

2018 and 2016 Prytania Street

Two variant forms of Greek Revival side-hall houses, the one in the foreground is more typical of the urban examples of the Faubourg St. Mary, since it is built at the banquette over which a cast iron balcony extends. It dates from 1855, built by J. E. Campbell for Benjamin Stelle for $5680.

Adjacent is one of Peter Conery's rental houses, also a side-hall house, but with wood columns running the full height of the facade. The second-level gallery railings are set between the box columns. The house was probably built in the late 1850s.

2127 Prytania Street

Alexander Harris had Day and Calrow, builders, build one of the city's most extravagant villa-style houses in 1857–1858. Thomas Kelah Wharton remarked, while visiting the building with designer James Calrow, "It promises to be the handsomest piece of work in the district." He was right; the opulence of decorative detail does not overpower the large center-hall house with its front gallery returning around the side to face what was once an elegant garden.

2343 Prytania Street. Photograph by Robert S. Brantley.

The Garden District: 1838-1878

W hen travel writer W. H. Sparks visited the Garden District in the 1840s he observed both the buildings and the English-speaking people who moved there as soon as they could gather the money to have a house built. After a quick look he summed up American New Orleans in his *Fifty Years of Memories* (1870).

"The Anglo-American commences to succeed and will not scruple at the means," he said. "And this is called enterprise combined with energy. Moral considerations may cause him to hesitate but never restrain his action."

Just as well that Garden District resident, Bishop Leonidas Polk of Trinity Episcopal Church, killed in the Civil War, was unable to contemplate Sparks' conclusion about his parishioners. Sparks went on with a vengeance: "The maxim is ever present in his mind; it is honorable and respectable to succeed—dishonest and disreputable to fail. It is only folly to yield a bold enterprise to nice considerations of moral right. If he can avoid the penalties of the civil law, success obviates those of the moral law."

Is this why the Garden District succeeded while the creole suburbs and the French Quarter languished during and after Reconstruction? As Sparks explained: "The Gallic or French American is less enterprising, yet sufficiently so for the necessary uses of life; he is more honest and less speculative, more open and less designing, more refined and less presumptuous."

Significantly, there were just two major creole households in the Garden District and neither lasted. Postmaster Michel Musson, who built **1331 Third Street** (see p. 147) in 1853, soon moved out. Antoine Jacques

Trinity Church at 1329 Jackson Avenue from the Henry Buckner House Gallery at 1410 Jackson Avenue. Photograph by Robert S. Brantley.

Mandeville de Marigny, son of Bernard de Marigny, built at **2524 St. Charles** (see p. 146), but his wife, Sophronie Claiborne, daughter of the American governor, left the Garden District and moved to New York with her children.

The Garden District was a project of Anglo-Americans for Anglo-Americans. American entrepreneurs led by Samuel Jarvis Peters, a Whig of Puritan Tory background, bought the strip of land in 1832 for $490,000 from Madame Jacques François Livaudais, living in Paris, to whom it had been awarded as part of her 1826 divorce settlement. Peters employed French refugee and former artillery officer under Napoleon, Benjamin Buisson, to lay out the new suburb.

Buisson had been in New Orleans since 1817, after attending the French Ecole Polytechnique. Yet he laid out the new faubourg as the simplest of suburbs. North–south streets were numbered. Historic associations were eschewed.

The utilitarian layout of the Garden District lacked amenities that had been beautifully conceived by Barthélémy Lafon in the Lower Garden District, although not executed in full. Perhaps it was developer Samuel Jarvis Peters' Puritan blood that kept him from demanding something creative. Only one square, named after Henry Clay, was laid out as a park and it was not centrally located. St. Charles Avenue, a continuation of Lafon's Naiades Street, was wide only because of the railroad tracks running in a "neutral ground" down the center.

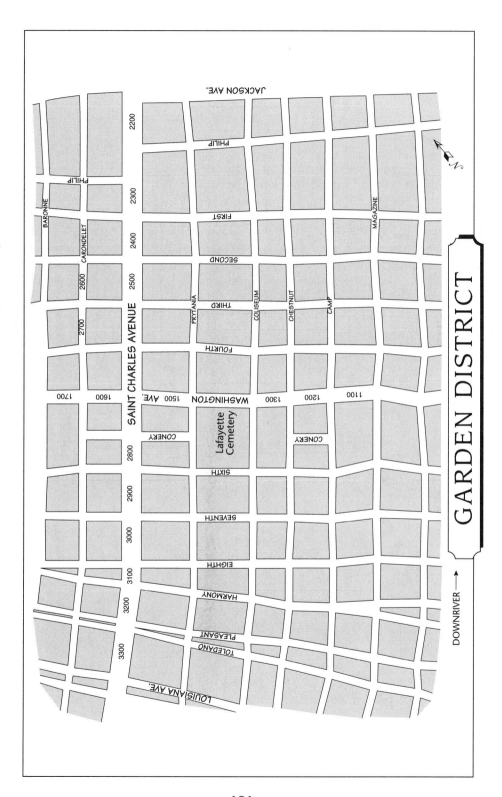

GARDEN DISTRICT

DOWNRIVER →

Ironically, Lafayette Cemetery became the central focus of Buisson's design. This cemetery is perhaps the city's most striking central element in any neighborhood except Jackson Square in the French Quarter. Nonetheless, the plain suburb Buisson laid out filled with fancy houses, while the exquisite and complex downriver suburb that Lafon had laid out earlier, the Lower Garden District, lost its cachet by the time Jacob U. Payne built his First Street house in Buisson's new suburb in 1849. Henry Buckner is not the only Lower Garden District resident to have moved upriver to the Garden District as soon as he accumulated sufficient wealth to commission the biggest house, at 1410 Jackson Avenue (see p. 145), on the edge of the Garden District.

The Garden District was settled by English-speaking Protestants who had made or were forging fortunes as factors, brokers, and providers, and as real estate developers, architects, and builders. According to economist James DeBow, in 1855, "New Orleans has more Maine natives than any Southern state except Mississippi, and twice as many New Yorkers as Kentuckians and Virginians combined." These are the men who agreed with Jefferson's sage prophecy about the lucrative future available in New Orleans. Most resided in the Garden District.

1410 Jackson Avenue. The Henry Buckner house, Lewis E. Reynolds, architect. Photograph by Robert S. Brantley.

They built similar houses up and down the streets, all costing about the same amount, $25,000 top dollar, except for a few ostentatious exceptions. The most expensive house of all, that of James Robb on Washington Avenue, cost $65,000 and was eventually demolished. Henry Lonsdale's house at the corner of Prytania and Third Streets, now a chapel, cost $40,000, while Henry Buckner's larger Jackson Avenue mansion cost just $30,000.

Portrait of James Robb. Attributed to George Peter Alexander Healy, ca. 1845. Courtesy of the Historic New Orleans Collection. Robb, the richest and most influential man in the Garden District, lost his wife to yellow fever, and his house was sold by Newcomb College for demolition and the lot became the Garden District's only subdivision.

Jacob U. Payne, whose 1849 house at **1134 First Street** (see p. 143) was one of the earliest five-bay double-galleried examples in the neighborhood and which set the style and the tone, had come from Kentucky via Vicksburg, where he had found a wife. A fellow Kentuckian, Colonel Robert Short, built one of the district's most luxurious three-bay side-hall houses, characterized by its cornstalk fence at **1448 Fourth Street at Prytania Street** (see p. 144) for about $24,000 in 1859. The Garden District's most interested architectural patron, Henry S. Buckner was also a Kentucky native (see p. 132).

A few Englishmen who retained their passports built major residences in the new suburb. One was Robert A. Grinnan, a commission merchant and cotton broker who arrived in 1850 to have Henry Howard design **2221 Prytania Street** (see p. 145), one of the Garden District's most original and sophisticated houses. Thomas Gilmour had the first assymetrical Italianate home in the city, built by Isaac Thayer at **2520 Prytania Street** in the early 1850s. Charles Briggs, also English, an insurance executive, broke with tradition by having Irish Protestant architect James Gallier, Sr. design a Gothic cottage at **2605 Prytania Street** (see pages 136, 146) in 1849.

1448 Fourth Street. Robert Henry Short house. Photograph by Betsy Swanson. Architect Henry Howard's most monumental works include this house, Belle Grove Plantation, and the Cyprien Dufour house at 1707 Esplanade Avenue. This cornstalk fence matches the one at 915 Royal Street.

2520 Prytania Street. Thomas Gilmour house. Photograph by Jerry Ward.

Henry Lonsdale, although born in Brooklyn, had English parents and had lived in England and Canada. He made his fortune as chief coffee broker from New Orleans to the American West, using Central American sources. The home he built at **2521 Prytania Street** (see p. 146) makes a trio of English residents at the corner of Fourth and Prytania Streets. Italianate-, Gothic-, and Classic-style houses, all built within six years with similar center-hall floor plans, make this one of the most striking corners in New Orleans.

How did the Garden District develop as a communal exhibition of Anglo-American wealth? The owners became wealthy about the same time and had houses built by the same few architects within a 20- year period. The architects and builders had for the most part come to New Orleans via Great Britain and New York, where they had seen the same prototypes, and they looked at the same pattern books by Minard Lafever and a few others. The owners also wanted houses that looked like their neighbors'. Contract after contract between architect or builder and client specifies "a home like the one at the corner," or "painted to match the color" of a neighbor's house, or "having a fence like that on Captain Leather's house."

2605 Prytania Street. Charles Briggs' house and carriage house. Photograph by Betsy Swanson, 1969. The carraige house or service cottage, always detached, is not in its original location.

County Cork native Henry Howard is the premier architect of the Garden District, designing at least two dozen of the houses. He lived at **1633 First Street,** which he may have designed but could not afford to buy. Although he designed more plantation homes in Louisiana than any other architect, as well as numbers of houses and commercial buildings in Faubourg St. Mary and the Esplanade, in addition to the Pontalba buildings in the French Quarter with James Gallier, Sr., Howard died in poverty in 1884. Unable to support his wife and 11 children, he experienced the collapse of his marriage and of his health. The money was in the building, not the designing of houses. Howard, for example, sometimes received only $150 for a set of plans and specifications.

Lewis Reynolds from New York is responsible for the most sophisticated designs in the Garden District. Scotch-Irish and Scottish builders such as Jamison and McIntosh, who established a firm using dozens of slaves as labor, along with Irish workers, knew where the money was, and their names appear on dozens of contracts as builders, not architects. Frederick Wing, whose center-hall Classic-style house remains at **1429 Seventh Street** (see p. 146), was known as a builder, not an architect.

James Gallier, Sr., on the other hand, after starting as a builder at Mountjoy Square, Dublin, was a careful designer and finished architect by the time he arrived in New Orleans in 1834, from County Louth via Dublin, London, and New York. Although known as an architect, he saw the advantage of owning a building yard in Faubourg St. Mary to build houses that others designed. He also had a sawmill along the river with slave labor to turn out the architectural elements so popular in the Garden District.

William Day, known primarily as a builder, built and lived in the Garden District and was apparently satisfied not to be called architect. London–born John Turpin lived at **2319 Magazine Street** in a house he designed. After working first as James Gallier's bookkeeper, he became his architectural partner in 1846, but by 1859 he gave up building and went into the wine business. New Orleanian William A. Freret, the Garden District's Parisian-trained architect, built his own house at **1524 Third Street** and many others.

These substantial homes in the Garden District were paid for with cash. If not cash, the standard note was not for more than five years. Yet most families had money left over to buy new furnishings, which added 20 to 40 percent to the cost of the house.

These interior furnishings were far more ornate and flamboyant than were the rhythmically proportioned exterior architectural embellishments. Even the interior decorative plasterwork, moldings, medallions, and woodwork specified by the builders and architects was far more ebullient inside than would be expected by a look at the outside.

Most of the Garden District houses were built between 1848 and 1865. Building continued apace even during the yellow fever epidemics. In 1853 the *Illustrated London News* wrote: "New Orleans has been built upon a site that only the madness of commercial lust could ever have tempted men to occupy." Twelve thousand were reported dead that year, and immigrants were as always the hardest hit, especially the vast numbers of Irish, many of whom were laborers for the houses under construction in the Garden District.

Yellow fever killed New Orleans' first surveyor and engineer, LeBlond de la Tour, in 1723. It hit America's most distinguished architect, English-born Benjamin H. Latrobe in 1820 on the third anniversary of his son's death of the same illness here, September 3, 1817. Yellow fever killed 28-year-old architect Charles Dakin in 1839 within a year of his arrival. Thomas Kelah Wharton, another noted English-born architect, arrived in New Orleans from Connecticut in the 1850s, after a stint in Holly Springs, Mississippi, and died here in 1862. Architect Lewis Reynolds saw six members of his family die of yellow fever. James Robb, the Garden District's richest resident, saw his wife and one of his four daughters die of yellow fever in September 1855.

Designed and built, then, by the same few people in the same few years, the Garden District is monolithic. There seem to be just three types of houses: center-hall villas, side-hall townhouses, and center-hall two story houses. The center-hall villa, raised on brick piers, is the least prevalent, but it seems most to fit into the neighborhood, associated as it is with gardens, such as Thomas Toby's 1838 villa at **2340 Prytania Street** in the Greek Revival Style.

Far more prevalent, however, is the Garden District's own vernacular version of the English side-hall townhouse. A Greek Revival–style example is **1238 Philip Street** (see p. 145), built for grain dealer John H. Rodenburg in 1853. Double galleries dominate as the significant exterior design feature of most side-hall townhouses. This creative expansion of an urban house type results in an indigenous and highly regional style of southern architecture. Repetitive as these double-galleried houses may be in type or style, they multiplied to create a neighborhood so singular that none other in the country boasts such a well- preserved array of single-family detached residences that cohere as a neighborhood. The side-hall townhouse, expanded into the Garden District double-galleried standard, has its luxurious epitome in the Robert Henry Short house at **1448 Fourth Street** (see pages 134, 144), one of the earlier houses to exhibit the Italianate decorative details on a plastered brick house with cast iron galleries.

The third most evident house type is the English center-hall two-story house, where a central door and a hallway on two levels is flanked by a room on each side at the front, each having two windows, usually full length, opening onto the double galleries. Such houses are two rooms deep at least, and the second set of identically sized rooms faces a rear gallery. Beyond the main house extends a service wing of two and sometimes three stories, less than half as wide as the house, so there is space along its side for a garden. This rear garden was available to residents of the house as well as to the entire service establishment. Across the back of such lots is often a stable or carriage house with rooms above for the male servants or the young men of the master household.

The center-hall house reached its apex of classical sophistication in the Garden District with the house Virginian Walter Robinson built with tobacco and banking money during the Civil War at **1415 Third Street** (see p. 147). The Italianate manner was applied to the standard center-hall type about 1870, when Samuel Jamison built the Joseph Carroll house at **1315 First Street** (see p. 144).

Galleries were the most essential feature of all types and styles of Garden District houses. In constant use as outdoor living and dining rooms, both front and rear, they often doubled as summer sleeping places and work areas for both resident family and their servants. Notice that some galleries, even of frame houses, have plastered gallery back walls complete with baseboards. After 1850 balconies and double galleries were of cast iron that had become available in mass-produced decorative patterns, imported from Philadelphia.

The hallways, too, were useful living spaces in the nineteenth century. The villas or center-hall raised cottages and the center–hall Greek Revival–plan houses, had identical doors both front and rear, so that a cross breeze made the hallways popular ancillary parlors. Often, bookcases and armoires lined them, and sets of furniture were placed to catch the breeze.

Galleries and halls, widely used spaces in the nineteenth century, are now empty symbols. On the other hand, the nineteenth century stairway continues to be a hallmark of style and wealth, according to the lavishness

1415 Third Street. Walter Robinson house. Photograph by Robert S. Brantley.

of its design. Similarly, chimneys were, in the English tradition, exhibitions of affluence. Therefore, chimneys went up and mantels appeared by the dozens: marble, cypress with a *faux marbre* finish, or cast iron. Brick chimneys, built for coal use, were major embellishments of house profiles; they have fancy brick work and corbeling as if they were an important and useful amenity, which they were not, in the semitropical climate.

A Garden District entrance door, continuing English tradition, made a definite statement. Usually, the door was recessed behind paneled reveals, hinged to swing shut for storms or privacy. Compare the bold Anglo-American entrance to any French Quarter example, where one cannot distinguish between door and window, where all exterior surface is flat and restrained. French Quarter residents hid wealth, invited mystery, and insisted on anonymnity. All amenities were centered around the rear courtyard and garden.

Side bays and projections with cast iron balconies signify Italianate designs grafted onto traditional Garden District floorplans. Sometimes these Italianate bays were added to earlier Greek Revival houses. Often faced with decorative cast iron and cresting above, the bays were usually a feature of the dining room.

Appendages, such as service wings and separate carriagehouses were an essential part of a Garden District complex from both design and management perspectives. The three-story slave quarters are an essential part of the overall design of the the Henry Buckner house at **1410 Jackson Avenue** (see pages 130-132) because they were visible from the back galleries of the main house and the rear windows of both the dining room and the bedrooms.

Charles Briggs' Gothic Revival house at **2605 Prytania Street** (see pages 134-136) has a two-story frame Gothic–style service cottage detached from the main house. His Irish servants lived there since the Englishman owned no slaves. Ogee arches, pediments, and verge boards provide sophisticated architectural amenities that repeat themes from the main house.

Similarly, the detached service building and carriagehouse at the Carroll house at **1315 First Street** (see p. 144) stands as an outstanding architectural element of the complex, and it looks more like Regency England than New Orleans Italianate.The outbuildings of the Robinson house at **1415 Third Street** (see pages 139-147) rank high in style and size. Unusual in arrangement, they extend to the side instead of to the rear of the main house.

Plus ca change, plus c'est la meme chose. Alphonse Karr's 1849 comment in *Les Guepes* is apt. "The more things change, the more things stay the same," in New Orleans' Garden District, at least. The following Garden District tour covers the most creative and robust years of construction, from 1838, when Thomas Toby built his villa at **2342 Prytania Street,** to 1872, when steamboat captains and plantation partners Bradish and Johnson commissioned their house at **2343 Prytania Street** (see p. 145) just across the street (McGehee School).

2343 Prytania Street. McGehee School, designed by Lewis Reynolds for Bradish Johnson. Photograph by Robert S. Brantley. Second Empire as it is, this house is far more Classic in style than it would have been had it been designed in New York at the same time, 1872.

2305, 2307, and 2309 Coliseum Street

Built in 1868 after Henry Howard designs for John Hall of Martinsburg, Virginia, these are fine examples of identical floorplans, one-story versions of the side-hall house, having galleried facades that alternate between Classic and Italianate decorative motifs.

2627 Coliseum Street

James Eustis, Henry Buckner's son-in-law, as well as a U.S. Senator and Ambassador to France, had the fanciful Swiss chalet with Gothic details built in 1876 and his family lived there through 1903. Until 1953 it was home to the family of Richard Koch, architect and historian. Three wide pediments distinguish the fanciful Garden District chalet.

2700–2726 Coliseum Street

This row of five once-identical, galleried, side-hall frame houses were built in 1861 by architect William Freret as a speculative building project. The Civil War ruined the investment but not the houses. Box columns on both levels of all the houses creates a pleasing rhythm along the street.

1313 Eighth Street

George Washington Cable (1844–1925) writer and early advocate of civil rights for African–Americans had this center-hall house built in 1874. He raised his family here and entertained such friends and literary contemporaries as Mark Twain, Joel Chandler Harris, Lafcadio Hearn, and Oscar Wilde.

2305, 2307, 2309 Coliseum Street. Photograph by Robert S. Brantley Such examples of facade architecture abound throughout American New Orleans.

2627 Coliseum Street at Fourth Street. James Eustis house, 1876, William Freret, architect. Photograph by Robert S. Brantley. The inspiration was a plate in **Holly's Country Seats,** published in 1863.

2700-2726 Coliseum Street.
Photograph by Betsy
Swanson. Five Classic-style
houses, 1861. W. A. Freret
(1833-1911), architech.

1437 Eighth Street

Daniel C. Byerly had his Second Empire version of the center-hall villa built in 1871. Different from the standard villa is the mansard roof, the oversized dormers, and the position on lowered piers. Former Confederate General John B. Hood moved to New Orleans into another Second Empire house at **1206 Third Street.**

1134 First Street

Jacob Payne's house set the standard for Garden District center-hall houses when it was built in 1849. Tower of the Winds capitals adorn the second-story columns above an Ionic order on the ground floor. Such progressions of column capitals were traditional to Garden District galleries.

Payne, a Kentuckian, charged a 2.5 percent fee for marketing cotton shipped to him from upriver. Like other cotton factors he extended credit to his clients for their supplies and equipment for the coming year, charging interest, thus becoming a personal banker.

1239 First Street

James Calrow and Charles Pride, builders, contracted in 1857 with commission merchant Albert Hamilton Brevard for this $13,000 side-hall brick house. It has a service wing, although he owned no slaves; he probably employed Irish immigrants to maintain the establishment. The double galleries feature a variation on the module, columns in antis, Corinthian columns above and Ionic columns below, set between square pillars or box columns at the corners. The cast ironwork has a rose pattern reflected in the rosette of the woven wire fence across the property line. This patented fence design is a forerunner of today's chain link fence. The library wing toward Chestnut Street postdates the main house.

1437 Eighth Street. Daniel Byerly house, 1871-1873. Photograph by Robert S. Brantley. The financial panic of 1873 saved the Garden District from the Second Empire craze imported from the Paris of Napoleon III via New York. The Second Empire signature emanates from the roof and from the rounded door and window moldings. But the house is just another villa-style cottage with a center hall raised on piers that have been filled in.

1315 First Street

This house dates from 1869 when Virginian Joseph Carroll, a cotton factor, contracted with Scotsman and builder Samuel Jamison to build the Italianate center-hall mansion. While the Carroll house is too exuberant to typify the Italianate in its Garden District interpretation, the house might be called a metaphor for Italianate in the area; all the forms seen throughout the neighborhood are evident on this one house. Yet the decoration succeeds as composition because of the large scale onto which the plethora of decorative detail was applied.

1213 Fourth Street

This is the essence of a relatively inexpensive, mid-nineteenth-century Classic-style Garden District house. Typical are the box columns, a cast iron gallery rail, and a simple cornice with dentils and small paired brackets. The service wing is to the side, somewhat unusual.

1448 Fourth Street (see p. 138)

A Baltimore builder, Robert Huyghe, built this 1859 Italianate version of the side–hall house after designs of Henry Howard, then in partnership with Albert Diettel. Wood and Miltenberger, the

New Orleans branch of Wood and Perot in Philadelphia, provided the cast iron fence in the cornstalk pattern.

1410 Jackson Avenue (see p. 132).

The Henry S. Buckner house (1856) by Lewis Reynolds is one of five houses Buckner commissioned in American New Orleans as he ascended the economic ladder. This house is the climax of his efforts. In its magnificent scale, with wide galleries on four sides, a projecting front portico with pediment, and side pediments, the house has a sculptural quality. Even the service wings and outbuildings are so well integrated into the house plan that they provide an essential element to a grandiose design.

1411 Jackson Avenue

Lewis Reynolds also designed the William Perkins house, unusual in plan and conceived in an entirely different manner from its neighbor, the Buckner house. A complex architectural mass, it presents varied forms on each exposure, whereas the sculptural Buckner house remains rectilinear and symmetrical. The Perkins house is national in its interpretation of the asymetrical Italianate mode rather than provincial and local like most of the Garden District, except for Howard's Grinnan House and the Bradish–Johnson extravaganza on Prytania (McGehee School).

1238 Philip Street

Grain dealer John H. Rodenburg's house (1853) exemplifies the Greek Revival style applied to the side-hall townhouse. Built of plastered brick with 18-inch–thick brick walls, it has 14-foot ceilings in the Victorian parlor measuring 18 by 40 feet. The two semioctagonal bays of the Chestnut Street wing were added in 1869.

2221 Prytania Street

The Robert Grinnan house, built in 1850 by John Sewell, is one of architect Henry

Howard's finest designs, with a plan unusual for the Garden District. A Classic-style gallery crosses only part of the front elevation and at the lower level only. Beside it a balcony projects at the second level. Bays and back halls as well as the absence of the usual long service wing distinguish the floor plan. The sophistication of Classic- style details with the Minard Lafever entrance reveal both Howard's successful apprenticeship with James Dakin and his access to Town and Davis work in New York.

2343 Prytania Street (see p.141).

The Bradish Johnson house (Louise S. McGehee School), designed by Lewis Reynolds in 1872, is the most monumental of the Garden District's center-hall houses, outdoing in decorative detail Reynolds's monumental 1856 Buckner Classic–style mansion on Jackson Avenue. Because of its French Second Empire decorative style, the house has long been attributed to William Freret, who studied at L'Ecole des Beaux Arts in Paris. The profusion of large projecting surfaces that ascend upward to a busy roofline with baroque rondels, sculptural chimneys, and French-style dormers differs sharply from the Carroll house at **1315 First Street** (see p. 144) which is an Italianate version of a chaste center-hall house dating from about the same time.

2507 Prytania Street

Newspaperman Joseph Maddox's center-hall, five–bay house was appropriate for the editor of the *Daily Crescent,* who had John Barnett, a prominent builder, design it in 1852, with John R. Eichelerger as builder. German immigrant Edward Gotthiel was the supervising architect. Maddox lost the house in 1854 through court seizure.

2520 Prytania Street (see p. 135)

London–born Thomas Course Gilmour, a cotton broker who purchased cotton from local factors on behalf of interests in Liverpool and other spinning centers of Europe for a fee commissioned his Italianate home in 1853, three years after his arrival in the city.

The architect selected, Isaac Thayer, planned a two-story brick house with kitchen and back buildings for $9500. The asymmetrical facade, with its paired and arched windows, represents an early use of the Italianate style. The carriage house was detached to the rear of the house and is now used as a residence facing **1417 Third Street.**

Gilmour's house with its six rooms (three over three) was enlarged to an eight–room house in 1892, when Mrs. John M. Parker, Sara Roberta Buckner, added the dining room, master bedroom and rear hall. The multilighted windows were replaced with large glass panes from the 1884 World's Fair Exposition. The present leaded glass entrance doors replaced the solid Greek Revival door. The present owners retained Mrs. Parker's exterior alterations and floor-plan while restoring and furnishing the interior to the 1853 taste of Thomas Gilmour's ownership.

2521 Prytania Street

Henry Lonsdale was born in New York of British parents and arrived in New Orleans in 1828 in time to make a fortune in gunnysacks and to lose it in the 1837 Panic. Londsdale made his second fortune as a coffee broker, which financed a towering center-hall mansion in 1856. The recessed door set behind an entrance with columns in antis is a restrained and elegant example of Henry Howard's Classic styling, flanked by full-length openings with deep molded cornices. The stepped gable ends, three-and-one-half stories in height, seen from Third Street, tower over a series of service wings in a progression of heights. His house is now used as the Chapel of Our Mother of Perpetual Help.

2605 Prytania Street (see p. 136)

The Charles Briggs house completes a triumvirate of center-hall houses built within six years of each other on this corner at Third Street. London-born Charles Briggs acquired this new Gothic-style house designed in 1849 by James Gallier.

The house is rare because the Gothic-style house never appealed to Garden District tastes, perhaps because it was associated with Catholic churches. But Briggs was English, and revivals of the Gothic style recalled the Tudor style. This chaste and restrained example, adhering to the traditional center-hall plan, is not starkly out of place in the Garden District. Pointed arches on the windows determine the Gothic mode, along with Elizabethan chimneys and a gallery with wide lowered and pointed arches, minimally Gothic in vocabulary. The interior continues the Gothic motifs with quatrefoil brackets, bunched rod Gothic columns and bosses. Few Garden District houses have matched interior and exterior motifs as does this house, no matter the style.

2524 St. Charles Avenue

This transitional style raised villa was part Classic, part Italianate built soon after 1856 for Louise Sophronie Claiborne, whose husband, Antoine Jacques Mandeville de Marigny, was son of Bernard de Marigny. A complex web of family affairs caused Mme. de Marigny to move uptown to the American neighborhood, then to leave it for New York.

2265 St. Charles Avenue

Lavinia Dabney was one of the few women to sign a contract for a Garden District house. James Gallier, Jr., designed her Greek Revival side-hall double-galleried house in 1856, but she only enjoyed it a year before she lost it in the recession of 1857. The contract for just $6600 specified frame construction. A change order called for brick.

1429 Seventh Street

Frederick Wing's own center–hall house is a delicate example of the Greek Revival style. Philadelphia–born Wing came up through the ranks as carpenter to become an architect, but he sold his newly erected house in 1862, soon after he enlisted in the Louisiana militia to serve the Confederacy. The galleries are supported by the kind of simple wood box column that became so characteristic of New Orleans' hundreds of rental houses.

1213 Third Street

Belfast-born Archibald Montgomery, president of the Crescent City Railroad, had Henry Howard build a conservative version of an "Italianate" Swiss chalet–style house soon after the Civil War. At last, even Howard had abandoned two–story galleries. That made possible the emphasis on the varied levels of the roofline with its pedimented eaves above brackets.

1331 Third Street

The original design of the Michel Musson house has been attributed to James Gallier, Sr., but the facade has been altered. The fine cast iron gallery is an 1884 replacement; the facade initially had two front bays, similar to the one on the garden side of the house, an unusual arrangement, but one with which Gallier, Sr. was familiar, as he had worked in the Grosvenor estate in London and in New York before coming to New Orleans in 1834.

1415 Third Street (see p. 139).

Walter Robinson came south from Virginia to establish himself as a cotton factor. But the Lynchburg native understood tobacco, and he went into perique tobacco, a curly black blending variant used in pipe tobacco, grown only in St. James Parish, Louisiana. Cuban cigar wrappers financed the elegant house that James Gallier, Jr., is said to have designed in the late 1850s. Unusual curved ends finish the double galleries of the center-hall five-bay house. Two stories of equal height, with 15–foot 8–inch ceilings, suggest the scale of the interior, which is among the most elaborate in the city. The service buildings extending out to the side and the sophisticated stable building are English in appearance and provide essential design factors to the *tout ensemble.*

1006 Washington Avenue

William H. McClellan, owner of a ship supply business, had this unusual side-hall house built in 1868. Encircled by double galleries, it a late example of this New Orleans' tradition. The Ionic colonnade below and the Corinthian second–story colonnade are Classic-style elements, but the large pediment with its bracketed eaves are Italianate and typical of the building date.

1126 Washington Avenue

This frame center–hall house, with its undulating double gallery, recalls a bowfront chest of drawers. It was built for iceman A. W. Bosworth, a native of Skowhegan, Maine. Like the University of the South at Sewannee, the house was designed by English-born Thomas Kelah Wharton, a protegée of Bishop Leonidas Polk. The magnificence of this house, which suffered from the absentee ownership of Harry Bruns of Fluvanna County, Virginia, may be seen from Magazine Street, where the rear elevation with its full galleries and the service wings are evident.

Washington Avenue at Prytania Street

Lafayette Cemetery No. 1 shows how high style a cemetery can be when it is the centerpiece for streets filled with fine architecture. Further, the marble, granite, and plastered brick tombs and monuments with their handsome ironwork and architectural design provide a city in miniature that exhibits nineteenth-century architectural styles.

The Irish Channel

Travel writers had given the Garden District its soubriquet by the 1850s. Here was New Orleans *nouveau riche* neighborhood. It had far fewer rental houses than other neighborhoods, although like Freret's examples at 1700 Coliseum, they were not unknown. In time Magazine Street emerged as a commercial strip and the houses toward the river became known as the Irish Channel. The custom had begun in the Lower Garden District and continued uptown. Today, the area from Jackson Avenue to Delachaise Street, from Tchoupitoulas Street to Magazine Street is called the Irish Channel National Historic District.

Repetition of building type and style and a rhythmical proliferation of architectural details gives the neighborhood pattern and composition. Shotguns abound from Greek Revival rows to late Victorian rows, interspersed among rows of earlier, Classic-style creole cottages, all inexpensive multifamily housing. The search for many types and styles of multifamily or double dwellings can bring the count to dozens. Another search is for the great variety of architectural decorative detail from local sash door and blind factories, including pierced work, turned work, pressed wood, shingles, and brackets of abundant variety. Since the Irish Channel is close to the river, secret remnants of early plantation complexes add to the area's charm and mystique.

2857 Annunciation Street at Sixth Street. Photograph by Robert S. Brantley. Creole cottages were usually relegated to the riverside of Magazine Street as the Irish channel marched uptown.

2857 Annunciation Street
at Sixth Street

This illustrates that creole cottages continued to be built, their canted gable ends extended to incorporate the ever-present overhang. Such houses date from the early 1830s on into the post–Civil War days when they went up to house freed slaves as well as the Irish.

2901–2915 Camp Street (see p. xxv).

Granite curbing, brick sidewalks, and wrought iron fences are amenities fronting this row of late Victorian double shotguns built for rent houses. Wide brackets supporting deep overhangs provide the main decoration on these 1880s examples. However, the drop siding and wood quoins are also standard.

1020 Fourth Street

Isaac Bogart had County Antrim native George Purves design this elegant small house in the Classic-style in 1849–1850, with Robertson and Shaw, builders. The Greek Revival front door leads directly to a side gallery. Delicate and chaste on the front elevation, it has an unusual but charming side overhang of a later date with giant brackets that cover a side gallery with louvered shutters.

1100 Jackson Avenue

This is a mid–nineteenth–century commercial building restored by Koch and Wilson, architects in 1973 for use as offices. It serves as an anchor for the neighborhood.

2353–2363 Laurel Street

This is a row of 1850s late Classic–style double shotgun houses. Notice the low hip roofs with the progression of brick chimneys. These early examples of the double shotgun type predate the similar three-bay, single examples in the Italianate style that Henry Howard designed at **2305–2329 Coliseum Street** (see p. 141) with their side halls.

904 Sixth Street

Charles Clark Gaines, a hardware importer, had this Greek Revival–style villa built in the early 1850s. Stenciled and

2331-33 Magazine Street. Double house designed by Henry Howard and Henry Thiberge in 1860 for Julius Forcheimer. Photograph by Robert S. Brantley.

hand-painted wall surfaces were found in the dining room wall and ceiling of the long-neglected house in the 1971 restoration.

2331–2333 Magazine Street

Louis Mayer, a tobacco merchant in partnership with Simon Forcheimer, had this elegant Classic-style rental property built in 1860 by Elijah Cox after designs of Howard and Thiberge, architects. It has all the charm and the same architectural forms as its detached center-hall and side-hall neighboring single–family dwellings.

436 Seventh Street

Near the levee rests this 1835 galleried cottage built for Mary Ann Grigson near the old Livaudais Plantation house, long demolished. This is a treasure that languished unrecognized, and unappreciated for decades. The canted roof, incorporating the front gallery and repeated at the back elevation of the gable- sided frame house, signifies its early date. The central arched entrance, flanked by one window on each side, adds a Regency touch, as did the work of builder Fitz Miller at the same time in the Faubourg St. Mary. This may be the oldest surviving building in the former city of Lafayette. Restored in the late 1970s by architect Charles F. Sanders, it has been furnished in the late–Federal style by owner James Didier with H. Parrott Bacot, cultural historian, as consultant.

Uptown, University, and Carrollton

I n the visually festive uptown area, life resembles a parade. Live oak trees parade down narrow fence-lined streets that are interrupted by wide avenues for variety every 10 blocks or so. Houses present files of closely spaced rectangles, those fronted with more rectangles in galleries, windows, and doors: the whole is an ever-repeated sequence of gracious galleries behind supporting columns.

A coherent whole permeates the lifestyle as well. Uptown has everything a city needs and much more: a world-class zoo, clusters of huge grain elevators, and the Mississippi River with its docks and tugboats, barges and ferries; institutions such as Tulane and Loyola Universities provide anchors and scale. As a legacy of benefactor John McDonogh, uptown also has all those McDonogh schools designed by James Freret. Nineteenth-century brick churches and convents by the dozens remain, their spires rising above the live oaks.

Restaurants and bars crop up at corners convenient to everyone, not to mention snowball stands, antique shops, and artisan factories, all housed in jigsaw puzzles of frame houses and storehouses, with a smattering of brick. Uptown has potholes, too, and few curbs, many of them simply slabs of granite or slate, and more than one car has rolled over on its side in the deep gutters, but who cares? It's part of the scene. One thing uptown has very few of is garages, because the area developed just before cars did and was laid out without alleys to adapt as driveways. This lack makes knowing where to park a minor but arcane science among the natives.

The site of the World's Industrial Exposition of 1884 has become Audubon Park, and behind it the Audubon Zoo is bound by the Mississippi River. The zoo and the river provide an unusual nightime uptown sym-

151

phony. Where else in an urban area do the brays of donkeys and zebras, the roar of lions, and the trumpet of elephants intermingle with the eerie sound of foghorns from tugboats chugging up and down the river? The squeal of a sea lion can make a resident's dog restless in the hot and humid nights of uptown New Orleans.

Hurst-De La Villebeuvre Plantation house. Formerly at Tchoupitoulas and Joseph Streets, built in 1832 for Cornelius Hurst and sold in 1837 to Jean De La Villebeuvre. Drawing by Thomas Kelah Wharton, 1855. Courtesy of the Manuscripts and Archives Division, the New York Public Library; Astor, Lenox, and Tilden Foundations. The working sugar plantation had its own railroad extending from the wharf on the Mississippi River to the cypress swamps that began near what is now Claiborne Avenue. The house was moved to No.3 Garden Lane in 1922.

Hurst-De La Villebeuvre house, 1832, at its original location facing the Mississippi near what became Joseph Street.

Portrait of Suzanne De La Villebeuvre, daughter of Jean De La Villebeuvre. Oil on canvas, by François Bernard, ca. 1850. Courtesy of John O. Toledano. She grew up in the plantation that her father bought from the Hurst family during the national financial crisis and panic of 1837, and from there she married Benjamin Toledano

Between the river and Magazine Street, a continuation of the Irish Channel upriver called for Catholic support and more frame rental shotguns. The Poor Clare Nuns anchor the corner of Magazine Street at **720 Henry Clay Street.** The old Public Health Service Hospital, long established at **210 State Street** near the river, is a complex of brick nineteenth–century buildings, now used as the Adolescent and Children's Mental Health and Substance Abuse Hospital. The mansard roof on the old section of DePaul Hospital at **1040 Calhoun Street** decorates an early twentieth–century uptown landmark.

The closely spaced uptown houses, mostly frame shotguns, have historically provided shelter for many social, economic, and racial strata. While houses built as modest rentals have become expensive owner-occupied homes, many remain rental property because uptown, indeed most of New Orleans, didn't grow urban. It started urban, even when the idea was *rus in urbe*, as in the Garden District.

After World War I, when it was conceded that the old Creole days had not only waned but were dying, even the Creole families moved upriver and intermarried among *les Américains.* They left the French language behind, retaining their fanciful names and their rituals of family and of church. They brought their recipes with them, too, along with their love of a good time and a gracious way of entertaining that is often confused with southern hospitality but is something different.

The hallmark of uptown, however, is the shotgun house or its camelback variant. This one-story frame house fits cozily on the standard 30–foot by 120–foot lot. Oriented front to rear, one room wide, usually without a side hall but with three to five equal-sized rooms extending to the rear, it is like a shotgun barrel. Whether they were two-bay or three-bay single houses or four-bay double houses, a front porch with a wide overhang or a full colonette supported gallery is inevitable. Chimneys march one behind the other on a low hip roof while doors and mantels inside progress front to rear. The shotgun kitchen is usually beside a bathroom at the back, the latter often a shedlike appendage.

The camelback is a shotgun with a second story over the back part, resulting from the need for more space. These two house types, shotgun and camelback, appear uptown by the hundreds, usually set back a few feet behind a low iron fence, with yard enough for a row of poinsettias or a riot of blue plumbagos. Shotguns have been repeated all over town in a panoply of styles, appearing as early as 1850, but they reached their apotheosis uptown in the 1880s.

Multiples of closely spaced frame shotguns on 30- and even 15- foot-wide lots alternate with a very few plantation houses and early suburban villas of the 1830s through the 1860s. All are overshadowed by the larger houses exhibiting juxtaposed massing of the heavy Eastlake style. Queen Anne multiple-story houses exhibit turrets, mansards, shingled sides, patterned slate, and jigsaw work gallery details, set on generous lots with side

7510 and 7514 Hampson Street between Cherokee and Hillary Street. Photograph by Betsy Swanson. Two of a row of five identical two bay shotgun houses.

galleries. The common denominator for all types and styles is the cypress construction, raised always on brick piers or a raised basement and the galleries with their plethora of jigsaw work, turned or sawed.

As early as 1850 seven little faubourgs, former plantations, were incorporated as Jefferson City from Louisiana Avenue upriver to Joseph Street. These included Faubourgs Plaisance, Delachaise, St. Joseph, and East and West Bouligny. The Boulignys had been the plantation of General Wade Hampton of South Carolina from 1816 to 1829 when he sold his 23.5 arpents fronting the Mississippi to Louis Bouligny, who subdivided. Upriver the Avart family subdivided, and then came Rickerville. Joseph Pilié, an *émigré* from St. Domingue, C. J. A. d'Hemecourt, a Frenchman in New Orleans with his family by 1831, Charles F. Zimple, and Henry Mollhausen contracted with the various plantation owners to lay out subdivisions beween 1835 and 1855. By 1870 the entire group was annexed to New Orleans.

As Jefferson Parish surveyor from 1832 to 1846, Benjamin Buisson, a former soldier in the French army, recalled Napoleon's battles when he named streets he surveyed between Toledano Street and Audubon Park. One of the little faubourgs, however, had been established as early as 1807 by the Joseph Wiltz family and laid out by Hyacinthe Laclotte, a native of Bordeaux, France; Faubourg Plaisance took in what is now Louisiana Avenue, which had been named Gran Cours Wiltz. The faubourg is memorialized in "Pleasant" Street. Nothing much happened there for decades,

3643 Camp Street between Amelia and Antoine Streets. Henry Rice house (Fink Asylum). Photograph by Betsy Swanson. This mid-nineteenth-century villa in the Italianate style has seen use as a residence, then an orphans' asylum, with a return to residential use in the 1970s.

1111 Milan Street at Chestnut Street. McDonogh No. 7 School, 1877, W. A. Freret, architect. Photograph by Betsy Swanson.

but the building inventory today illustrates that it has uptown's earliest and grandest center-hall villas, including **3643 Camp Street** (see p. 156) and two-story, side-hall houses, continuing the Garden District tradition.

Upriver from Jefferson City at Joseph Street, little communities developed, such as Hurstville, between Joseph and State Streets, subdivided in 1837 by Cornelius Hurst. Hurst, however, kept enough land with his house to sell a working sugar plantation with its own private railroad that transported cypress and sugarcane to the docks; Jean de la Villebeuvre bought it that year, and Thomas Kelah Wharton sketched the bucolic scene with the house built in 1832 under the superintendance of William Cochrane. The house is gone now, moved upriver in 1922 to No. 3 Garden Lane, near Longue Vue gardens.

Then came Bloomingdale; Burtheville, extending to Audubon Park, was cut into lots in 1854 for Dominique François Burthe. Next came Greenville, which extended upriver to the edges of the city of Carrollton, beginning at Lowerline Street. Carrollton was a development project of the New Orleans Canal and Banking Company, conceived under the charter of the New Orleans and Carrollton Railroad. Laurent Millaudon, arrived from France in 1802, Senator John Slidell from New York, and Samuel Kohn of Germany, all immigrants, banded together to buy the Spanish colonial plantation owned by Barthélémy Macarty since 1781. Surveyor Charles Zimpel divided the tract in 1833 and it was named after William Carroll, a general under Andrew Jackson during the Battle of New Orleans. A key to their project was the charter of the New Orleans and Carrollton Railroad the same year.

The developers were powerful men, and in 1854 the seat of Jefferson Parish was moved to Carrollton Avenue. Architect Henry Howard designed the courthouse, now used as a school at **719 South Carrollton Avenue** (see p. 159).

St. Charles Avenue became the location of choice for the wealthier Anglo-Americans, and their parade of eclectic building styles for a successful turn-of-the-century population follows the bend in the river to present a lavish display of monumental and gaudy two-story houses.

For the first time eclectic taste in New Orleans architecture was expressed, ranging from the 1907 neo-Italianate mansion at **5120 St. Charles Avenue,** built in 1907 for Mark Isaacs (Latter Memorial Library since 1948), to architect C. Milo Williams' turreted and shingled frame Edwardian at **7030 St. Charles Avenue.** In between were Second Empire cottages and mansions, such as **5604 and 5624 St. Charles Avenue.** Wealth financed the Romanesque Revival-style houses built of rock-faced stone, such as **3804 St. Charles Avenue,** dating from 1890, built for the widow of Charles Newman. This florid style took; Favrot and Livaudais, architects, designed **4717 St. Charles Avenue** in 1904 for cotton magnate W. P. Brown, and they used it again at Tulane University. It took, but it didn't fit.

719 South Carrollton Avenue between Hampson and Maple Streets. Jefferson Parish Court House, 1852, Henry Howard, architect. Photograph by Betsy Swanson,1969.

Garlanded cornices and attenuated reeded columns applied in pairs often indicates neo-Classic Revival or City Beautiful houses of the turn of the century through World War I. One example is the Round Table Club, which in 1917 moved into **6330 St. Charles Avenue,** with its Tiffany stained glass staircase window.

Sully and Toledano, then Toledano and Wogan, built houses with some Shingle-, Craftsman-, and Prairie-style details and others with Queen Anne motifs, such as **4114 St. Charles Avenue** (see p. 171) Checkered tile, lattice work in arabesque forms, and decorative verge boards identify several of the houses they designed on St. Charles Avenue.

Thomas Sully, however, must be the king of uptown architecture. Son of a local cotton broker and great nephew of the noted painter, he opened his architectural practice in 1883 after apprenticing in New York with George Slade and Henry Rutgers Marshall. He could rock along on the St. Charles streetcar to his office and look at more buildings that he had designed than most architects could manage everywhere within a lifetime.

The first New Orleans architect to abandon the service wing, he went back to the colonial plan, relegating the service building to the rear of the lot. He also abandoned the front-to-rear linear orientation. Instead of halls, Sully designed large reception rooms or "living halls" open to all the major

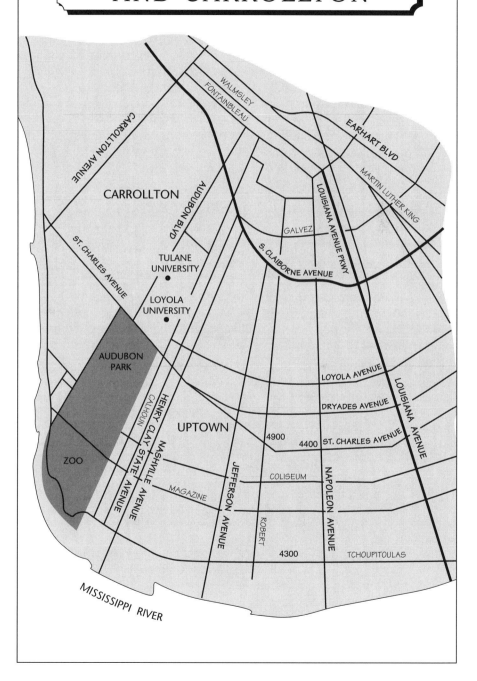

UPTOWN, UNIVERSITY, AND CARROLLTON

WALMSLEY

FONTAINBLEAU

EARHART BLVD

CARROLLTON AVENUE

MARTIN LUTHER KING

CARROLLTON

AUDUBON BLVD

LOUISIANA AVENUE PKWY

GALVEZ

ST. CHARLES AVENUE

S. CLAIBORNE AVENUE

TULANE
UNIVERSITY

LOYOLA
UNIVERSITY

AUDUBON
PARK

LOYOLA AVENUE

LOUISIANA AVENUE

DRYADES AVENUE

CALHOUN

HENRY CLAY

ZOO

UPTOWN

NASHVILLE AVENUE

STATE AVENUE

4900

4400

ST. CHARLES AVENUE

JEFFERSON AVENUE

COLISEUM

NAPOLEON AVENUE

MAGAZINE

ROBERT

4300

TCHOUPITOULAS

MISSISSIPPI RIVER

first-floor rooms. They dominate his houses. He abandoned second-floor galleries, wanting his chimneys, towers, bays, pitched roofs, gables, and dormers to have dramatic effect. He liked inset porches, too. Sully's houses are derived from northern summerhouses, not townhouses, and this makes them stand out in urban New Orleans. He built so many of them that they fit in the *tout ensemble* because of the sheer numbers as well as because of the frame construction and the porches and galleries.

Today uptown, the university area, and Carrollton have melded into a long neighborhood that follows the river through its bend at Carrollton. Most houses date from the end of Reconstruction in April 1877 to World War I. The Carrollton Railroad of 1833 spurred the subdivision of plantations. The World's Industrial and Cotton Centennial of 1884 thrust the largely vacant suburbs into development. Baldwin Wood's huge pumping system, one that he exported to Holland, overcame by 1914 the horrendous drainage problems to make uptown a livable area.

All About Magazine and Carrollton Shopping

Besides driving by car, there are four ways to experience uptown: streetcar, bus, a ride on the river from the aquarium to the park, or walking. The St. Charles Avenue streetcar is an outgrowth of the New Orleans and Carrollton Railroad. For a $1.00 fare, travel uptown from the Garden District past Sacred Heart Academy at Cadiz Street, Loyola University, Holy Name Church, and Tulane University on the right, with Audubon Park on the left. Follow the bend at Carrollton, continuing along the intermixed commercial and residential Carrollton Avenue to Claiborne Avenue. Turn around and come back to see it all from the other direction; there's enough to look at both ways.

Step down at the bend in the river at Carrollton Avenue for a stop at the restaurants and shops between the levee and St. Charles Avenue, such as Mignon Faget's at **710 Dublin Street,** with her original cast gold and silver jewelry. You might try **Maple Street,** with its Maple Street Book Shop at **7523** and bars and restaurants that the university students and faculty use. Try little restaurants in old houses under the levee, including Café Volage at **720 Dublin Street** or Dante Street Deli and Patio Bar at **736 Dante Street.**

Ride through the antique shop strip and see the mix of residential turned commercial and commercial district as it appears today after over a century of continual use. The antique shops include a cluster in the 3400 block including the Blackamoor at **3433 Magazine Street,** Didier, Inc. at **3439 Magazine Street,** and others as interesting. Another cluster centers around **3900 Magazine Street** where Casey Willems throws his pots at **3919 Magazine Street.** Mario Villa at **3908 Magazine Street** exhibits his iron furniture and lamps that have garnered numerous awards. Jean Bragg at **3901 Magazine Street** specializes in George Ohr and Newcomb Pottery. Her textiles and white linens are outstanding, too.

Stop at Reginelli's for lunch at **3923 Magazine Street.** Jerry Bremermann has a showroom at **3943 Magazine Street.** In the next block at **4038 Magazine Street,** Neal Auction Company has grown like Topsy in the uptown location.

Another enclave of activity begins at Jefferson Avenue, You'll see the historic Lewis Reynolds–designed Poydras Home from 1857 at **5354 Magazine Street,** bereft of its upper level but still an uptown landmark, in front of the Lawn and Tennis Club, setting of some of Ellen Gilchrist's award-winning short stories.

The New Orleans Academy of Fine Arts and Academy Gallery at **5256 Magazine Street** was established in 1978 by Auseklis Ozols with the active support of Dorothy Coleman. You'll find the original P.J.'s Coffee and Tea Company at **5432 Magazine Street,** so popular that she has franchised. For takeout New Orleans food, don't miss Chez Nous Charcuterie, Inc. at **5701 Magazine Street.** Wirth More Antiques at **5723 Magazine Street** has eighteenth- and nineteenth-century French Antiques that the owners are able to find in the French provinces. Nina Sloss at **6008 Magazine Street** concentrates on the "State Street Look," inaugurated in the 1930s by Henry Stern, whose French Quarter antique shop set a standard for English imports for uptown residences. If you're looking for the typical New Orleans look in

4521 St. Charles Avenue (see p. 171) (see p. 171) Sacred Heart Academy, 1900. Photograph by Robert S. Brantley.

men's clothing, stop at Perlis, **6070 Magazine Street.**

By the time you get to the **6500 block of Magazine Street,** the street will have widened and live oaks will shade you as you go upriver toward Carrollton Street. The oak trees signify that you have reached Audubon Park, with its 55 acres of oak trees on the site of the 1884 Exposition and the Etiènne de Boré Plantation. On the river side of Magazine Street are the Audubon Zoological Gardens, where you may have to spend the rest of the day. Walk along the river here at the Butterfly behind the Zoo. You can arrange a steamboat ride on the *Cotton Blossom* back downtown to the aquarium from this point, or head toward Carrollton and Riverbend where there's another informal spot for hiking along the levee.

Magazine is the Street of Dreams, six miles of special things to see and do and eat. Not many areas in the United States display such a variety of talent as found in the old shotguns and commercial buildings along Magazine Street. After all, *Magazine* is the French word for both warehouse and shop: *magasin*. It's appropriate here.

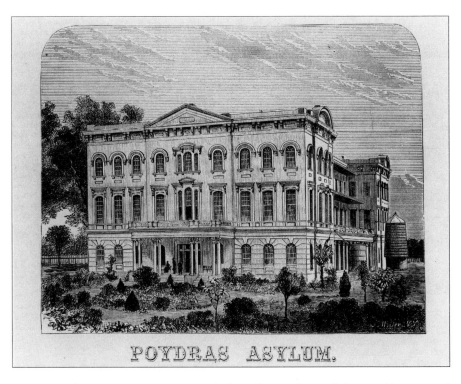

POYDRAS ASYLUM.

5354 Magazine Street. Poydras Asylum, designed in 1857 by Lewis E. Reynolds. Engraved by J. W. Orr, 1873. Courtesy of the Historic New Orleans Collection. This historic building was mutilated by the removal of the top two floors in the 1960s but remains in use as a home for the elderly.

R ecent visitors to New Orleans attended a wedding reception at Sacred Heart Academy and were guests at a historic uptown home on Arabella Street near the villa that Judah P. Benjamin bought for his sister to live in at **1630 Arabella.** The visitors enjoyed New Orleans cuisine at Gautreau's at **1728 Soniat Street** in a renovated and adapted drugstore. They saw the nearby raised villa at **5027 Dryades** (see p. 165) at the corner of Soniat that was built in 1851 by W. O. Denegre on land that Mme. Amelie Delassize Avart gave her daughter, Louise Almais, wife of Valmont Soniat Dufossat.

Next day, after running in Audubon Park with a visit to the zoo and a walk along the levee, they had poor boys at Domilise's at **5340 Annunciation Street.** Their final meal at Clancy's at **330 Webster Street** at the corner of Annunciation Street concluded the perfect uptown experience for them.

Touring the District

1630 Arabella Street

Built in 1850 to face St. Charles Avenue, the Greek Revival villa has four cast iron Corinthian capitals between corner box columns that support a fine dentiled entablature. Senator Judah P. Benjamin, later in Jefferson Davis's Confederate cabinet and Queen's Counsel to Victoria of England, and his brother Joseph bought the house in 1852 for their widowed sister, Rebecca Levy. Seized by the quartermaster of the Union army in 1865 because of its association with the rebel Benjamin, it was never reclaimed by the family.

1530 Calhoun Street

This small center-hall gable-ended house had an earlier life as a plantation, moved here from upriver. Three dormers, high brick chimneys, and the elliptical arched entrance set the scene for the columned gallery and an Anglo-American provenance.

3427 Camp Street

Hugh Evans, a builder, purchased the lot in 1863 and built this unusual three-bay raised cottage with its late Classic decoration. The house, owned by the Evans family until 1979, retains its cistern and the street its brick sidewalks and open gutters. This area has a number of these Italianate three-bay, galleried cottages, some built by Evans for his neighbors.

3643 Camp Street (see p.156).

Fink Asylum, the raised villa in the Italianate style was built in 1866 for Henry Rice, an importer. With brick additions in the rear it was used from 1875 to 1973 as an asylum for Protestant widows and orphans.

3627 Carondelet Street

Cuthbert Bullit commissioned this "Swiss villa," as it was called by the *Daily Picayune* in 1868 when they announced its completion according to plans of German-born architect Edward Gottheil. It was moved here from 3811 St. Charles

Avenue in 1883 to make way for Simon Hernsheim's mansion, now the Columns Hotel. Like most Swiss villa–style houses, popular with the romantic picturesque movement in the mid-nineteenth century, it has a wide projecting gable ornamented with a jigsaw verge board, a pattern repeated over the windows. Picturesque style or not, the house, New Orleans style, has its center-hall floor plan.

4319 Carondelet Street

This masonry Art Deco building was built as a Post Office after designs of Albert Theard during the 1930s. The wide bas relief in the frieze was inspired by the Mayan studies of Tulane University's Middle American Research Institute. The Junior League has adapted it for use as headquarters.

719 South Carrollton Avenue (see p. 159)

The Jefferson Parish Courthouse, now a school, was designed in 1854 by Henry Howard and built by Frederick Wing and Robert Crozier for $59,000, to include a jail. Howard hallmarks include the projecting pedimented portico with Ionic columns. The exterior, according to the building contract, was to be plastered and jointed to imitate masonry, the joints being lined off with chocolate-colored oil paint. The entrance doors were to be grained or bronzed. The bases and capitals of the columns and of the pilasters at each corner of the building are of cast iron.

1015 South Carrollton Avenue

The Tudor Gothic villa built in 1850 for Nathaniel Newton Wilkinson illustrates the Gothic Revival style with a cruciform plan. This floor plan is even less common in New Orleans than the Gothic style, also very unusual.

4422 Coliseum Street

This delicate galleried three-bay side-hall house with its entrance recessed

behind pilasters dates from 1869, when Theodule Martin had it built. It relates in style to the Evans house at **3427 Camp Street** (see p. 163).

4219 Constance Street (Faubourg East Bouligny)

This unusual mid-1870s building was built for the German-based Society of Sisters of Christian Charity. After serving as the rectory of St. Henry's Roman Catholic Church until 1987, the frame building with its cross timbers, decorative verge board, and hammer arch has become Stella Maris, an archdiocesan center for seamen.

4868 Constance Street (Faubourg West Bouligny)

This was built in 1852 for commission merchant Samuel L. Ewing. The Greek Revival raised plantation-style house, surrounded by galleries with box columns on three sides, has four full-length openings across the front. The Avart Plantation house was built earlier in an adjacent square but has been demolished, leaving this house as evidence of the antebellum rural period of Jefferson City.

5027 Dryades Street

Soniat Dufossat house. This raised basement Greek Revival country villa with box columns reflects a touch of late Classic style in the bracketed cornice. Banker William O. Denegre, whose family had come to New Orleans as refugees of the French Revolution via St. Domingue, built it between 1851 and 1854. The name *Soniat Dufossat* refers to the property ownership by François Robert Avert's heir Mme. Valmont Soniat Dufossat, who sold the unimproved land to Denegre.

1234 Henry Clay Avenue

Thomas Sully designed this cottage for Susie M. W. Ellermann in 1895. It has Sully's typical one-story gallery over part of the front elevation, with his signature

1530 Calhoun Street at Benjamin Street. Photograph by Betsy Swanson. An example of a small plantation house moved from a plantation upriver and set in an urban uptown scene near Tulane University.

3427 Camp Street between Delachaise Street and Louisiana Avenue. Hugh Evans house, ca. 1864. Photograph by Betsy Swanson. A relatively unusual house type, three bays with gable ends, raised on piers with a full gallery in the Italianate style.

3627 Carondelet Street. Cuthbert Bullit house, built 1867, moved to this location 1883. Photograph by Betsy Swanson.

1016 South Carrollton Avenue. Nathaniel Newton Wilkinson house, 1850. Photograph by Betsy Swanson. One of the city's three important Gothic-style buildings.

projections and pediments, shingles and bays. The interior shows his large living hall with rooms ranging off it in every direction.

1334 Henry Clay Avenue

Continuing the local tradition of the raised basement, the cottage with its bays, its shingled and sunburst pediments, and its one-story gallery recalls Sully's 1890s Uptown designs.

1500 Henry Clay Avenue

Judge John Howard Ferguson had this Gothic Revival cottage built in 1870 in Burtheville, and the family remained there until 1920. It features every characteristic of the type and style: shingles and slate, pointed gables juxtaposed one against the other, deep eaves with icicle jigsaw work hanging down, casement openings, and latticework; all conforms to the southern vernacular, with live oak trees and monkey grass.

5520 Hurst Street

This unusual cottage may be a remake of the overseer's cottage of the Cornelius Hurst Plantation, but if so, it has been moved, which is not unusual. The original four-bay cottage with a front gallery was built or moved by 1850, and when architect William A. Freret bought it in 1901 he reportedly added the two mansard towers, brackets, cast iron crestings and a new gallery.

Louisiana Avenue (Faubourg Plaisance)

904 Louisiana Avenue at Laurel Street

One of the earliest remaining houses in old Jefferson City, this Classic-style raised villa with its center hall and wide wood steps was built for Clement Wilkins, a stock dealer who purchased the land from a Delachaise heir in 1853,

1334 Henry Clay Avenue at Pitt Street. Photograph by Betsy Swanson. At the turn of the nineteenth century as a diverse population moved uptown, the architecture diversified, became less regional, and began to reflect national trends. Raising the house on brick piers, however, remained constant to most types and styles.

the year of the terrible yellow fever epidemic, and built the house immediately. The cast iron railing pattern and the Tower of the Winds columns were typical of the period.

912–914 Louisiana Avenue

This large gable-ended double house dating from the early 1880s resembles a raised villa except for the pair of central entrances. Joseph Gitzinger, feedstore owner near the Faubourg Plaisance stock landing during the 1860s and 1870s, bought the lot and probably built the house soon afterward.

1010, 1016, and 1020 Louisiana

These three once-identical early galleried double-shotgun houses, were built in 1869 for developer Joseph Kohn as rental property. Faehnle and Kuntz were builders for the "three double attic dwellings to cost $11,200." A building contract specifies that the cypress steps were to be "painted in imitation of granite," front door to be "grained in imitation of oak." The kitchen buildings, now demolished, were to have "bells with best springs and copper wires extending to the front gates." The numbers of the houses were to be "painted and gilded on the glass front door headlights" or transoms, minute details for rental property.

1205 Louisiana Avenue

Charles W. Wilson, architect and builder, built this Greek Revival center-hall house for his family by 1861 on land he purchased in Faubourg Plaisance in 1859. They lived there until 1875, just as Reconstruction was about to end. The house has been used by Our Lady of Good Counsel Parish for many years, and the pair of service wings have been preserved, making this an important architectural document.

1413 Louisiana Avenue

This house illustrates that the Garden District architectural vocabulary translates well into an 1872 double house.

The segmental arched openings and the bracketed cornice with parapet are Italianate, but the Classic-style box columns on two levels suggest some economy. Edward Beebe had Henry Bensel build the house, but Beebe died within a year of its construction. Author Kate Chopin and her husband, Oscar, a cotton factor, lived here from 1876 to 1879. The National Society of the Colonial Dames of America in the State of Louisiana bought the house in 1974 and restored it.

1424 Louisiana Avenue

Eugene Schmitt had this Italianate center-hall raised villa built in 1870, his family living there until 1909. Jules Monroe bought it and his heirs live there now.

1525 Louisiana Avenue

The Freret mansion is probably the most widely recognized house from the days of Jefferson City. James Peter Freret, sheriff, legislator, and owner of the New Orleans Cotton Press, bought six lots in 1854, and the Jefferson City Council minutes document that Freret's house was going up in 1857. Originally, there were galleries along both sides and across the back, enclosed after 1896. Three windows flank the central entrance on each side, instead of the usual two.

Freret and his wife Livie D'Arensbourg, of the German coast upriver from New Orleans, had 17 children. Their oldest son, William, studied Beaux Arts architecture in Paris in the early 1860s, returning to serve the Confederate army as engineer, then to design some of New Orleans' more distinguished buildings.

7835 Maple Street

This monumental Greek Revival plantation-style house with its columns and heavy entablature seems out of place in the modest neighborhood today. The Reverend John Bliss Warren had the house built in 1844; surely with its New York references and the plantation look

1205 Louisiana Avenue. Builder Charles W. Wilson's house, front elevation and rear courtyard with service wings and rear elevation. Photographs by Betsy Swanson,1969.

James Dakin or Henry Howard had a hand in its design. Its monumental style suggests the work of architect James Dakin. **See pages 160-162 for Magazine Street.**

1111 Milan Street (see p. 152)

McDonogh No.7 is one of the original 19 schools built with a $700,000 bequest by John McDonogh, who also left land for City Park. This three-story Gothic-style building was designed by architect William A. Freret, who designed a number of the McDonogh schools that feature fine brickwork.

1903 Milan Street at Dryades Street

Uptown corner cottages often received the bay and turret treatment, along with galleries that continue around the exposed side, such as this one. They are most common in the 1890s and lend a picturesque, lacy, and sculptural effect to the basic double-parlored house that the galleries and turrets mask. A suprising number of such facade decoration was added in the 1880s and 1890s, to earlier cottages, such as the one added to the 1877 example at **4003 Carondelet Street.**

738 Napoleon Avenue

John Bourdet bought the containing lots and was living in his center-hall villa-style house in 1858. The oversized dormer is a later addition.

927 Napoleon Avenue

Built in 1876 as McDonogh No.6, this William A. Freret–designed building is the earliest black public school in the city.

l025 Napoleon Avenue at Camp Street

St. Stephen's Church was begun in 1871 but was not ready for its first Mass until 1887. Englishman Thomas W. Carter designed the Gothic revival brick church and the builder was Thomas O'Neil. Carter also designed Our Lady of Good Counsel Church on Louisiana Avenue. The spire at St. Stephen's, the highest of any church in the city, was added in

1903 Milan Street at Dryades Street. Photograph by Betsy Swanson.

1905 according to designs of Favrot and Livaudais. Vincentian Fathers established the parish in 1849.

1314 Napoleon Avenue at Prytania Street

St. Elizabeth's Children's Home. Thomas Mulligan, a native of County Donegal, Ireland, designed and built the central mass of the building in 1865. It appears Italianate, with its cast iron hood moldings and two-level galleries supported by Corinthian columns. However, the convex mansard roof identifies an early example of the Second Empire style. In 1883 Albert Diettel designed and Albert Thiesen built the brick section along Prytania for $10,000, and the following year a similar addition was put up toward Perrier Street. The chapel, 100 feet long, occupies the second-floor wing on Prytania Street. Author Anne Rice has renovated the complex.

2108 Palmer Avenue

The Toby Hart villa, built in 1873, was probably designed by the owner, who was a house painter and decorator. It epitomizes the picturesque style applied to the usual New Orleans raised center-hall house. The combination of Gothic revival with stick style, Queen Anne, and Italianate makes it a whimsical fit into the tropical New Orleans scene, with the exuberant jigsaw work reflecting the lavish look of the abundantly planted garden.

2115 Palmer Avenue

The Joseph Fornaris house, dating from 1897, is a two-story version of the corner turreted house, similar to an illustration in the 1888 edition of *Shoppell's Modern Houses* catalog. Here the turret becomes a shingle-clad part-octagon primary section of the dwelling.

4721 Perrier Street

This delicate center-hall villa with its box columns having spandrels to form lowered arches on the front gallery dates from about 1870, when Charles Pascoe, a builder, probably built it for himself. The importance of the house was recognized by the 1940s, when Miss Sally Dart had architect Richard Koch renovate it. For 30 years it was the home of the Paul Blanchard family.

3900 St. Charles Avenue

Rayne Memorial Methodist Church was designed in 1875 by German-born Lewis Hillger and built by James Cox. The neo-Gothic brick church was named after William Rayne, killed in the Civil War. His father gave the site and much of the $17,000 cost of construction to the St.Charles Avenue Methodist Episcopal Church. Gothic motifs executed in red brick combined with shingle-style elements work successfully in one of the more interesting Protestant churches uptown.

4114 St. Charles Avenue

Sully and Toledano were architects for this Queen Anne house. Shingles clad the house and blue and white tiles define a string course. Latticework creates arches on the gallery in an East Indian motif. John S. Wallis, president of the Louisiana Sugar Refining Company, commissioned the house for his daughter, Mrs. L. E. Griffin, in 1885.

4521 St. Charles Avenue (see p. 161)

Sacred Heart Academy, established in New Orleans in 1887, was first housed on this site in an 1847 villa-style galleried house, where Samuel J. Peters, major uptown developer, died. The building here was designed by local architects Collins Diboll and Allison Owen in 1900, with additions by them in 1906 and 1913. While the concept was a Colonial Revival style, the effect is quintessentially New Orleans, set behind the 1847 fountain from the Peters house. Giving the establishment a New Orleans look are the arched windows with their louvered shutters and the balustrade

1314 Napoleon Street at Prytania Street. St. Elizabeth's Children's Home, 1870, named after the daughter of benefactor Dr. William N. Mercer, who lived at 824 Canal Street in the house designed by James Gallier, Sr., now used as the Boston Club. Recently purchased for restoration by the novelist Ann Rice..

3900 St. Charles Avenue at General Taylor Street. Rayne Memorial Methodist Church, 1875. Photograph by Betsy Swanson.

extending across the front elevation above paired white columns.

5005 St. Charles Avenue (Faubourg Avart)

The Orléans Club, an uptown landmark, was built in 1868 for Ann Elizabeth Wynn Garneron on a lot her father, William Lewis Wynn, had given her and her husband, Col. George Garner. One of the two oldest houses on St. Charles in the Jefferson City section, it is New Orleans' conservative effort at a sophisticated French style, with three high-style dormers piercing the roof. Otherwise, the building is standard center-hall Italianate, true to its region, comfortable, and predictable.

5806 St. Charles Avenue

The Werlein–Villere Italianate villa, one of the best-sited houses on the avenue, dates from 1870–1871.

5824 St. Charles Avenue

The Antonio Palacio villa was designed by Henry Howard in 1867 for the native of Bilbao, Spain, and built by Daniel Frazer. These two adjacent villas make an interesting comparison of similar Italianate dwellings in the New Orleans manner.

Audobon Park (see p. 178)

Audubon Park, snuggled between the Mississippi River and St. Charles Avenue with its streetcars, and bisected by Magazine Street with its buses, is an accessible urban park. Directly across St. Charles Avenue from Tulane and Loyola universities, Audubon Park is loaded with historic associations and picturesque views. The site and the great live oaks draped with moss harken back to the time when Etienne de Boré established a plantation on part of the Bienville, then Jesuit, land grant.

Carpetbag Governor Henry Clay Warmouth's cronies Malet A. Southwork and Robert Bloomer purchased an option on the old de Boré Plantation for $2500 from the widow of Louis Frederick Foucher, who was living in France in February of 1871. Without putting up more money, they agreed to buy her entire planation for $600,000 and by August 1871 had sold one half of the tract to the city for a park for $800,000, a $200,000 profit, plus future profits on the second half of the old plantation, from St. Charles Avenue toward the cypress swamps (site of Tulane University and adjacent neighborhoods).

The World's Industrial and Cotton Centennial Exposition in 1884–1885 on the site propelled the development of the park and stimulated uptown residential development, so that most houses between Napoleon and Carrollton, except the older villas, may safely be dated after 1885.

In 1893, after Tulane and Loyola universities had relocated to the area, Frederick Law Olmsted received a letter from New Orleans park commissioner J. Ward Gurley, an attorney and former District Attorney, stating, "I am directed . . . to enquire whether you desire to submit an estimate . . . for a plan for the laying out and embellishment of Audubon Park . . . .upon a basis of, say, . . .one million dollars." That was the beginning of a relationship with Olmsted, Sr., who influenced, indirectly at least, uptown's City Beautiful movement. Then in 1897 John Charles Olmsted, nephew as well as stepson to the great park planner, visited the park and became active in its planning for 23 years. During that time private donations funded the park's special features, such as the formal entrance from St. Charles Avenue with the Gumble Fountain, the Newman bandstand, the Popp gardens, and the Hyams wading pool.

Frederick Olmsted, Jr., came to the park, too, and his great contribution was the Zoological Garden. In 1919, Daniel D. Moor, editor of the *Times-Picayune,* formed the New Orleans Zoological Society. The most important architectural addition to the zoo came

5806 St. Charles Avenue at Nashville Avenue. Werlein-Villere villa. Photograph by Betsy Swanson,1969.

in 1928 when Sigmund Odenheimer donated the sea lion pool, designed in the Beaux Arts tradition by Samuel P. Stone, Jr., architect and park commissioner.

Moise Goldstein, architect and board member, worked with the park staff to prepare a proposal to the Works Progress Administration to construct a new zoo after plans by the Olmsted firm, and the Merz Memorial Zoo opened in May 1938. By 1970 the Audubon Zoological Society, following the leadership of the family of William B. Wisdom, Jr., spearheaded the Audubon Park Zoological Study. For the first time in the park's history, volunteer efforts, including the Friends of the Zoo, with a membership of 32,000 families, coincided with political support, and Audubon Park Zoo was rebuilt under the directorship of Ronald Forman.

Frederick Law Olmsted, Jr., had understood how the river was neglected as the city's major visual, natural, and environmental resource. "It is amazing and deplorable . . . that on the banks of the greatest river of the continent, no river-bank park has been provided. . . . I am fired with enthusiasm for the possibilities it presents." He failed in his efforts, but finally a riverfront park was built in 1968–1969. Today, a steamboat takes visitors from the aquarium at the edge of the French Quarter to the landing at the park.

6226 St. Charles Avenue

Holy Name of Jesus Catholic Church, built in 1914, was designed by DeBuys, Churchill and Labouisse, who emulated the English Perpendicular Gothic style for the uptown edge of the Jesuit complex.

6300 Block of St. Charles Avenue

Loyola University moved to the present campus in 1911, when DeBuys, Churchill and Labouisse designed the red brick and terra cotta–trimmed Tudor–Gothic buildings that line the quadrangle.

6823 St. Charles Avenue

Tulane University, founded in 1834, later incorporated into the University of Louisiana, was endowed as a private university in 1884 by real estate entrepreneur Paul Tulane, of French Huguenot background, born in Princeton, New Jersey. Harrod and Andry, architects, designed the base for the uptown campus in 1894 in the Richardsonian Romanesque style. The Middle American Research Institute, established in 1924, exhibits its extensive pre-Columbian collection in Dinwiddie Hall. The Southeastern Architectural Archives is quartered at the Tulane Library.

Behind Tulane University at **1229 Broadway Street** is Sophie Newcomb College with Newcomb Hall, Josephine Louise House, and the Art Building built in 1918 after plans of New York architect James Gamble Rogers. Founded in 1886 by Josephine Louise LeMonnier Newcomb (1816–1901) in memory of her daughter Harriott Sophie Newcomb (1855–1870), the college was first located in the former Thomas Hale house on Lee Circle and on Washington Avenue in the James Robb mansion, both James Gallier designs and both demolished.

Audubon Place

Adjacent to Tulane University is a private street with 28 houses, most built in the revival styles of the early twentieth century. Developer George Blackwelder of Fort Worth, Texas envisioned a millionaires' enclave behind the iron arch entrance, flanked by turreted and tiled stone gatehouses. A similar arrangement is Rosa Park at **5800 St. Charles Avenue,** which dates from 1891.

No. 2 Audubon Place

The Georgian Revival house built in 1907 for William T. Jay is associated with United Fruit Company magnate Samuel Zemurray, who lived in the house for decades. Starting in business in the area by shipping bananas to grocers in Mobile, Alabama, he became chairman of the board of United Fruit. He donated the house as official residence of presidents of Tulane University.

7214 St. Charles Avenue at Broadway. Greenville Hall, St. Mary's Dominican College, now part of Loyola University of the South, 1882, William Fitzner, architect. Photograph by Betsy Swanson.

Even though Audubon Park is a tourist attraction and has over a million tourists visitors a year, it remains a refuge of busy uptown life. "I live Uptown just so I can watch the sun rise through the moss under the live oaks at Audubon Park," explains a Newcomb College graduate who lives on Henry Clay Avenue. "Remember the look of the mist rising up from the ground into the live oaks, with the sun piercing the veil of moss? There's nothing quite like Audubon Park anywhere. Just look at the spire of Holy Name above the live oak canopies."

Uptowners spend long hours in the zoo with their families and with guests. It's just such things as the relief carving in brick on the Tropical Bird House, executed by Works Project Administration workers, that make the zoo's architectural elements as exciting as the animals and the oaks. The brick elephant barn, with its chimney and belvedere, its pilasters and arches, looks as if it could be the home of le Duc du Maine.

7214 St. Charles Avenue

Greenville Hall of St. Mary's Dominican College (now part of Loyola University) was built in 1882 for the girls' school established in 1861 by Dominican nuns from Cabra, Ireland. Architect William Fitzner designed the frame center-hall building. It recalls steamboat Gothic prototypes and fits perfectly into the uptown setting, with its two-level galleries and cupola. The ogee-shaped dormers were added later.

Tchoupitoulas Street

The Tchoupitoulas bus is not a pretty ride, but it's lively and will take you to the world of *The Confederacy of Dunces*. On one side the river seethes with docks and rows of brick warehouses, formerly cotton presses and sugar sheds, where once there were plantation houses and sugar mills and the great brick factories of the Avart family, who worked their plantation for about five generations.

4109 Tchoupitoulas Street

Still owned by the building family, this center-hall Greek Revival villa with its modest details was the master house for the Montgomery farm from about

1845. The fine Greek key front door frame is the most sophisticated architectural detail on the building, which has become surrounded by heavy industry mixed with commercial and small, late nineteenth–century houses and shops.

4608–4610 Tchoupitoulas Street

This enormous complex of brick warehouses was built for the Lane Cotton Mills, which began operations in 1856, but most of these buildings date from the 1880s. Even so, their survival is astonishing.

4701 Tchoupitoulas Street

This is a rare surviving example of an 1870s commercial building, many of which once lined the street.

4901 Tchoupitoulas Street

Hansen's Sno Bliz Sweet Shop in its frame corner storehouse is a feature of the New Orleans lifestyle. Mr. and Mrs. Hansen make huge barrels of each flavor every day in season to pour over the snowballs, but the Nestlé's and Cream, with its pink color and almond flavor, is the most typical of New Orleans.

Entrance to Audubon Park. These entrance gates follow American Renaissance designs of the Olmstead firm in New York. Photograph by Robert S. Brantley.

LAGNIAPPE

Garden District scene at Seventh and Coliseum Streets. Photograph by Robert S. Brantley.

Architecturally Speaking

Since you want to learn how New Orleanians live through studying their architecture, consider the following interiors and museums. They are listed chronologically according to architectural style or museum interpretation period.

Ursuline Convent (see p. 27) at 1114 Chartres Street.(529-3040) Built in 1745 using a stairway and other materials from the earlier convent of 1727-1734, this is the oldest building in the Mississippi Valley and the only complete French colonial building standing in the French Quarter.

Madame John's Legacy at 624 Dumaine Street. (568-6968) Louisiana State Museum complex. When it's open this property of the Louisiana State Museum illustrates Spanish colonial life from 1788.

Pitot house (see p. 79) at 1440 Moss Street.(482-0312 open Wed-Sat. 10:00-3:00) The Louisiana Landmarks Society runs this Spanish colonial *maison de maitre*. Built in 1799, it reveals the continuing French colonial building and cultural traditions.

Hermann-Grima house, (see p. 41) at 820 St. Louis Street.(525-5661) An example of American building styles invading the old French Quarter, the house William Brand designed for Samuel Hermann has been interpreted

by The Christian Women's Exchange to show the life-style of the 1830s. Cooking in the open hearth and in the period ovens is a special presentation unique to this museum house. The museum shop, established in the original stable, sometimes has good antiques and silver. The stable is the best preserved such outbuilding in New Orleans.

Beauregard-Keyes house at 1113 Chartres Street. (523-7257) also known as Le Charpentier house. From 1944 until her death in 1970 writer Frances Parkinson Keyes lived in this historic house. The 1826 house is now a museum with extensive gardens.

1850 House at 523 St. Ann Street facing Jackson Square (part of Louisiana State Museum Complex)(568-6968). Both James Gallier Sr. and Henry Howard worked on designs for the two rows of townhouses that Micaela Almonester, Baroness de Pontalba, commissioned in 1850 to revitalize her extensive holdings in the old French Quarter. The Louisiana State Museum now owns and administers the Lower Pontalba buildings. One of the houses is authentically furnished using fine pieces aquired from the creole families that lived in such houses in the mid-ninteenth century. The first floor is the museum sales shop.

Gallier house (see p. 40) at 1132 Royal Street.(523-6722) James Gallier Jr. married creole Aglae Villavaso, which must be why he chose the French Quarter for his own home, self-designed in 1857. Although Gallier Jr. captured the commission for the fabulous French Opera House, most of his clients were from the English-speaking community. The interpretation reveals many of the housekeeping secrets of mid-ninteenth-century inhabitants, such as the summer covers, the medicine cabinet, mosquito nets, and the correct flooring for a mid-ninteenth-century interior bathroom.

New Orleans Pharmacy Museum at 514 Chartres Street.(524-9077) *La Pharmacie Française* opened as a museum in 1950 in the pharmacy located in an 1823 Transitional period storehouse built by the country's first pharmacist, Louis Joseph Dufilho Jr., licensed by examination in 1816. The building is owned by the city, and the museum is operated by the Friends of Historical Pharmacy. The courtyard is available for parties, receptions and special events.

Judge René Beauregard house at Chalmette Unit, Jean Lafitte National Historic Park and Preserve. (La. Route 46, six miles downriver from New Orleans: follow St. Claude Avenue to St. Bernard Highway, which is La. Route 46). The 1832 creole plantation house, remodeled in 1856 and again in 1865 is used as a visitors center, with an emphasis on the Battle of New Orleans in 1815, but you can learn about plantation life and river culture.

Louisiana State Military Museum at 6400 St. Claude Avenue.(271-6262) Jackson Barracks is not only a fine collection of Louisiana Greek Revival buildings built in 1835, but a visit there shows how military personnel lived in the lower South climate.

Doullut house (Steamboat House). (949-1422) At 400 and 503 Egania Street at Douglas Street near the St. Bernard Parish line are a pair of frame houses built in 1905 for steamboat Captain Paul Doullut. They are almost follies and were influenced by the Japanese exhibit building at the St. Louis World's Fair of 1904. One house is open to the public Wednesday through Sunday from 10 to 4.

Kemper Williams house, enter through 533 Royal Street.(523-4662) Part of the Historic New Orleans Collection, this house illustrates how an Anglo-American couple accustomed to all the refinements of southern culture and taste lived in the French Quarter in the 1940s and 1950s. Eclectic, but with an interest in the English taste, fabric and lace with modern influences in decoration and fixtures, the Williams house also reveals their interest in Louisiana history and art.

Longue Vue house and gardens at No.7 Bamboo Road.(488-5488) Edith Rosenwald Stern gave her house and gardens to the city of New Orleans to be presented as "an example of mid-20th century living at its best from which the visitor could draw both ideas and inspiration." Her husband, Edgar Bloom Stern (1886-1959), a native New Orleanian, joined his father's cotton firm Lehman, Stern and Co., Ltd. and expanded into diversified business interests all of which impacted New Orleans: banking, lumber, oil, publishing and real estate. He and his son Edgar, Jr. founded the first television franchise in Louisiana, WDSU-TV.

The Stern's lifelong adventure into architecture and landscape gardening began in 1935, when Ellen Biddle Shipman, a student of Charles Adams Platt, planned their eight acres of fountains and gardens. Shipman introduced the Sterns to architect William Platt, FAIA (1897-1984) and his brother Geoffrey (1905-1985), who began work in 1939 on a Classic Revival-style house with a low hipped roof covering a symmetrical organization with flanking dependencies linked by colonnades in the Palladian manner. Side elevations are based on Shadows-on-the-Teche, a National Trust property dating from 1831 in New Iberia, Louisiana and the 1826 Beauregard-Keyes house on Chartres Street in the French quarter. The estate shows what wealth combined with education, good taste and intelligent planning can achieve at a certain point in the history of architecture and American culture.

Museums

The major museums have portraits, landscapes, genre paintings, decorative arts, and furniture that will broaden your understanding of New Orleans history, culture and lifestyle.

New Orleans Museum of Art at City Park, No. 1 Lelong Avenue. (488-2631) The Kuntz Collection of Southern Furniture and the Louisiana paintings and silver collections illustrate New Orleanians' taste and preferences through the centuries. The collections of Louisiana provenance indicate the kinds of arts and crafts that appealed to wealthy inhabitants and to the series of museum directors. A recently completed addition expands exhibition space and the museum shop and provides for a garden cafe.

Cabildo and Presbytère, Louisiana State Museum (see p. 24) on Jackson Square,700 block of Chartres Street.(568-6968) The pair of buildings flanking the cathedral at the old Place d'Armes or Jackson Square has been the repository since the 1930s for furniture, paintings, decorative arts, and collections of the old creole and American families. The Arsenal, facing 615 St. Peter Street; Jackson House, 619 St. Peter Street, and the Creole House, at 616 Pirates Alley, are historic buildings used as administrative offices or for special functions and are entered from the Cabildo.

A premiere collection of children's portraits has been assembled as well as Spanish colonial and early American period family portraits. The Louisiana State Museum collection reveals over 250 years of Life in New Orleans. *Friends*

of the Cabildo Walking Tours of the French Quarter are available from the 1850 House, and at the Presbytère. The Friends of the Cabildo Museum Shop is highly recommended, too, and profits go to a good cause.

U. S. Mint (see p. 69) at 400 Esplanade Avenue and Decatur Street. (568-6968) The 1835 Mint building by William Strickland has become part of the Louisiana State Museum complex. Mardi Gras and jazz exhibitions introduce two of New Orleans' native art and music forms.

The Historic New Orleans Collection (see p. 35) at 533 Royal Street (523-4662). This is essential for the scholar and the conscientious visitor to New Orleans. The front room always has a sophisticated and detailed exhibition, changing bimonthly. Informative guided tours and a research library are available. While the rooms of the eighteenth-century Merieult house have been transformed into ten history galleries, the patio and the floor plan illustrate much about creole life in the early American period. The manuscript and art collections illustrate Louisiana in a depth far more detailed and more subtle than that of any other New Orleans museum. This is a private institution established and funded by the L. Kemper and Leila Williams Foundation.

St. Peter and Chartres Streets. Street scene showing Le Petit Théatre du Vieux Carré, the Cabildo and St. Louis Cathedral (see p. 24). Drawing by A.R. Waud, 1871. Courtesy of the Historic New Orleans Collection. The Cabildo at Jackson Square and the Presbytère, flanking the cathedral, are the keystones of the Louisiana State Museum, a facility that administers the most impressive array of historic buildings in the south.

184

Great Places to Go

Aquarium of the Americas at No. 1 Canal Street in Woldenberg Park. (861-2538) The aquarium is a 16 acre riverfront park leading past the Moonwalk to the French Market. Administered with Audubon Park by the Audubon Institute.

Audubon Zoo at 6500 Magazine Street. (861-2537). Take the Aquarium Zoo cruise aboard the John James Audubon Riverboat between the zoo and the Aquarium. Four round trips daily. Reservations 1-800-233-2628 and 504-586-8777.

Jean Lafitte National Historic Park and Preserve headquarters at the Folklife and Visitor Center in the French Market at 916 North Peters Street. (589-2636) This National Park Service section administers nine units or centers focused on a particular facet of Louisiana's cultural and natural resources. It offers historical walking tours in the French Quarter from headquarters at 10:30 daily. Themed *tours du jour* leave at 11:30 daily and Garden District tours begin at 2:30. Reservations required.
Louisiana Office of Tourism now shares offices in the Lower Pontalbas with the New Orleans Welcome Center.

The main office is in the Superdome. They have entire packets of information on any subject you might want to pursue related to New Orleans and Louisiana.

Le Petit Theatre du Vieux Carré (see p. 42) at the corner of St. Peter and Chartres Streets at Jackson Square is a careful historical reconstruction of the 1797 building on the site. The theater began in 1916 and moved to this location in 1919. The courtyard is old world, and between September and June the theater presents seven plays. Other events such as the Tennessee Williams/New Orleans Literary Festival during late March use the theater as well.

Williams Research Center, a division of the L. Kemper and Leila Williams Foundation, at 410 Chartes Street. (523-4662) The restoration by architect Davis Lee Jahncke, Jr., of an abandoned courthouse and police station designed in 1915 by E. A. Christy brings together the Historic New Orleans Collection's three research divisions. The history and culture of French and Spanish Colonial Louisiana and New Orleans and the region to the present becomes available in a historic setting under the most efficient research conditions available. The Williams

185

Reseach Center joins the Huntington, Newberry and Folger research libraries, focusing, however, on the south.

Confederate Museum at 929 Camp Street. (523-4522) The oldest museum in Louisiana and the second-oldest Confederate museum in the south, the building was designed by Sully and Toledano in 1891 for the Association of Confederate Veterans to be used as a museum for war relics and as a meeting place. It includes the collection of the Louisiana Historical Association, beginning in the 1840s.

Louisiana Children's Museum at 428 Julia Street. (523-1357) All kinds of hands on activities for children, situated in historic buildings.

Contemporary Arts Center at 900 Camp Street. (523-1216) Changing exhibits of avant garde art and two theaters for alternative theater and music. Housed in an historic warehouse of the late nineteenth century, it is in the heart of the Arts District, with over 17 galleries, schools and auction houses.

New Orleans School of Glassworks at 727 Magazine Street, 70130. (529-7277). Jean du Pont Blair is the energy behind this contribution to the southern art scene. Visitors and students watch glass blowing demonstrations daily, except Sunday. Children and adults study glass blowing. Unusual glass is sold, too.

Ya/Ya at 628 Baronne Street. (529-3306) "Ya/Ya" stands for "Young Artists/Young Aspirations" and has provided educational arts opportunities for talented young inner-city artists. Their art works, furniture, and paintings are available at the gallery.

New Orleans Academy of Fine Arts at 5256 Magazine Street. (899-8111)

Founded in 1978 by Auseklis Ozols with the leadership of Mrs. Dorothy J. Coleman for the serious study of traditional drawing and painting, the Academy offers exhibitions as well as instruction in the rehabilitated historic house they use as headquarters.

Isleño Museum on La. Route 46 about nine miles south of the Chalmette Battlefield at 1357 Bayou Road, St. Bernard Parish. (682-0862) Part of the Jean Lafitte National Historic Park and Preserve, devoted to the history of immigrants from the Canary Islands who came to St. Bernard and Plaquemines Parishes from the Spanish colonial period, encouraged by Governor Galvez. Most were fishermen and they developed their own isolated and distinct Spanish derived culture in the lower reaches of the Louisiana marshlands around the Mississippi and along Bayou Terre Aux Boeufs.

Red Streetcar Ride from the Warehouse District at the Riverwalk and the Hilton Hotel at Poydras Street through the French Quarter to the U.S. Mint area.

Louisiana Nature and Science Center, at 11000 Lake Forest Boulevard in Joe Brown Memorial Park in New Orleans East. (246–5672)

Fort Macomb on Highway 90 at Chef Menteur Pass. Built in 1818 under contract with Bennett and Morte of Washington, D.C. Like Fort Gaines and Fort Morgan in Alabama, Fort Macomb and Fort Pike were part of a chain of fortifications built after the Battle of New Orleans.

Fort Pike on Highway 90 at Rigolets Pass. This fort is in much better condition than Fort Macomb, built at the same time by the same builders. Abandoned as a fort in 1890, it is now part of the state park system and is worth a picnic and visit.

Cemeteries

Mark Twain proclaimed that New Oreans' best architecture is found in its cemeteries. It is a fact that fewer architecturally notable tombs have been demolished than historic buildings. The group leading the preservation effort is Save Our Cemeteries, P. O. Box 15770, New Orleans, LA 70175.

Although New Orleans does lie about four feet below sea level, that is not the reason for the aboveground tombs. The Spanish brought the tradition from Andalucia with its Roman system of wall vaults and funerary monuments. The Spanish established St. Louis Cemetery No.1 in 1789 on the city commons, a distance from the center of population around the church, site of the first French cemetery.

New Orleans' celebrated cities of the dead reflect the exotic along with a grace and a grandeur unknown in other American cities. The brick, granite, slate, marble and the ironwork, fashioned after all the prevailing styles of architecture project New Orleans' own attitudes about death.

New Orleanians have a lighter touch about death, precisely because they were threatened constantly and in a more violent form than elsewhere in the United States. In 1853 yellow fever killed 11,000 in five months. Life in New Orleans in the eighteenth and nineteenth centuries was a roller coaster. If it wasn't yellow fever, it was Asiatic cholera, or a break in the levee. These dramatic and dangerous crevasses were a threat when the water was high. As a result there's a sort of whimsy about death, transformed into a kind of friend so that the bereaved could sustain life among the living. Jazz funerals illustrate this attitude.

Because New Orleans was a Catholic city, where protestant graves were shunted for over a century into a secluded area, burial rituals differ from those elsewhere in the United States. Mourning portraits painted in oil were *de rigueur* in the nineteenth century, with grouped subjects dressed in black, the bereaved widow or widower wearing or exhibiting a miniature of the deceased. Death notices were printed as broadsides and posted on street-corner poles and prominent buildings. Often niches at the tomb held likenesses of the deceased. Jazz funerals are common, and All Saints' Day, November 1, is a festival when the living visit the deceased in their tombs throughout the city. Even today, due to the efforts of Save Our Cemeteries the cemeteries are a place to enjoy, to stroll, to promenade, and to visit old friends and family.

St. Louis Cemetery No. 1 on Basin Street at St. Louis Street, 1796. Benjamin Latrobe designed monuments to the first and second wives of Governor W. C. C. Claiborne in 1811, in the rear of the cemetery.

St. Louis Cemetery No. 2 on North Claiborne Avenue between Iberville and St. Louis Streets. Several important monuments were designed by J. N. B. DePouilly, whose grave is located in one of the wall vaults. Many jazz funerals occur here.

St. Louis Cemetery No. 3 at 3421 Esplanade Avenue. Established by the city in 1835 and acquired by St. Louis Cathedral in 1856. The cemetery's marble tombs seen from the nearby expressway commemorate what one viewer observed as "a sea of Catholics". A monument to architect James Gallier, Sr. is notable.

Cypress Grove Cemetery on Canal Street at City Park Avenue. Established by the Firemen's Charitable Association, the cemetery was designed in 1840 by Frederick Wilkinson, who designed Jackson Barracks.

Lafayette Cemetery No. 1 (see p. 202) on Washington Avenue at Prytania. Established in the 1830s as a cemetery for the city of Lafayette.

Metairie Cemetery on Pontchartrain Boulevard. This impressive cemetery on the site of the old Metairie Race Course was planned in the 1870s by Benjamin Morgan Harrod, architect.

St. Roch's Cemetery at St. Roch and Derbigny Streets. The small Gothic style St. Roch's Chapel designed in 1875 by Father Peter L. Thevis is the centerpiece of the cemetery.

Mardi Gras

Mardi Gras is not associated with any place or building in New Orleans— It engulfs the entire city. Mardi Gras could not happen in an Anglo-American city. It's too celebratory, takes too much time away from business, and disturbs the family life of populations that are historically Protestant. It's just too much fun and sometimes too sinful. Traditionally a Roman Catholic custom, in Catholic New Orleans, Mardi Gras has become a way of life for the population. The carnival season lasts from Twelfth Night (Epiphany) on January 6 to Mardi Gras Day, "Fat Tuesday," the day before Ash Wednesday. Some say that New Orleans has become one ongoing Mardi Gras, where life becomes a pageant and the people mask reality.

The Twelfth Night Ball catapults the city into the carnival season. These and other dances or carnival balls and the public parades are sponsored by Krewes, civic organizations, secret "societies," marching clubs, fun-loving neighborhood groups, and truck paraders. Increasing in numbers and lavishness as Mardi Gras Day approaches, carnival balls are sumptuously staged pageants complete with tableaux. Krewe members don elaborate costumes and masks, and provide special Krewe favors for the women to whom they have sent invitation.

The public parades flood the streets, beginning about two weeks before Mardi Gras Day. The festivities climax on Mardi Gras Day, "Fat Tuesday," with masking and a gigantic public party taking over the city. New Orleans becomes a solid mass of masked and decorated humanity. Groups enter the streets tied together. Crowds pack Canal Street, extending shoulder to shoulder across the width of the vast throughfare. Public and private parties, usually with New Orleans jazz and creole cooking, fill the "neutral grounds," squares, and private residences.

New Orleans is the only city in North America, one wag said, where men of the business, civic, and social community concern themselves for more than three hundred days of the year with the production of carnival season — the parades and balls replete with costumes, pageants, tableaux, big bands, miles of decorated floats, marching bands, flambeaux (marching and whirling torch carriers), and horses carrying costumed "dukes." This enormous extravaganza of events consumes the seasons after Easter until the onslaught of the carnival season, when New Orleanians "laissez les bons temps rouler."

Whether you consider carnival season as formal ritual or as amusing spoof, it affects life in New Orleans and reinforces tradition. Locals can take it as a festive season or as an inconvenience in their driving and work schedule. One curious effect is that New Orleans youngsters get used to costumes and regalia. My own son doesn't rent a tux or full dress for the weddings he participates in; he wears his own and is as comfortable as if he were in his football jacket and jeans.

Imagine my amazement one Sunday afternoon at my father-in-law's house when I opened the door in response to the bell to a group of men in full dress, with capes, top hats, and gloves. After prearranged "secret negotiations," the Krewe captain and committee had arrived to inform my father-in-law that he had been selected to be king of a particular Krewe. Was it Oberon, or was it Mithras? Cocktails and hors d'oeuvres carried on silver trays appeared instantly, and mysteriously the headwaiter for the club associated with the Krewe arrived to serve. The captain proposed appropriate toasts to celebrate the honor and the occasion. This was months before Mardi Gras, and preparations for the oncoming event animated the year.

2503 St. Charles Avenue, Thomas Sully, architect. Photograph by Robert S. Brantley.

Literary New Orleans

Tennessee Williams was not the first writer to catch the humor and irony of New Orleans. Where else could you catch the streetcar named Desire, transfer to Cemeteries, and get off at Elysian Fields? The early travelers to New Orleans from other parts of the United States usually found more copy here in the Crescent City than anywhere else.

Travel writers held sway over the perceptions about New Orleans in the eighteenth and nineteenth centuries, but suddenly, in the 1920s, by which time America was All-American, the creative literary authors of fiction found the one place in the south that had atmosphere, mystique, and lots of whiskey. They found the few locals who wrote, and they made friends with the staff at the old *States Item,* many of whom lived in the French Quarter. This meant Albert Goldstein, who published these *arrivistes* in the *Double Dealer,* and Sherwood Anderson, who attracted a number of authors to the French Quarter, as did Roark Bradford, an editor of the *Times Picayune* who employed William Faulkner to write articles for the newspaper. Lyle Saxon came back to New Orleans, where he had visited as a child, to live in the French Quarter and write for the newspaper, subsequently heading up the WPA team.

But the French Quarter wasn't the only place for writers to capture the feeling of New Orleans. The Lower Garden District was George Washington Cable's childhood neighborhood. Young women who came to Newcomb College, uptown, became writers as did Tulane University professors. New Orleans influenced an array of authors: Elma Godchaux, Kate Chopin, Grace King, and Tennessee's Evelyn Scott (Elsie Dunn) and more recently Lillian Hellman, Shirley Ann Grau, Valerie Martin, James Feibleman and Pierce Butler, all of whom lived in the American sector. The differing neighborhoods were usually reflected in some aspect of their works.

624 Pirates Alley. William Spratling, the architect and noted jewelry designer, shared this apartment with William Faulkner in 1925. Faulkner's *Soldiers Pay* was written here.

536 Royal Street. Lyle Saxon rented and renovated 18 rooms here in the 1920s when he entertained Thomas Wolfe, Edmund Wilson, Sinclair Lewis, John Steinbeck, and John Dos Passos.

613 Royal Street. Hervey Allen wrote part of his *Anthony Adverse* here

640 Royal Street. William Faulkner stayed at the LeMonnier House intermittently.

711 Royal Street. Truman Capote rented a room here in 1945. He was born in New Orleans at Touro Infirmary while his family was staying at the Monteleone Hotel.

715 Governor Nicholls Street. Sherwood Anderson and his wife, author Elizabeth Pratt Anderson, lived here and in the Pontalba buildings on Jackson Square.

613–615 Dumaine Street. William March, author of *The Bad Seed,* stayed here.

1014 Dumaine Street. Tennessee Williams rented rooms here and elsewhere in the French Quarter.

719 Toulouse Street. This 1799 house built for Joseph Bizot was the home of regionalist writer Rouark Bradford and his wife, and here they entertained William Faulkner and Ernest Hemingway. Bradford's *Old Man Adam an' His Chillun* became a Pultizer Prize winning Broadway hit, *The Green Pastures,* by Marc Connelly.

722 Toulouse Street (see p. 45) Tennessee Williams rented rooms above the restaurant here, in 1939.

516 Bourbon Street. Lafcadio Hearne rented rooms here and at 813 Baronne Street, No. 68 Cleveland Street in the American sector, and at 1458 Constance Street in the Lower Garden District.

623 Bourbon Street. Thornton Wilder once rented a place in this building, the home of U.S. Congresswoman Lindy Boggs.

823 Decatur Street. O. Henry and Eugene Field were often seen at Madame Begué's historic restaurant here in the early twentieth century.

536 Madison Street. Lyle Saxon lived here and John Steinbeck married his wife, Gwen, here in 1943.

1113 Chartres Street. Frances Parkinson Keyes was enchanted with New Orleans when she came here, and she bought this house, where she lived for many years.

2900 Prytania Street. F. Scott Fitzgerald is associated with this house.

1313 Eighth Street. George Washington Cable lived here.

1749 Coliseum Street (see p. 120) Grace King owned this house.

1407 First Street. Edward Larocque Tinker lived here.

1413 Louisiana Avenue. Kate Chopin lived in this one-time double house with her husband Oscar from 1876 to 1879, and the National Society of Colonial Dames in America in Louisiana has restored it as their headquarters.

Take a literary walking tour to find out all the details and so much more about "Literary New Orleans," by calling Ed Boardman or *Bookstar. (525-8360)*

Hotels and Lodgings

N ew Orleans is one of the few American cities to offer a number of good independent hotels and chains that have adapted to the architecture of the place. Those presented here have respected the historic aspect of their neighborhood; most are adaptive uses for old houses or commercial buildings, warehouses, and even factories. Those that are contemporary infill where old buildings were destroyed have historic buildings as some part of the complex. The **Monteleone, Roosevelt,** and **Le Pavillon**, the old-time, full-service hotels, were put up before there were demands to preserve the integrity of the extant neighborhood. The **Omni Royal Orleans,** at 621 St. Louis Street, replicates in footprint, location, name, and spirit one of America's foremost mid-nineteenth–century hostelries, pulled down in 1915, but the present hotel dates from the 1960s. You can see a segment of the original walls on Chartres Street near the garage.

The 600-room **Monteleone Hotel** at 214 Royal Street (523-3341; 1-800-535-9595) replaced an historic square in the days when history was not a consideration. Designed by Toledano and Wogan, architects, in 1907 on the edge of the Quarter near the central business district, the Monteleone continues as it has for generations as the privately owned hotel of choice for southern families visiting the French Quarter. The lobby is bustling and baroque, and you'll find old-time bellmen who've worked there for decades. $115–$165 in season. $$$$$

The **Omni Royal Orleans** at 621 St. Louis Street (529-5333; 1-800-843-6664) is a gracious luxury hotel with a lobby that's exciting and full of places to eat, drink, listen to music, and enjoy New Orleans' atmosphere. Room views on the riverside give you an idea of nineteenth-century New Orleans. After all, the Royal Orleans has to live up to its antecedent, the Royal St. Louis, designed as the creole lodging par excellence by Frenchman J. N. B. DePouilly. With its demolition in 1915 and the burning of the French Opera House in 1919, creole

1100 block of Governor Nicholas Street. Photograph by Betsy Swenson, 1969.

society and French Quarter culture ebbed into a decline. $$$$$

Grenoble House at 329 Dauphine Street, (522-1331) saved three Greek Revival townhouses, one dating from the 1830s. The service wings and rear stables of each townhouse surround deep patios to provide an idea of residential complexes of the early nineteenth century. Seventeen furnished apartments with one or two bedrooms start at about $185 per night. $$$$

The **Olivier House Hotel** at 828 Toulouse Street, (525-8456) is owner operated, with Katherine and James Danner on site to assist you in their casual way to enjoy the 28-room, 12-suite complex. The main house dates from 1836, a design of J. N. B. DePouilly in the transitional style, with a subsequent Greek Revival renovation by the same architect. A corner creole cottage has been added to the complex, complete with original furnishings from a plantation in Labadieville, the estate of an elderly creole lady who had lived there most of her life. $$$

The **De La Poste Hotel** at 316 Chartres Street, (581-1200; 1-800-448-4927), conforming infill on Chartres Street for three decades, has expanded to incorporate adjacent historic buildings, with one section facing Decatur Street to offer 87 rooms with 13 suites. On-site parking is an asset, as is **Ristorante Bacco**, listed as one of the 20 best restaurants in New Orleans by food critic Gene Bourg. $$$

The **Prince Conti** at 830 Conti Street, (529-4172; 1-800-366-2743) has about 50 rooms and two suites furnished with antiques, and their **Bombay Club** restaurant has the best martinis in town, according to those who know. Caldwell's New Orleans Bathhouses occupied the site in the 1830s, but the hotel took over a more recent building and adapted it for use as the hotel. $$$

The **St. Louis Apartment Suites** at 521 St. Louis Street, (522-5014; 1-800-348-3888) was a Greek Revival family home with a *porte cochère* entrance leading to its service wing and rear carriage house. Located two residences from the **Napoleon House** at Chartres and St. Louis Streets, it shares a property line with an almost identical owner-occupied residence. Both were built by Gurlie and Guillot for Etiènne Debon and rebuilt after 1840 for Jean Adrien Delpit, tobacconist. $$$.

The heart of the quarter, downriver from Jackson Square, will give you the feeling of French Quarter residential living.

Maison De Ville at 727 Toulouse Street, (561-5858; 1-800-634-1600), a romantic and sophisticated place, recalls an historic residence filled with antiques. Member of Small Luxury Hotels of the World, Maison De Ville has 16 rooms on Toulouse, and on Dauphine between St.Louis and Toulouse are seven brick-between-post creole cottages, in one of which John James Audubon lived while working on the *Birds of America*. **Le Bistro**, one of the top 10 restaurants of 1993, adds cachet to the Maison de Ville, with its bentwood chairs and bistro setting. $$$$$

The **Provincial Hotel** at 1024 Chartres Street, (581-4995; 1-800-621-5295), not far from the Ursuline Convent in the lower French Quarter, is locally owned. It incorporates some historic, nineteenth-century buildings and service wings on Ursuline and Decatur with on-site parking. $95–$175.

Le Richelieu at 1234 Chartres Street, (529-2492; 1-800-535-9653) deep in the lower French Quarter, is housed in one of five identical, Greek Revival, galleried frame houses, built in 1845, plus a macaroni factory built in 1902 by the Cusimano family. Rates start at $85 in this reasonably priced 88-room hotel. $$$

The **Soniat House** at 1133 Chartres Street, (522-0570; 1-800-544-8808) built in 1829 for a prosperous plantation owner, Joseph Soniat Duffosat, is included on the National Trust list of Historic Hotels of America. The gracious ambiance around a patio recalls traditional French Quarter life. The Old U.S. Mint, part of the Louisiana State Museum complex, the French Market, lively Flea Market and Farmer's Market are nearby attractions. Rates start at $115 for the 17 rooms and seven suites. $$$$

621 Esplanade Avenue, adjacent to the French Quarter, has one of the earliest bed and breakfast establishments in town, the **Lamothe House** (947-1161; 1-800-367-5858), built in 1839, and renovated in the 1950s by Mrs. Edward P. Munson. Now the unusual double house has been transformed again into an opulent inn with 11 rooms and nine suites full of antiques. A visit to Lamothe House will show you just what author Kate Chopin experienced when she came downriver from St. Louis to marry her creole husband. $$$

Melrose Mansion at 937 Esplanade Avenue (944-2255) joined the lists of Esplanade restorations for bed and breakfast in 1990 when the nine-room bed and breakfast opened. The 1884 Second Empire–style house has a square side tower housing four rooms and four suites. The complimentary chauffeured limousine is an asset for devoted building watchers. $$$$

The Dufour-Baldwin house at 1707 Esplanade Avenue (945-1503) is an alternative experience in high style and architectural space as presented on the Esplanade Ridge.

Faubourg St. Mary Central Business District

All the great hotel chains have been flocking to New Orleans over the past decade, and more will descend with gambling. The oldtime, centrally located favorite is the **Fairmont Roosevelt**, 123 Baronne Street near Canal Street, (529-7111; 1-800-527-4727). Originally called the Grunewald, the Roosevelt maintains the opulent lobby that passes from Baronne Street to University Place, where you can see the historic **Blue Room** and the famous **Sazerac Bar,** with murals by Paul Ninas. The 660-room hotel has served as home to some of Louisiana's most colorful political figures. $$$$

Two early-twentieth-century landmark hotels have recently undergone revitalization in the business district near Poydras Street, not far from the Superdome, the River, the flourishing Arts District, and the Warehouse District, where the World's Fair stimulated exciting development.

Le Pavillon at 833 Poydras Street at Baronne Street,(581-3111; 1-800-535-9095) was built as the Denechaud Hotel by Toledano and Wogan, architects, assisted by Rathbone DuBuys for $350,000 in 1906. Marble floors, massive Sienna marble columns and pilasters, and bronze and mahogony railings were preserved in the 222-room remodeling of 1971 by Seiferth and Gibert and now by architect Peter Trapolin.$$$

The five-story **Lafayette Hotel** at 600 St. Charles Avenue (524-4441; 1-800-733-4754) was built in 1908 in the heart of the business district. Restored with 24 rooms and 20 suites when Faubourg St. Mary became stylish again, it has received kudos for its fine restaurant, **Mike's on the Avenue,** regarded in 1993 as one of the best restaurants in the city. $$$$

The **Lower Garden District** is a New Orleans neighborhood where rehabilitation commenced in the 1970s after publication of *New Orleans Architecture: The Lower Garden District.* It has taken the joint effort of the Junior League, the Preservation Resource Center, and leadership of the residents with the associations they have initiated to wrest this vicinity from annihilation. Now it is a National Register District and a local Historic District.

The **Terrell House** at 1441 Magazine Street (524-9859; 1-800-878-9855) represents this success. The 1858 galleried side-hall house was built for cotton broker Richard Terrell, and Fred Nicaud restored it in 1984 as a guest house with six rooms and three suites. Furnished in creole-style antiques suitable to the period of the house with a presentation of the finest light fixtures in New Orleans. $$$

Another Lower Garden District triumph is the **Maison St. Charles,** at 1319 St. Charles Avenue near Lee Circle (522-0187; 1-800-831-1783). As managing partner for this effort, I purchased all the available buildings and lots on the containing square. Five 1850s-period Greek Revival townhouses were rehabilitated by architect Peter Trapolin as 30 suites and a restaurant in a 130– room complex, now a Quality Inn. The infill architecture designed by Trapolin and Allen Bacquet provides contemporary hotel rooms with galleries around a series of patios and gardens. $$$

The **Prytania Park** at 1525 Prytania Street (524-0427; 1-800-862-1984) is a renovation project involving a Classic-style townhouse and two double townhouses in the Greek Revival style complete with front cast iron balconies and service wings. Associated with it is a well-regarded cafe across the street at 1600 Prytania Street. Numerous international visitors use the place, popular for proximity to the streetcar on St. Charles and antique shops along Magazine Street. $$$

Fairchild House at 1518 Prytania Street (524-0154; 1-800-256-8096) offers seven rooms with private baths in an 1841 Greek Revival residence. $$

Josephine Guest House at 1450 Josephine Street (524-6361) at Prytania Street in the Lower Garden District is Italianate perfect, built in 1870, now restored and furnished with period antiques. The six guest rooms with private baths are offered at rates from $135

The **Columns**, at 3811 St. Charles Avenue (899-9308; 1-800-445-9308), an 1883 mansion for a tobacco magnate was, during the 1940s and 1950s, a much-remembered, glorified boarding house for visitors to Tulane and Loyola universities and for Newcomb students who arrived early for rush. Large rooms, odd shaped, with high ceilings and well lit from vast windows were essential to the look and feel of the Columns. Claire Creppel has restored the residence as 19 romantic rooms with a popular restaurant. $$ to $$$$$

Antoine's Restaurant with couple looking at the bill of fare while waiter looks on. Photograph by Charles Genella,1939. Courtesy of the Historic New Orleans Collection.

Restaurants, Bars, and Nightclubs

Antoine's at 713 St. Louis Street.(581-4422) Antoine Alciatore opened a small boarding house on St. Louis Street soon after his arrival in New Orleans from Marseille in 1840. Five generations of his children have run Antoine's, each generation returning to France to learn more about cuisine and the restaurant business.

Restauranteurs worldwide know Antoine's, and so do all the provincials who recognize New Orleans as their mecca for special occasions. They come by private jet and by train. Some even take the Greyhound Bus, but there's always a meal at Antoine's.

Waiters are your guides and your friends, there to ease you into the customs of Antoine's. You will not be overwhelmed if you understand their importance to the ritual of a good meal.

My waiter Marshall helps me decide, but I usually start with Oysters Ellis, after Dubonnet (red) with a twist of lemon. Despite the temptation of seafood, I have a "nice *tournedo*." Souffled potatoes are a must, and Antoine's is the only place where sauces are essential to the dining experience. Turtle soup and Sweetbreads Financière are the Proteus Day luncheon favorites on the Monday before Mardi Gras.

Bacco at 310 Chartres Street (522-2426) in the De La Poste Hotel has captured the imagination of French Quarter diners and has been listed in the top 20 restaurants for 1993.

Bayona at 430 Dauphine Street (525-4455) is the project of award-winning chef Susan Spicer. A tiny place, pleasant, very European, Bayona has lovely presentations of good food. Her garlic soup is a *non pareil*.

Bistro at the Maison de Ville, 733 Toulouse Street (528-9206), is an alternative lunch and dinner place, quite intimate with beautifully presented French-style food.

Brennan's (see p. 34) at 417 Royal Street.(525-9711) The need for expansion of their popular restaurant business brought the Brennan family to 417 Royal in 1955. The family business has become history in New Orleans because of their efforts to create a distinctive cuisine and operation. Here is the New Orleans Irish success story, out of politics and architecture.

Galatoire's at 209 Bourbon Street doesn't take reservations. Line up with the locals at ll:30 every morning or try for the second seating. Lots of New Orleanians go straight to Galatoire's right after work. My grandmother Maude Monnier Gewin rode over on the Hummingbird from Mobile to meet me just so we could go to Galatoire's while I was a student at Newcomb. She invariably ordered Trout Almandine and a salad. I might get more adventurous with Crabmeat Ravigotte. You can't get that anywhere else. Ask for a demitasse of dark roast coffee if you're not brave enough for a cup of the bitter chicory. The waiters are an essential part of the Galatoire's experience, as are the mirror-covered walls reflecting the white tablecloths, waiters dressed in black and white, and the linen-clad Orleanians, the women with their pearls. I've driven straight through from West Texas, or from Charlottesville, Virginia to meet friends at Galatoire's.

Peristyle, deep in the Quarter at 1041 Dumaine Street, (593-9535), is an important place to eat, and the setting, with murals of City Park, is very New Orleans. Another young chef with creative talent presides, for dinner only.

Tujague's (spelled with a *g* and pronounced with a *q*) at 823 Decatur Street (525-8676) has been in business since 1856, presenting its brisket of beef in a six-course, *prix fixe* French-style presentation after shrimp remoulade. It's casual, but you don't order, they bring it, and it's just what you wanted even though you may not have known it.

Less Expensive French Quarter Food

Acme Oyster and Seafood House at 724 Iberville Street (522-5973) is accessible to both the French Quarter and the central business district. Stop shopping and relax with the best fried food and sandwiches you can find.

Brocato's at 537 St. Ann Street is Angelo Brocato's family pastry shop, a long-time Quarter institution. Try the granita; it's the real thing.

Café du Monde at 813 Decatur Street. Although the location had to change, as did the management during various French Market renovations, the Café du Monde has been packed with locals and tourists for generations, 24 hours a day. Order café au lait and beignets since it's all you can get, except for orange juice and regular coffee for the unadventurous.

Croissant d'Or at 617 Ursulines Street is the place for breakfast in the old Brocato's building. Look down and see the sign in the tile for the "ladies' entrance." It's been awhile.

Gumbo Shop at 630 St. Peter Street. (525-1486) The owners may change every lifetime or so, but the gumbo and the place remains just as much fun as it was in the 1950s, and it's in a Spanish colonial building, dating from 1795.

La Madeleine at 547 St. Ann Street (568-9950) in the Lower Pontalba apartments is recent and owned by French people from France. Bread, coffee, and atmosphere with light meals, like the Caesar salad and the Croque Monsieur.

Napoleon House at 500 Chartres Street (524-9752) is not only a great setting (they haven't spent a cent on decor since 1814) but has great muffelettas and offers small portions of all the great Creole and cajun specialties. It's been going strong since the 1930s, at least as a bar with food.

Faubourg Marigny has developed some interesting places to eat in attractive historic buildings, such as the **Praline Connection** at 542 Frenchmen Street (943-3934). Open for three meals a day with late hours, this corner neighborhood restaurant concentrates on soul food and sweets from the adjacent sweetshop.

Feelings, also known as **Cafe d'Aunoy,** after the former plantation in the area at

2600 Chartres Street, has a residential setting with good food.

City Park and Esplanade Avenue have **Gabrielle**, for dinner, at 3201 Esplanade Avenue (948-6233), where 40 guests at a seating enjoy food cooked by the owner who trained under Paul Prudhomme at **K-Paul's Louisiana Kitchen** at 416 Chartres Street. The waiters are mostly friends of the owners.

Lunch at **Degas** at 3127 Esplanade Avenue, (945-5635), named because in 1872 Edgar Degas stayed at the Musson house across the street at 2306 Esplanade Avenue in 1872.

Dooky Chase at 2301 Orleans Street is the most famous African-American restaurant in New Orleans, where Leah Chase and her husband, Dooky, have been preparing great lunches and dinners for decades.

Eating American

Bon Ton Café (see p. 101) at 401 Magazine Street.(524-3386) When, in the early 1970s, the Bon Ton restaurant moved to the historic brick building at 401 Magazine Street, the preservationists know that a battle had been won. The challenge was to save downtown, Faubourg St. Mary. Now at 401 Magazine Street brick walls with wide folding doors and high ceilings envelop the guests. Crawfish bisque or *étouffée*, bread pudding, and whiskey sauce are essential parts of the casual dining scene, for lunch or dinner.

The Warehouse District in Faubourg St. Mary has burgeoned with restaurants since the World's Fair and the success of the Arts District catalyzed by the Preservation Resource Center, with their headquarters at a townhouse on Julia Street.

Emeril's at 800 Tchoupitoulas Street (528-9393) is owned by the chef, Emeril Lagasse, who has won national awards.

He has recently furthered the preservation movement by purchasing a historic townhouse across from St. Patrick's Cathedral on Camp Street where he lives.

Mother's at 401 Poydras Street (523-9656) is a mainstay for everyone from businesspeople to longshoreworkers, who stand in line to pick a poorboy or hot, hot lunch New Orleans style.

The Garden District

The Garden District features **Commander's Palace** at 1403 Washington Avenue (899-8221). Every neighborhood has its institutions and all the things that give it wholeness. In the Garden District it's all rolled up on Washington Avenue around Prytania Street with Lafayette Cemetery and Commander's Palace. Opened in 1880 by Emile Commander, the restaurant was bought by the Brennan family in 1974. It works because of their flair for ingenuity and good food.

Commander's is an occasion itself, but take time to walk around the neighborhood a bit. Look at the bollards, great cast iron standards sticking out of the brick pavement. They kept the carriages from going down in the deep granite drainage ditches, also worth a careful perusal. Look through the screens of shrubs to catch glimpses of architectural details in fairytale settings, cast iron lyre-pattern railings, corinthian column caps, and entablatures, eyecatching because of their very misproportion. Imposing facades hide chaste gable sides, and the service wings are always longer than the houses. You'll see new combinations of classical decorative design. But it works, both individually and as a collective whole of Classical and Italianate motifs, jumbled and combined to create special houses in a special neighborhood unique to the south. Here is a neighborhood that seemed to have been built almost entirely during the Civil War and the harsh days of reconstruction. That's New Orleans, the city that care forgot, whose citizens tried to forget to care.

Save Our Cemeteries, under the leadership of Garden District writer Mary Louise Christovich, has spent over $250,000 in city-owned Lafayette cemetery. The organization understands perfectly Mark Twain's comment that the best architecture of New Orleans is in its cemeteries. They want to recycle everything. How about the abandoned wall vaults? It took an act of the legislature for them to get permission to reuse those that had been abandoned for generations. Save Our Cemeteries, understanding that genealogists are ancestor worshipers, have proposed that each society or organization of genealogists save and restore one tomb per year as a project.

If you think it strange to preview lunch at Commander's with a cemetery tour, you must understand that the philosophy of Save our Cemeteries is in keeping with the history of New Orleans. Death is an occasion—for eating, drinking, and for jazz funerals. A walk through the cemetery is the best architectural lesson available to revue the history of the temple and the development of architectural styles in America.

Uptown

Uptown eating means restaurants in little commercial buildings in residential areas, such as **Gautreau's** at 1728 Soniat Street (899-7397), a drugstore building with tin ceilings and an unglazed tile floor. Gautreau's was the project of Ann Avegno Russell, who began it despite the distraction of six children; it barrelled to international fame in a short time.

Upperline at 1413 Upperline Street at Prytania Street (891-9822) combines a corner commercial and a residence behind it. Owner-manager JoAnn Clevenger came to the restaurant business via flowers, cotumes and vintage clothing, and theater, good training for restaurant work.

Clancy's at 6100 Annunciation Street at Webster Street (895-1111) is in one of those old-time frame cottages that has changed through the years from the old corner hangout to an upscale dining experience, reasonably priced.

Casamento's at 4330 Magazine Street (895-9761) specializes in oysters. Some member of the Casamento family will serve you while you enjoy the shiny white walls, tile floor, and the oyster stew. Even the sidewalk out front is covered in tile, and you'll see gunnysacks full of newly delivered oysters or oyster shells set out to haul away.

When you find a corner bar and restaurant between Magazine Street and the river, you can figure its run by an Irish or Italian family and the food is good. This includes **Franky and Johnny's** at 321 Arabella Street, (899-9146), worth a trip to see the neighborhood and enjoy a po-boy and a beer. **Domilise's Bar**, at 5240 Annunciation Street (899-9126), has some of the best po-boys, along with friendly folks of the neighborhood.

Parasol's, a bar and family restaurant at 2533 Constance Street (897-5413), is in the heart of the Irish Channel, and it's an old-time substitute for the "club" for the Irish constituents.

Carrollton has **Brigtsen's** in an old house near the levee at 723 Dante Street (861-7610). Rated as one of the 10 best restaurants in 1993, Brigtsen's also has a great uptown location among wonderful shops such as Ballin's for dresses and Mignon Faget for original jewelry, all in picturesque old cottages.

Camellia Grill at 626 South Carrollton Avenue (866-9573). Where else can you eat at a counter and have big cotton napkins? Your hamburgers, omelettes, and waffles, your coffee and mocha freezes, are served by professional waiters in pressed white jackets.

Mid-city means New Orleans's urban sprawl, out Canal Street and out Carrollton Avenue. It's worth the ride to experience lunches and dinners with beer in great cold stemmed glasses along with your po-boy at **Liuzza's**

Restaurant and Bar, 3635 Bienville Street and 234 North Telemachus Street (482-9120) near Carrollton Avenue.

Mandina's at 3800 Canal Street (482-9179) offers a similar experience. Only in New Orleans will you find Italian restaurants with "Wop Salad" written on the menu.

Christian's at 3835 Iberville Street (482-4924) is beautifully situated in a former church but named after the owner, Chris Ansel of the Galatoire clan. He opted for his own restaurant after learning the business in France and at the family restaurant. They serve lunch Thursday and Friday, and dinner Monday through Saturday.

The original Ruth's Chris Steakhouse is going strong way out on 711 North Broad Street.(486-0810). There you meet laid-back waitresses who are great businesswomen, good at repartee, and know just how to serve the gigantic steaks and vegetables that only Chris knew how to cook to please the local politicians.

Music

Jelly Roll's, named after jazz great Jelly Roll Morton, at 501 Bourbon Street (568-0501) is home base for trumpet player Al Hirt.

Lafitte's Blacksmith Shop (see p. 19) at 941 Bourbon Street (523-0066) is a good piano bar in a great building, and it's been there a long time.

Palm Court Jazz Café at 1204 Decatur Street (525-0200) has old-time jazz musicians, good food, and a bar with a great jazz brunch. Live music Wednesday through Sundays.

Pat O'Brien's at 718 St. Peter Street (525-4823) is in one of the French

Quarter's Spanish colonial buildings dating from 1792. The courtyard, the singing, and the drinks have been famous for generations.

Preservation Hall, 726 St. Peter Street (522-2841). No drinking and eating, just listening to old-time jazz.

The Esplanade in the Royal Orleans at 621 St. Louis Street (529-5333) is great for Irish coffee or a drink, with Roger Dickerson and others at the piano.

Faubourg Marigny presents Snug Harbor at 626 Frenchman Street (949-0696) with some of the best jazz in town, with Ellis Marsalis and Charmaine Neville when they're in town.

Faubourg St. Mary with its spacious warehouses has attracted Michaul's at 701 Magazine Street (522-5517) and Mulate's at 201 Julia Street (522-1492) with Cajun food from southwest Louisiana, Zydeco music, and Cajun dancing.

Pete Fountain's Nightclub at the Hilton Riverside No. 2 Poydras (523-4374) is in a contemporary building, but the river view is as old as New Orleans and the clarinet is old-time New Orleans.

The Garden District has the Bayou Bar at the Pontchartrain Hotel, 2031 St. Charles Avenue, (524-0581), with piano music Thursday through Saturday nights.

Uptown it's Professor Long Hair's Tipitina's, 501 Napoleon Street (895-8477). All kinds of live music, seven days a week, with the Neville Brothers when they're in town, the Meters, and the Radiators.

Carrollton has the Maple Leaf Club at 8316 Oak Street (866-9359). Thursday is usually Cajun night dance time.

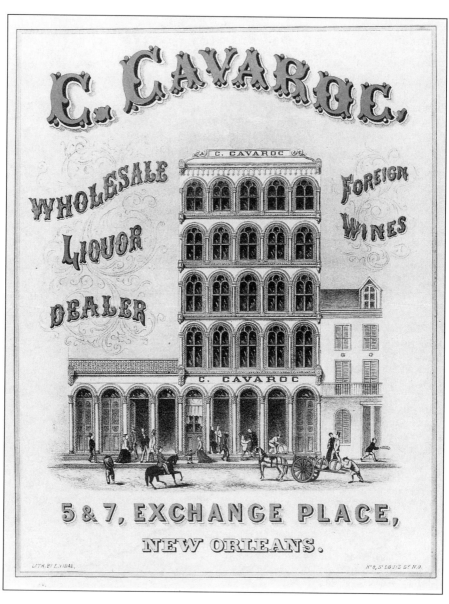

Cast iron building at 113-115 Exchange Place. Printed by Simon Benedict, 1869-1871. Courtesy of the Historic New Orleans Collection.

Ragtime and
Dixieland Jazz
New Orleans' Own

rchitect Benjamin Latrobe took his usual careful look at life in New Orleans . . .this time at the dances on Congo Square early in the 1800s. He saw black Africans with "hardly a dozen café au lait faces in the crowd." Many of the dances had sacred undertones, related to voodoo ritual, some of it imported by the *émigrés* from St. Domingue, either directly or via Cuba, like the calinda and the carabine, or the frenetic bamboula and counjaille.

Thirty years after slavery had ended, Congo Square, renamed after New Orlean's Civil War General Beauregard, remained the site of Sunday bamboulas and ancient dances and music among the black population. Chants and drumbeats were interrupted by the shouts of *calas* (rice cake) and *estomacs mulatres* (gingerbread) vendors. Others hawked good-luck charms and voodoo mixtures that could bring bad luck to whomever its secrets were directed.

Still today the Second Line, a band parading to a jazz funeral, winds and twists its way through the streets of Faubourg Tremé to the St. Louis cemeteries. Street music slides from dirges and wails to joyous beats such as "When The Saints Go Marching In" after the graveside service. Blaring outbursts rack into insistent beats as men and women join the band weaving through the aisles of the cities of the dead at St. Louis II. Members of fraternal organizations, benevolent societies and burial clubs swing out to the rhythms and the sounds to send their brother to heaven, God knows, a better place at least.

It's not too different from what Latrobe saw. Jazz, New Orleans style, is the product of a music-mad populace reaching back to the founding years when the French brigantines lent the captain's band to play *motets* at the parish church for weddings. After all, the word jazz, they say, comes from a French word, too, jaser, "to prattle". Even the word dixie, as in "Dixieland," comes from New Orleans, where the French word *dix* was printed on 10 dollar notes.

Jazz and Dixieland music are the end products of a couple of hundred years of musical tradition. Governor Vaudreuil introduced the *soirée dansante* in the 1740s. For the next 150 years no visitor to a New Orleans home failed to be honored with one. Entrepreneur Bernard Coquet initiated Blue Ribbon Balls in 1809; these became the celebrated Quadroon Balls, held twice weekly for *femmes de couleur libres*. Significantly, *hommes de couleur libres* were not allowed to dance, but the musicians at these events were black.

The French Opera House opened to *William Tell* in 1859 in the building designed by James Gallier Jr. which burned in 1919. There was a balcony for the slaves, and a visitor to New Orleans was amazed to hear African slaves singing opera arias as they hurried about the streets of the French Quarter on errands.

From the turn of the century until 1917 Storyville, the restricted and legal red light district, along Rampart and Basin Streets, very near the old Congo Square, brought the piano to jazz and Dixieland. Without the red light district the African-American musicians who entertained in the "Madames' houses" would have had no access to the expensive pianos. With Storyland, piano music began to rock along with the sound of cornet, trumpet, and drum.

Spencer Williams immortalized Lulu White's "house of ill repute" with his "Mahogany Hall Stomp." Tony Jackson, entertaining at the house of "Octoroon Countess Willie V. Piazza" countered with "Elgin Movements in My Hips, with Twenty Years Guarantee." Ferdinand LeMenthe (Jelly Roll Morton), a barber apprentice, was one of the first "piano men," entertaining at Tom Anderson's Arlington Annex. On Sundays during the day, he and many other boys played their way to Milneburg on Smoky Mary, the railroad train, belting out his "Milneburg Joys" along the railroad to Lake Pontchartrain.

Misery, mosquitos, and heat meant New Orleans to the poor African-Americans who eked out a life on Perdido Street in hovels, tenements, and broken-down shacks. Even the name *perdido* means "lost" in Spanish. But there was music, and even money enough to buy music instruments at the pawn shops.

Everything about these people was improvised: their clothes from rags, shoes from sacks, houses from cardboard and tin, food from scraps, and so was the music they played. Louis Armstrong was born on Perdido Street, and there he listened to Buddy Bolden, the barber who blew his horn to fame and madness. In music and music alone the American blacks and the creoles of color joined forces and the result was jazz—they called it ragtime at the black dance halls such as Big Easy and Funky Butt, where

Buddy Bolden played and Louis Armstrong listened. White musicians, including Papa Laine in the 1890s, caught the fancy. They started the "Spasm Band" and they called their music "Dixieland."

World War I brought controls by the U.S. government which succeeded in closing Storyville, and the Iberville Housing project went up in its place in 1939. Urban renewal in the 1950s wiped out the homes and stomping grounds where much of jazz and Dixieland developed. Irony plays its own music: now New Orleans has Louis Armstrong Park where the old houses of jazz musicians once stood.

As for funerals, you may attend your own if you enter St. Louis Cemeteries I or II alone, unless you arrive at a very public time like a jazz funeral, or on Sundays when Save Our Cemeteries offers tours. (588-9357) Some bus tours include the cemeteries near the old ramparts. (Rampart Street) Because of crime these two cemeteries had been off limits to both tourists and residents over the past decade.

Not so in Benjamin Henry Latrobe's day; people died fast in New Orleans—from duels, like Micajah Lewis, Governor Claiborne's brother-in-law and secretary, to yellow fever and Asiatic cholera, both of which ran rampant four months of the year. Street vendors came to the cemeteries to sell *calas,* delicious rice cakes, along the aisles of the cemetery to the crowds whitewashing and painting the tombs and visiting their family graves. The cities of the dead were filling up, and the living were there to see it.

The New Orleans Jazz and Heritage Festival has been so successful under the aegis of Quint Dairs, a founder of Jazz Fest, that it has moved to the fairgrounds. The ten-day event the last weekend in April and the first one in May brings over 4000 performers, cooks, and craftsmen plus the tourists who flock to New Orleans for Jazz Fest. Book your hotel a year ahead and call 522-4786 or 800-488-5252 for tickets and informtion.

Photograph by Ben C. Toledano.

Bookstores and Books

The Bookstores of New Orleans

When you arrive in New Orleans, after finding your lodgings, visit a bookstore in the neighborhood because a bookstore proprietor is one of the best resources for learning about a city, its people, and its history. **Bookstar** at 414 **North Peters Street,** has a huge selection of new books in the vicinity of the old Jax Brewery along the riverfront on Decatur. Proprietor Ed Boardman can arrange literary tours of the French Quarter, or call Heritage Tours, 949-9805. A walking tour is a must if you are interested in late nineteenth and early twentieth century literature, and these tours are far more factual and entertaining than most.

Harold and Bonnie Kate Leisure are long gone from the French Quarter, but Joe DeSalvo and Rosemary James, a local journalist, have restored the historic building where William Faulkner once lived at 624 **Pirates Alley** and have an antiquarian bookstore, the **Faulkner House**. Joe covers the local greats, including Tennessee, Bill, and Truman. **Dauphine Street Books** at 410 **Dauphine Street** specializes in jazz and local interest. There's **Beckham's Book Store** at 228 **Decatur Street** for old books. In fact, there are more out-of-print book shops in New Orleans than ever before.

Edwin Blair is the proprietor of **Blair House of Books,** Factor's Row, Suite 302 at 806 **Perdido Street,** in the historic building where Edgar Degas painted his New Orleans relatives at work in 1872. The internationally noted painting, "Cotton Market in New Orleans," was bought by the Municipal museum at Pau, France.

But you may have to go to the Historic New Orleans Collection, the Williams Research Center, the Louisiana State Museum Library, or to the Southeastern Architectural Archives in the Howard Tilton Library, Tulane University to find some of the best books on New Orleans. The Historic

New Orleans Collection library has memoirs of many early travelers to the city and a shop with an extensive collection of contemporary books.

For new books, De Ville's **Books In Print** is on the riverwalk and at 344 Carondelet street. **The Garden District Book Shop** is in the historic old Rink at 2727 Prytania Street diagonally across from Lafayette Cemetery No. 1. Uptown, it's Rhoda Faust's **Maple Street Book Shop,** at 7523 Maple, a kind of collateral descendant of Tess Crager's book shop and publishing firm. **Beaucoup Books** at 5414 Magazine Street is Jefferson City's neighborhood bookstore with a good selection of children's books in French and Spanish. The octagon–shaped **Uptown Square Books,** 299 Broadway, is presided over by Mark Zumpe. One uptown bibliophile and author calls Mark her "book shrink" because his eclectic reading and patience make him a nonstress anecdote-rich advisor on the right books for family or friend.

New Orleans, bookwise, has come a long way since Monsieur Berquin-Duvallon visited in the 1790s when Manuel Gayoso de Lemos was governor. "A book-seller," he wrote, "would die of hunger in the middle of his books unless he sold a book of interest to his readers on how to double your money in one year."

The **Preservation Resource Center** at 604 Julia Street (581-7032) is your headquarters for preservation methodology. Under the guidance of director Patty Gay, this umbrella organization for areawide preservation has, since the 1970s, thrust New Orleans into the forefront of the preservation movement.

The **New Orleans Historic District Landmarks Commission** at 830 Julia Street (565-7440) offers literature and advice on preservation ordinances and policy. Offered are published lists of the landmarks in city-administered historic districts as well as restoration and renovation guidelines.

The **Vieux Carré Commission** at 334 Royal Street in the historic Bank of Louisiana Building (529-3950) was created by the first statewide legislation on preservation in the United States (1936). The Vieux Carré Survey, the research project to document the French Quarter, is available there and at the Historic New Orleans Collection.

Books on Food, Jazz, and History

The most extensive published architectural resource on New Orleans is the series funded by the Friends of the Cabildo and published by Gretna's Pelican Publishing Company, the seven–volume *New Orleans Architecture.* Conceived in 1970 by photographer Betsy Swanson, founder of the Friends of the Cabildo Mary Louise Christovich, and me, the ongoing series covers the city neighborhood by neighborhood. In 1975, Volume V of the series received the Society of Architectural Historians' Award for the "most distinguished work of Scholarship in the History of Architecture published by a North American scholar, November 1, 1973–October 31, 1977."

Samuel Wilson, Jr., the architect, historian, and founder of the Louisiana Landmarks Society, made restoration of historic buildings the right thing to do in New Orleans. One of his many useful works is *The Vieux Carré: New Orleans, Its Plan, Its Growth, Its Architecture,* a volume of the Vieux Carré Historic District Demonstration Study, published for the city of New Orleans in 1968.

Impressions Respecting New Orleans, Benjamin Henry Latrobe's diary and sketches written between 1818 and 1820, was edited by Wilson and published by Columbia University Press in 1951.

New Orleans, Its Old Houses, Shops and Public Buildings, by Nathaniel Courtland Curtis (Philadelphia: Lippincott, 1933), is an early effort by an architect to record what makes New Orleans architecture unique in the United States. Ironically, Curtis's firm, Curtis and Davis, designed the Superdome and the Rivergate, at the river near the foot of Canal, the latter now demolished by the gambling interests.

New Orleans and Its Environs, The Domestic Architecture 1727–1870, by Italo William Ricciuti, includes photographs by Rudolf Hertzberg and an introduction by Talbot Faulkner Hamlin (New York: Bonanza Books, 1938). Ricuitti, an architect, sought a reference work for architects and draftsmen on historic New Orleans architecture; he couldn't find one, so he produced one himself.

Southern Comfort, The Garden District of New Orleans, by S. Frederick Starr, with photographs by Robert S. Brantley, was published in 1989 by MIT Press. Starr, past-president of Oberlin College, then director of the Aspen Institute, and always a jazz musician, wrote enthusiastically about New Orleans in at least three books during his five years in the city. *Southern Comfort* has as much information in the footnotes as Starr presents in the evocative text about the Anglo-American arrival in New Orleans and their establishment of their own suburb, the Garden District.

Martha Ann and Ray Samuels' *Great Days of the Garden District* with its walking tour, sponsored by the Louise McGehee School, remains a handy guide, available at the bookstore at the Rink, a Garden District renovation project of Martha Ann Samuels.

Historic Jefferson Parish from Shore to Shore, by Betsy Swanson (Gretna: Pelican Publishing Company, 1975), was funded by the Jefferson Parish Council and the Jefferson Parish Environmental Development Advisory Board. Neighboring parishes would do well to continue the series.

Fabulous New Orleans by Lyle Saxon, illustrated by E. H. Suydam, was published locally in 1958 by Robert L. Crager. Saxon had been the director of the Louisiana and New Orleans guides for the Works Progress Administration during the Great Depression, when he worked with many of the artists, writers, and photographers who lived in the French Quarter.

New Orleans Yesterday and Today, A Guide to the City, is a handy book published by Louisiana State University Press (1983, revised in 1988). The contributors, Walter Cowan, John C. Chase, Charles L. Dufour, O. K. Leblanc, and John Wilds, artists and journalists well acquainted with their city, know what's what and present it in a topical way. The librarians at the Historic New Orleans Collection recommend it for easy reference.

New Orleans City Guide (New York: Houghton Mifflin, 1938) was written and compiled by the Federal Writers' Project of the Works Progress Administration for the city of New Orleans, chaired by Lyle Saxon. It's still a valid read, and the Historic New Orleans Collection has recently reprinted it with a foreword by Pat Brady.

Stuart M. Lynn's photographic portfolio *New Orleans* (New York: Hastings House, 1949) is the product of his 1938 visit to the city, when he caught the French Quarter at the moment in time when indifference turned to interest and awareness of potentialities and responsibilities surfaced. Rooms above the courtyard of the Napoleon House, reached by the exquisite winding stair under the galleries, became his home.

Truth can be stranger than fiction, but fiction with Grace King was also the truth as she saw it. When she criticized George Washington Cable's fiction to publisher Richard Watson Gilder, he challenged her to write about the New Orleans she knew. Her story, *The Pleasant Ways of St. Medard* (1916), is a fictional account of her family's experience during Reconstruction. You can learn about Reconstruction in the history books, but you understand it with Grace King (1852–1932).

Liliane Creté came from Paris to New Orleans almost every summer during the 1970s. She roomed in the dormitory at Dominican College in the old building on St. Charles Avenue, walking to Tulane to do research. Louisiana State University Press published her book *Daily Life in Louisiana 1815–1830,* translated by Patrick Gregory, in 1981. Perhaps because she's French, she depicts the creole with full understanding, and she clarifies the difference between French culture and creole culture in New Orleans.

Les Aventures du Consul de France de Nouvelle Orléans a Carthagène, edited by Max Dorian and Dixie Reynolds (La Rochelle, Editions Navarre, 1981), presents in French trenchant descriptions and reflections on American enterprise by the resident French consul in New Orleans Armand Saillard, with letters dating from 1808 to 1835.

BAGATELLE

Beauregard-Keyes house courtyard and servants' wing. Photograph by Robert S. Brantley.

N'Orlyunseeze:
A Glossary

It's been 230 odd years since Louisiana was a French colony, but even today French culture and the language hang on tenaciously in small ways. Architecture, religion, and vocabulary are the most obvious hints of the Gallic roots of the city. Then, too, the well-documented French penchant for entertaining and being entertained accounts for the development and growth of Mardi Gras, of jazz and Dixieland music, and of creole cuisine and fine restaurants.

Most of all, though, New Orleans French culture is a gift from French women. First of all, they put up with the place all those years: the Asiatic cholera, the yellow fever, the duels, the *placées,* the stylized way of life. The women came knowing full well that a child or more would be dead of yellow fever or the surviving children orphaned if the odds proved true. The French women, undaunted by the cession of Louisiana to Spain in 1762, promptly married Spanish officers. Madame Panís, the widow of an executed French leader, Joseph Milhet, of the rebellion against the incoming Spanish regime, married one of the Spanish officers, who had just arrived to quell her husband's efforts to keep New Orleans French.

There's some evidence that when Spanish colonial *Alferez Real*, Royal Notary, and wealthy realtor Señor Don Andrés Almonester y Roxas, married his French creole bride, Louise De La Ronde, he had to speak French. She wasn't about to learn Spanish, and their daughter Micaela Almonester's dowry agreement with the French creole Baron de Pontalba's son was itemized in French. The executed Frenchman M. Milhet, then, need not have worried, for New Orleans did remain French in spirit and in language throughout the 40 Spanish colonial years. The Spanish notaries had to speak and write French, as did the city guards and police.

After the Louisiana transfer to the United States in 1803, newspaper advertisements indicate that police hired by the city had to speak both French and English. Nothing is said about Spanish. Notarial documents, by law Spanish from the 1760s to 1803, reverted immediately to French recordation, and records abound in both French and English until the time of the Civil War. John Slidell, Edward Livingston, and Judah P. Benjamin understood that French was essential to success in the legal profession. Surely that's not why each married into prominent New Orleans creole families or *émigrés* from St. Domingue.

Tradition has it that the 1919 burning of the French Opera House at the corner of Bourbon and Toulouse Streets in the French Quarter spelled doom for French culture. That or World War I, when creoles came back Americans. Perhaps the Sicilians who took over the lower half of the French Quarter beyond St. Ann Street in the 1880s and 1890s added to the decline of the use of French in New Orleans.

Here are some handy words that you will be hearing in New Orleans that you may not hear anywhere else; some are French, others Spanish, English or just N'Orlyunseeze:

Abat Vent: The little overhang extending out from the cornice level of creole cottages, sometimes supported by iron bearers.

Arpent: A linear measurement of 11.5 rods, about 192 feet, used locally in Canada and early Louisiana to mesure river frontage. A square arpent is equal to 0.84 acre. Arpentage is like acreage. An arpenteur is a surveyor.

Bagatelle: French for a trifle, nonsense, and even lovemaking. In New Orleans it means just a little something. There are plantations named Bagatelle, too.

Banquette: The sidewalk.

Bayou: A natural canal created by the overflow of a lake or river or the draining of a marsh. The word is Choctaw for river or creek.

Bousillage: Mud mixed with moss and used for infill between timber framing, begun by the French in the 1720s and used even in the early nineteenth century. It was always covered with plaster.

Box Columns: Wood pillars used to support galleries in Greek Revival and Classic-style houses.

Briqueté entre poteaux: Brick-between-post construction. Bricks were used to fill the space between timber framing by the French from the 1720s after the Company of the Indies established their brickyard on Bayou Road.

Cajun: French for Acadian, referring to the descendants of exiles from Acadia, renamed Nova Scotia by the British when they won it from the French. More than 10,000 of these exiles found a permanent home in the Atakapas Indian country of then-Spanish Louisiana after 1765. Now that area comprises the nine Acadian parishes south and west of New Orleans.

Colombage: Framing system using heavy cypress timbers, mortised and tenoned, as jambs and window frames. Sears Roebuck used the idea a couple of centuries later because the framing of each side could be assembled on the ground, raised and set on sills or piers. The French filled between with *bousillage*, mud mixed with moss and animal hair or shells. The more permanent method was using brick as infill between the posts or *briqueté entre poteaux*.

1630 Arabella Street. Cornice and column of Benjamin-Schlesinger house. Photograph by Betsy Swanson.

Concession: Land grant from the king of France.

Creole: From the Spanish word *criollo*, having roots in *criar*, to breed or to create. In eighteenth- and nineteenth-century New Orleans the word designated birth in the New World of European parentage or American-born offspring of European parents. The term *creole of color* distinguished persons of creole and African or African-American parentage. Recently the "of color" has been dropped, so that creole also refers, ironically, to a "person of mixed blood, Caucasian and African-American of French cultural heritage and racial background." *Creole* has become a word to designate emanation from French traditions, such as creole cuisine, and even creole ponies, chickens, and tomatoes.

Engagé: French person indentured for three-years .

Entresol: French mezzanine. Locally, an *entresol* house has a 16-foot-high first floor with the upper space behind the arched transoms of the facade used for storage.

Fais do do: A family dance in Cajun country. It comes from the French words *faire*, to make and *dormir*, to sleep.

Faubourg: French word used in New Orleans for suburb.

Flambeaux: The torches carried in Mardi Gras parades by the special *flambeau* carriers, who weave and dance with their torches.

Garconniere: A plantation outbuilding, detached from the master house, used as bedrooms and lodging for the older boys of the family.

Garde de frise: The wrought iron guards that separate the balconies of common-wall buildings at the second level and upward. These charming railings that project out in a semicircle, each rod terminating with a "devil's pitchfork," keep trespassers from hopping from balcony to balcony. You'll probably only see them in

New Orleans and Puerto Rico among U.S. holdings.

German coast: Doesn't refer to Germany, but the banks of the Mississippi between New Orleans and Baton Rouge, home of the descendants of the first Palatinate settlers, who arrived between 1719 and 1731.

Gris gris: Pronounced "gree gree." Refers to a charm, statuette, or amulet provided by a voodoo specialist to bring luck or conjure evil on enemies. A little gris gris can help a situation or it can cause disaster, whichever its purpose.

Habitation: Plantation.

Krewe: An organization that masks and parades or performs the skit for a carnival parade or ball.

Lagniappe: A little something extra, like a baker's dozen.

Louvered shutters: Cypress shutters having working cross pieces to control light and air. These did not appear until about the 1830s. Previously, shutters were of the **batten** variety, solid, with vertical beaded boards or paneled. Even into the twentieth century, more modest creole houses and commercial establishments used batten shutters.

Maison de maître: Master house, usually a large Creole cottage with outbuildings on a square of land or a plantation.

Mardi Gras: French for Fat Tuesday, the last day of feasting before Lent. Mardi Gras is 46 days before Easter and can fall as early as February 3 or as late as March 9. Mardi Gras season begins on **Twelfth Night,** the feast of the Epiphany, the night the three kings visited Bethlehem.

Parishes: Louisiana political subdivisions called counties in other states are called parishes, a holdover from the Roman Catholic origins of the state where church parishes paralleled political geographical divisions.

Personne de couleur: An historic term used in notarial documents to distinguish a person of partial African heritage. Inventories and wills, marriage, death, and birth certificates and church registers would distinguish between *personnes de couleur* and *Africains.* They also distinguished among *negre, mulatto, octoroon, quadroon, and bricté* in such documents, and individuals would so distinguish themselves on official documents. *Homme de couleur libre,* abbreviated in official documents as h.c.l., means a free man of color. *Femme de couleur libre,* f.c.l., means a free woman of color. *Pardo* was the Spanish for light skinned. *Moreno* meant dark skinned. There were during the Spanish colonial period *pardo* militia units and *moreno* militia units. They were never mixed.

Picayune: Means a triviality, but it was what the French called the smallest Spanish coin, worth 6¼ cents.

Pigeonnier: Dovecote, an architectural feature of a plantation complex, often octagonal or square, usually situated in pairs equidistant from the rear sides of the masterhouse.

Trashold: Means "threshold" to a New Orleans carpenter, and when you think about it, why not?

Uptown, downtown, and river and lake corner: Terms often heard in New Orleans to give directions. Everything is either on the river side of a street or the lake side (Pontchartrain) if a street runs roughly east to west. A house may be on the uptown river corner (somewhat southwest) or the downtown lake corner (somewhat northeast) or the downtown river corner or the uptown lake corner, or on the riverside or the lake side of the street. Forget north, south, east, and west; it's too confusing since the river winds around so much that while New Orleans is referred to as located on the Eastbank, parts are on the Southbank, and the Westbank is not what it's supposed to be. The possibilities are not endless, but they seem to be.

Downtown has also become a way of life, as has uptown. There are books comparing growing up downtown or back o'town to growing up uptown. Wherever it was, it was bound to be interesting since it's New Orleans.

Voodoo: Comes from the African *Dahomey word,* vodu, a deity. This African cult, once an animistic religion with emphasis on the snake as a symbol, was brought to New Orleans by slaves and free persons of color from the French Caribbean islands, especially St. Domingue and Martinique.

Zinc: "Sink" in New Orleans, perhaps because they used to be made of zinc and it's the French word for bar and counter.

1500 block of Dumaine Street. Photograph by Betsy Swenson.

The Palace Cafe on Canal Street. Photograph by Robert S. Brantley.

New Orleans Creole Cooking Means Shopping too

William Makepeace Thackery wrote home that he was in New Orleans "just when the orchards were flushing over with peach blossoms and the sweet herbs came to flavor the juleps. It seemed to me the city in the world where you could eat and drink the most and suffer the least." He would still be right if he wrote that today. New Orleans has its creole home cooking and its famous creole restaurants. Sometimes it's one and the same. Either way, New Orleans just may consistently present the best food to be found in North America.

Shopping, of course, is one secret, and there was the French Market where Choctaw Indians stolidly sat to offer their *filé*, or sassafras root. From the early French days Frenchmen leased their guns and powder to nearby Indians to hunt game while the French farmers and their *engagés* plowed the fields. There's still the **French Market** along Decatur Street not far from the U. S. Mint on Esplanade. Go there at dawn and have breakfast at **Fiorella's** with the market men and women.

If you don't want to get up so early, just take the trek to **Zara's** in the Garden District or **Langenstein's** uptown to see how the locals buy their groceries. After they shop, they go home and start on the roux. Without a good roux, you have nothing. It's the base of about everything, along with chopped onions, green onions or shallots, celery, green pepper, parsley, and garlic.

A roux cannot look insipid but must be rich and very dark brown. My mother-in-law Beecye Casanas Toledano explained that to me—in an urgent voice. You can brown the flour in a dry skillet and then add it as needed to your butter or oil and sauteed vegetables. Or you can brown it a little darker by adding a soupçon of butter to the olive oil and white unbleached flour, stirring with a wooden spoon, but keep stirring. If you've been influenced by the Sicilians and add tomato or tomato paste, be sure you sauté the paste in an iron skillet. Nothing is to read "red." Red is not allowed. The same goes for finely chopped garlic from which you have removed the greenish center; sauté it a good long time. You must add a whole bayleaf or more and thyme to everything.

Your base, though, to about any main dish is chopped green peppers, celery, shallots or green onions with their stems, onions, and parsley. Who cares about the specific amount, although Joseph Augustus, who'd known cooks who had been slaves, adjured me to cut down on the parsley. "Makes the gumbo and the grillades bitter," he said. The idea is that you use whatever you have in the icebox (that's New Orleans for refrigerator): the whole green pepper or the entire bunch of celery. Just be sure you have a good chopping knife, and chop not too coarse and not too fine, although these days with all the emphasis on health, a little coarseness adds finesse. You can use your Cuisinart, but stand there and buzz it off and on. No mush, please.

Now that you've chopped up everything you bought and it's simmering in the big iron skillet with the olive oil mixed with a little butter, it's time to get serious. There's still time to change your mind. Will it be gumbo, shrimp stew, grillades, creole chicken, jambalaya, or red beans? The roux and the vegetable base can be the same for these dishes, even for crawfish bisque or etoufée, stuffed eggplant, or delicate mirleton picked up from the street vendor or out of the backyard.

Old Creole Recipes

————————

Pralines are round, caramelized sugar candy full of pecans. Here's how you make them. In one small cast iron skillet heat a big kitchen spoon of white sugar to caramel-colored liquid while stirring with a wooden spoon. In another heavy cooking pot, ¾ cup milk and 2 cups sugar must be mixed and stirred above low heat until bubbles occur on the sides of the pot. Then add a pinch of baking soda and stir. When the mixture boils again in the heavy cooking pot on top of the stove, add the liquefied sugar from the small skillet, stirring until the caramel liquid mixture is well blended. Continue to cook on medium low, boiling softly for at least 7 minutes. Continue up to 3 minutes more or until the mixture begins to roll away from the sides of the pot. Take the pot off the stove and add one-third stick of butter, 1 tablespoon of vanilla and 2 cups of pecans. Beat until creamy and spoon onto rounds on waxed paper. The trick is not to have the mixture turn to sugar before you've spooned out about 30 small pralines. If they stay gooey, you haven't cooked it enough or you haven't beat it in the pot long enough; just use it over ice cream if it doesn't work as pralines. Usually, it takes a helper to get the pralines out of the spoon onto the wax paper. Wrap individually in aluminum foil after they've cooled.It's easier to go to **The Old Time Praline Shop** at **627 Royal Street.** It's been run by the same family for 35 years, and they don't seem to have spent 2 cents on decorations. They cook pralines.

Café au lait is strong New Orleans coffee made of dark roast beans often mixed with some chicory. It is usually made in a porcelainized French drip pot. Steaming milk is added, sometimes half and half. If you really want something good on a hot day, pour cooled coffee over ice cubes; add milk to get the right color. Pour a teaspoon of vanilla in and you've got a creole treat.

Beignets are creole doughnuts, made without a hole, like *sopapillas*, and after they're fried in hot oil, beignets are dusted with powdered sugar.

Jambalaya is the Louisiana version of *paella*. Season a chicken and boil it: pull off all the meat afterward and set aside. Brown in a skillet some andouille or hot sausage, cut into bite-size pieces, pouring off the fat. Meanwhile use a huge cast iron skillet and sauté two chopped bunches of shallots or green onions, two big yellow onions, two green peppers, a bunch of celery with leaves, three cloves of garlic, and a half bunch of parsley (preferably the flat Italian kind). Add a big can of peeled tomatoes or some fresh tomatoes and simmer some more. Pitch in 2 cups of raw long grain rice, or use some already cooked rice, adding the broth from the chicken to be absorbed. Throw in the cooked pieces of chicken, sausage and some peeled raw shrimp if you have them, and let simmer until the rice is done and the liquid is absorbed. Season with salt and with Adobo or Tony's Chachere and spoon onto a plate. Serve with salad and French bread.

Gumbo comes from the African word for "Okra," brought to Louisiana from the Cote d'Ivoire. You can make gumbo with okra or you can leave out the okra and add a half spoonful of filé powder, which is the ground-up root and leaves of sassafras that the Choctaw Indians sold at the French Market. Gumbo has the same ingredients as jambalaya but needs crab-meat and a whole lot of seafood broth (cook the discarded shells from your shrimp with seasoning and strain) or chicken broth; even duck broth will do. I skip the tomatoes, and I don't add my sliced, raw, fresh, or frozen okra until the end because I don't want it to become stringy. I prefer the look and taste of stew with some fresh vegetables. You have to cook your rice separately and steam it. Just before serving add some good fresh crabmeat and some fresh shrimp to your gumbo pot even though you may have blue crabs that have boiled in the pot for hours. Serve in a soup bowl over rice. Some people add some chopped parsley and chopped green ends of green onions over the top for garnish.

Po-boys are made with French loaves split down the middle and but-tered, filled with fried oysters, shrimp, roast beef and gravy, or ham and cheese, or other meats. Dressed means to top with chopped lettuce and tomatoes. Benny and Clovis Martin, from the Acadian parishes, invented them and sold them for 10 cents a piece in the French Quarter.

Crawfish bisque, crawfish etoufée, or **crawfish pie** is more Cajun, a South Louisiana dish, than a Creole or New Orleans one. I'm not up to stuffing crawfish heads, but I sure can buy a pound of prepared fresh craw-fish tails with lots of orange gooey fat. Add them to sauteed green peppers, onions, green onions, parsley and celery with garlic. Pour the mixture into a pie shell, cover the top with another, and cook it until the shell is done. It makes a good crawfish pie.

This **ravigotte sauce** is not like Galatoire's but it's still good with crab-meat. To 1cup mayonnaise, preferably homemade (otherwise Hellman's), add juice of one lemon, 1 teaspoon of capers, 3 teaspoons of chopped parsley, 2 teaspoons of chives, 1 chopped shallot including green ends, black pepper, and three small sour pickles finely chopped. Add 2 table-spoons of cream to blend. Cook in a casserole with seafood or serve cold with cold seafood.

Plantains or bananas flambé are a favorite dessert in New Orleans. You can buy the plantains at Schwegmann's for sure. Peel and slice three ripe plantains lengthwise into three or four slices each. Sauté in a skillet with pure butter. Set plantains aside and add a cup of sugar to the skillet to caramelize. Add either a little water with lemon juice or some banana liqueur depending on whether this is vegetable or dessert. Throw the bananas or plantains back in the skillet and simmer until the syrup is thicker. Dribble brandy over them and set afire if you like, and spoon over vanilla ice cream for dessert.

Heavenly hash is as New Orleans as pralines, but since Holmes and Maison Blanche have disappeared or cut back, there's a real problem. The hero of **The Confederacy of Dunces** gobbled it up. To 2 pounds of bulk milk chocolate, add 12 tablespoons of vegetable oil and mix over very low fire to melt in double boiler. I add a spoon of vanilla, carefully so that the chocolate does not get stringy. If it strings I have to add more oil. Add 2 cups of chopped pecans (not very chopped). Pack whole marshmallows side by side in an oblong buttered pyrex pan. Pour the melted chocolate mixture from the double boiler over the marshmallows. Cool to set and cut into squares.

Brioche is the wonderful slightly sweet egg bread that you have for breakfast instead of croissants with your café au lait. Croissants may be French, but they're not New Orleans. McKenzie's bakery still has the best New Orleans' style brioche, in a small loaf, pointed at both ends and dusted with sugar. You can still get Creole cream cheese at Langenstein's and Zara's. Put some sugar on top and enjoy it with your brioche and café au lait. That's what my father-in-law, Fred Toledano, and I did every morning in 1960 when I was writing my thesis and finishing at Newcomb College.

I like light brioche and here's how I do it.

Scald 2 cups of milk and add two sticks of butter and 1/4 cup of granulated sugar. Cool enough to add two packages of dry yeast with 2 teaspoons of salt. Add three beaten eggs and stir in 7 cups of unbleached flour to make dough. Knead dough with additional flour for about 3 minutes to achieve a smooth but still tacky dough. Put big ball of dough into an oiled bowl and turn. Allow to triple in bulk, about 2 hours or more. Punch dough down and let rise again until doubled. Make baby oblong loaves and let formed loaves double and bake at 375 for about 15 minutes after sprinkling with a little sugar.

Pain perdu is "lost bread" or French toast. When the French bread from Leidenheimer's Bakery is no longer fresh, slice it at angles and soak in a mixture of three lightly beaten eggs, a heaping tablespoon of sugar, a teaspoon of vanilla and a splash of brandy. Brown in a skillet where you have melted some fresh butter. Dust with powdered sugar.

King's cakes are popular from Twelfth Night (Epiphany, January 6th),and are breakfast and snack fare until Mardi Gras day after which the bakeries do not make them until the next year. Gambino's, McKenzie's,

Haydel's, and other bakeries have their own recipes for the yellow-colored egg bread shaped into circles of different sizes and covered either with sugar or dollops of icing colored purple, green, and yellow—Mardi Gras colors. Inside the king's cake is a fava bean or a tiny statuette of a baby, usually plastic now. Whoever gets the baby or the bean has good luck the rest of the year, is the queen of the ball, or has to buy the next day's king's cake. **Haydel's Bakery** has a king's cake mix complete with Mardi Gras video.

Mirleton is a tropical squash, called a *chayote* in Spanish, which grows on a vine, and you treat it like a delicate eggplant. After boiling or microwaving mirleton until soft, take out the insides, discard the very hard little middle. Make a stuffing of the mirleton insides, sauteed onions, chopped garlic, parsley, and celery, and mix the stuffing with ham or shrimp and crabmeat. Put back in the shell and bake or heat until hot.

The **cocktail** and its name were invented in New Orleans,. An essential ingredient to a number of New Orleans favorite drinks has New Orleans roots. Antoine Amédée Peychaud was an emigré from the uprising in St. Domingue in 1793. At the pharmacy he established in New Orleans at **437 Royal** he manufactured his **Peychaud bitters**. The bitters, good for any stomach malady, also added zest to cognac or brandy. Peychaud bitters became essential to a French brandy drink and the concoction found a ready market in the New Orleans coffee houses, the origional sazerac.

The **Sazerac** is a New Orleans favorite. In 1859 John B. Schiller, local agent for the cognac firm of Sazerac de Forge ct Fils, of Limoges, France, opened the Sazerac Coffee House at 13 Exchange Alley. Over the decades the brandy and bitters changed to rye whiskey and Peychaud bitters. Eventually, a dash of **pernod, herbsaint** or **absinthe** was added. The absinthe innovation has been credited to Leon Lamothe, who was a bartender for the former cabinetmaker and furniture importer, Emile Seignouret, at 520 Royal Street.(The patio is open for viewing.)

The **Ramos gin fizz** was developed by Henry C. Ramos, who arrived from Baton Rouge in 1888 to open a bar in the American sector. Ramos' blend of egg white, powdered sugar, vanilla, and orange flower water make it an amazing drink.

Mix in a tall bar glass 4 drops of orange flower water, juice of one-half lime and one-half lemon, one jigger of dry gin, one teaspoon of powdered sugar, one egg white, one jigger of cream, one squirt of seltzer water, and 2 drops of vanilla. Shake well with crushed ice until the mixture has some body and strain into a tall, thin, cold glass. Better yet, just go to the Fairmont-Roosevelt where they've made them for years.

Index

NOTE: Generic lists of information presented in the front and back matter are included in the index, but specifics are left to the reader. Both of these sections are filled with relevant research information and advice to the traveler.

Creole usage and American custom have caused the French "de," "du," or "des" to be combined sometimes with the sir name or place name, as in DePouilly. The index follow notaries' spellings in documents in the New Orleans Notarial Archives.

To clarify names and relationships, I have used both married and maiden names of women in the index, using Mr. and Mrs. for Monsieur and Madame.

This index has been prepared for the traveler, both armchair and on-site, historian, genealogist, sociologist, architect and builder as well as architectural and art historian. It elucidates the role of women and it informs relative to the role of the African American in New Orleans history.

Beauregard-Keyes House, 26, 43, 45, 181. *See* Le Charpentier-Beauregard house
Beauregard Monument Association, 82
Beauregard, Pierre Gustave Toutant, 39, 118; superintendent at Custom House, 97; statue of, 82; portrait of, 92
Begué's Restaurant, 30
Belidor, Bernard Forest de, author, 27
Benevolent Societies, 23
Benjamin, Judah P., Senator, Judge, 17, 163
Bensel, Henry, builder, 168
Berdou's Restaurant, Gretna, 108
Bernard, François, artist, 158
Bienville, Jean-Baptiste Le Moyne, Sieur de, 85. 88. *See* LeMoyne
Blackamoor Antiques, 160
Blair, Jean du Pont, glassworks of, 186
Bloomingdale, Uptown suburb 157
Bogart, John, and Culyer, park designers, 80
Boisdorè, François, architect-builder, 27
Books on New Orleans, recommended, 211–212
Bookstores, recommended, 209–210
Bousillage, 12, 13, 20
Boutet, Hilaire, architect-builder, 42, 45, 79
Brand, William, architect, 15, 17, 21, 41, 65, 86
Brennan's Restaurant, 26, 34
Brick-between-post, 12, 13, 19, 56, 57.
Briggs, Charles, English-born insurance executive, 134, 136
Briqueterie, 13
Brocato, Angelo, ice cream, 18
Buckner, Henry S., 77, 130–133, 145
Building contracts, 69, 135
Buisson, Benjamin, surveyor, 11, 130, 155
Bullard, John, director, New Orleans Museum of Art, 82
Burtheville, Uptown suburb, 157
Butterfly, a river walk, Audubon Park, 162
Byrnes, James, director of Delgado Museum, 82
Bywater, creole suburb, 59

Cabildo, 7, 10, 11, 24, 28, 65, 80
Cabinets, 12, 14, 21, 41, 65, 78
Cable, George Washington, author, 31, 115, 141

Café Volage, 160
Calrow, James, builder, 127, 143
Cambiaso, Reverend John, architect of Jesuit Church, 94
Camelback house, discussed, 154, 155
Campbell, J.E., builder, 127
Canal Street Historic District, 93
Canary Islanders, 59
Cantillon brothers, bankers in Paris, 4
Carlos III, King of Spain, 6
Carnegie Foundation, 20
Carondelet, Baron de and Governor, 7
Carroll, General William, honored by Carrollton, 157
Carroll, Joseph, contractor, 144
Carrollton Avenue and Bend in River shopping, 160
Carter, Thomas W., English-born architect, 170
Casey Willems Pottery, 160
Cashio, Cochran, landscape architects, 30
Castaing, Alexander, builder, 73
Cathedral, St. Louis, 6, 10, 11, 23, 28
Celebration in the Oaks, at City Park, 81
Cemeteries, discussed, 187, 188
   Lafayette (cemetery no. 1), 132, 147, 201, 202
   St. Louis Cemeteries, 2, 23, 41, 64
Chalmette National Historical Park, 59, 60, 182. *See* Beauregard, Judge René house
Charity Hospital, demolished, 89
Chattel property, 59
Chez Nous Charcuterie, 161
Chopin, Kate, Mrs. Ocscar, author, 168
Christian Woman's Exchange, 42. *See* Hermann-Grima House
Christovich, Mary Louise Mossy, preservation leader, 202, 210
Churchill and Labouisse, architects, 176
Churches, 6, 23, 27, 28, 43, 60, 61, 62, 64, 78, 85, 94, 96, 110, 114, 118, 120, 122, 146, 165, 168, 170, 171, 173,
City Park Improvement Association, 80
City Park, 80–82
Civil War, 11, 62
Cizek, Eugene D., architect, 57
Claiborne, Governor W.C.C., 8, 11, 38, 39, 43, 48, 75
Clairain, Louis, builder, 56
Clancy's Restaurant, 163